THE HILLFORTS OF Iron Age Wales

THE HILLFORTS OF Iron Age Wales

Toby Driver

LOGASTON PRESS

FRONTISPIECE: Tre'r Ceiri hillfort, Llŷn Peninsula, Gwynedd, rising from a freezing winter cloud inversion in January 2022. (© Crown copyright: RCAHMW. NPRN 95292. AP_2022_0236)

First published in 2023 by Logaston Press
The Holme, Church Road, Eardisley HR3 6NJ
www.logastonpress.co.uk
An imprint of Fircone Books Ltd.

ISBN 978-1-910839-67-6

Designed and typeset by Richard Wheeler in 11 on 15 Minion.
Cover design by Richard Wheeler.

Printed and bound in Poland www.lfbookservices.co.uk

Logaston Press is committed to a sustainable future for our business, our readers and our planet.
The book in your hands is made from FSC® (Forest Stewardship Council®) paper.

British Library Catalogue in Publishing Data.
A CIP catalogue record for this book is available from the British Library.

CONTENTS

for

Aric & Charlie

PREFACE

Hillforts were the commanding hilltop homes of the people of prehistoric Wales for centuries before the Roman Conquest. Many continued in occupation throughout Romano-British times and into the Early Medieval period. These great structures, more than a thousand of which still stand today, show the emergence of monumental prehistoric architecture and engineering on a grand scale. Together they reflect the spread of innovation and cultural ideas across Britain and the continent.

The hillforts of Wales – or that part of western Britain which later became the country of Wales – were home to leaders and their communities of craftspeople, warriors, religious specialists and farmers. The names of some of these regional peoples have survived, among them the Ordovices, the Deceangli, the Silures, the Gangani and the Demetae. This book tells the story of these hillforts from their beginnings in the Late Bronze Age around 1150BC, to their rise during the Iron Age from 800BC as defended homes, early villages and formative towns and their transformation or reoccupation under Roman rule after AD 80.

Hillforts show us the importance of complex networks of alliance and exchange which existed among the rural prehistoric communities of Wales, and of the roles of architects and visionary leaders, both women and men, who were able to build homes so durable that they survive today as significant landscape features. Hillforts were founded, developed, rebuilt and abandoned; generations of people lived, worked and died within their walls. Hillforts ranged from small, defended family farmsteads to larger early villages and vast regional centres exerting territorial and economic control. The construction of hillforts reflected a critical change in society after the Late Bronze Age with communities coming together to live closely in bounded settlements for the first time. Conflict and rivalry also became more ingrained in society from the Late Bronze Age onwards with competitive raiding undoubtedly forming part of everyday life in the Iron Age.

Nor is there simply one type of 'hillfort' in Wales. This catch-all term encompasses a variety of different defended farmsteads, long-lived settlements, early villages, seasonal meeting places and even ceremonial and ritual sites built over a period of 1,000 years and more, with marked regional differences. Some are on hills, whilst others commanded valley junctions, escarpments and coastal cliffs. The Iron Age communities of Wales only encountered the brutality of a professional army and siege warfare with the coming of the Roman legions in the mid first century AD. Two thousand years later these ancient defended hilltops still fire the imagination.

Despite their presence in the landscape – it is hard to drive more than a few miles in Wales without passing a hillfort – and a century or more of archaeological enquiry, scientific investigation and excavation, these great prehistoric defended settlements remain something of a mystery to most. While there is lively academic debate and much new research among archaeologists, the same searching questions remain among the wider public: how old are the hillforts? what did they look like? how wild was the countryside? how did people live in such exposed positions? and what happened when the Romans swept through Wales?

This book sets out to answer these searching questions and many others. It is not a textbook, nor is it a description of every hillfort in Wales. Instead I have tried to draw out some of the core themes and stories about hillforts which deserve to be more widely known, to ignite an interest in these ancient structures. Within these pages I will take the reader on new journeys to special locales in the Welsh countryside, that are all too easily overlooked in our modern world. I will shed light on new avenues of research and direct the reader towards some of the best monuments to visit.

In revisiting many of these hillforts during the writing of this book I have had my enthusiasm fired again, seeing both 'old friends' but also making my first ascents up to some 'new' summits. Along the way I have been guided, inspired and educated by friends and colleagues who share the same interest in these ancient places and to whom I owe a great debt of gratitude. I hope that, on reading this book, many more people in Wales and beyond may also develop an interest and a passion in these very special ancient places.

Toby Driver, December 2022

ACKNOWLEDGEMENTS

At the outset this book was designed to introduce the subject of hillforts and the Iron Age of Wales to a wide audience, with an aim to address many of the common questions which are still asked about this distant period. During the writing process I have relied heavily on the generosity and expertise of several friends and colleagues who have willingly read and commented on chapter drafts. My sincere thanks to Dr Simon Rodway, Dr Julian Whitewright, Dr Oliver Davis and Dr James January-McCann who have all given me detailed comments on particular chapters, significantly improving the book. In addition I have had valuable discussions with Dr Jeffrey Davies about the Romans and their campaigns, with Alice Thorne about Garn Goch hillfort and the Iron Age of southern Powys, with Dr Kate Waddington and David Hopewell about Tre'r Ceiri hillfort and with Louise Barker about Craig yr Aderyn/ Birds' Rock and the coastal promontory forts of Pembrokeshire. My thanks to my mother Lyn Pugh who copyedited the first draft of the entire manuscript. Sincere thanks are also due to Richard and Su at Logaston Press for all their help and professional guidance along the way in bringing this book to fruition. Any remaining errors or omissions are entirely my own.

I am indebted to a number of people for many years of discussions and fieldwork days, over the course of which my ideas on hillforts have developed or changed. I'd particularly like to thank Louise Barker at the Royal Commission who has surveyed and interpreted many archaeological sites in Wales and with whom I've enjoyed years of site visits and conversations about hillforts. I have learnt a great deal working with Louise, Dr Bob Johnston and Dr Oliver Davis over several years on the Skomer Island Project. The words of my PhD supervisor, Professor Andrew Fleming, are also never far away when I'm writing about hillforts. It's

Emerging from 2,000 years of windblown sand. A great Romano-British roundhouse dating to the 2nd–3rd centuries AD under excavation by the Gwynedd Archaeological Trust at Dinas Dinlle coastal hillfort, Gwynedd, in the summer of 2021. Research by the EU-funded CHERISH Project confirmed that the soft cliff edge (RIGHT) is eroding at an average rate of 40cm a year and the roundhouse will, in time, collapse over the edge. The roundhouse has now been preserved inside the hillfort by the National Trust as a 'climate change indicator' of ongoing cliff loss. Compare with Fig 6.7 (© Crown: CHERISH PROJECT 2022. Produced with EU funds through the Ireland Wales Co-operation Programme 2014–2023. All material made freely available through the Open Government Licence. NPRN 95309)

been a pleasure and a privilege to have been involved in the EU-funded CHERISH Project since its inception in 2015/16 and to have worked with such a brilliant joint-nation team, including on the archaeological sites of Ireland with Anthony Corns, Rob Shaw, Dr Sandra Henry and Dr Edward Pollard and in Wales with Dan Hunt, Hannah Genders-Boyd, Professor Sarah Davies, Dr Patrick Robson and Dr Hywel Griffiths. It's also been a pleasure to work more recently with Dr Julian Whitewright and Dr Jayne Kamintzis at the Royal Commission.

On the subject of hillforts and later prehistory I would like to thank various individuals from whom I have learnt a good deal over the years including Ken Murphy, Fran Murphy, Professor Harold Mytum, David Hopewell, Fiona Gale, Professor Niall Sharples, Professor Barry Burnham, Mark Lewis, Professor Andrew Fitzpatrick, Chris Musson, Heather James and the late Terry James, Dr Adam Gwilt, Dr Evan Chapman, Professor Ray Howell, Professor John Grattan, Dr Rachel Pope, Frances Lynch, John Roberts, Tomos Jones, Delun Gibby, Dr Erin Lloyd Jones, Scott Lloyd, Kathy Laws, Michael Freeman, Carrie Canham, Jessica Domiczew and Luke Jenkins. It's been good to re-engage with many of these people for the recent Research Framework process. I've also been fortunate to get to know many colleagues in the Hillfort Study Group (HFSG) over the years. A high point was the busy HFSG visit to the hillforts of Ceredigion in 2022.

Research for this book would have been far more difficult during lockdown without the online databases of the Royal Commission (*Coflein*), the Welsh Archaeological Trusts (*Archwilio*) and 175 years of the journal *Archaeologia Cambrensis* online. Twitter has also been invaluable, especially during the Covid lockdown, to stay in touch with the rest of the Iron Age world. Via Twitter I have built contacts with Manuel Gago in Galicia, Spain, Dr Miles Russell at Bournemouth University and PhD researchers including Dr Tiffany Treadway, Dr Adelle Bricking, Dr Reb Ellis and Andrew Reynolds.

I extend my utmost thanks to various people who have helped to provide images for this book. To Christopher Catling and Penny Icke for permission to use various Royal Commission images from the National Monuments Record of Wales and Kay Kays for various National Museum Wales images. To Delun Gibby and Brian Southern of Pembrokeshire Coast National Park Authority for Figs 1.4 and 8.4. To Manuel Gago for Fig 5.34 and for putting me in touch with Franjo Padín for Fig 7.7. To Oliver Davis for Fig 1.7. To Andrew Davidson at the Gwynedd Archaeological Trust for Fig 6.7, to Ken Murphy at the Dyfed Archaeological Trust for Fig 7.6, and to Paul Belford and Gary Duckers at the Clwyd Powys Archaeological Trust for Fig 1.20. To Adelle Bricking for her excellent photo in Fig 2.14. To Dr Miles Russell at Bournemouth University for Figs 2.5 and 4.2. To several individuals who helped to track down the original Brian Byron (Giffords) reconstruction paintings for Anglesey (Figs 2.4, 4.14, 6.1, 6.4 and 6.15), particularly Robert Williams, Llansadwrn, and to Dafydd Gruffydd at Menter Môn for permission to reproduce them. To the Editor and Trustees of the Cambrian Archaeological Association for allowing me to reproduce several historic illustrations from *Archaeologia*

Cambrensis. To Lucinda Walker at the Historic England Archive for Figs 3.1 and 5.1. To Brenda Craddock and Ioan Lord for permission to reproduce Fig 5.5. To Julie Edwards at West Cheshire Museums for sourcing Fig 2.8 and for translation of the inscription and Ian Jones at Oriel Môn, Anglesey, for kindly photographing the replica Llyn Cerrig Bach weapons in Figs 3.8 and 4.4.

I also gratefully acknowledge funding from the Mark Fitch Fund towards the acquisition of several images for this publication from some of the main museums and picture libraries; the help of the fund has been invaluable. My final thanks to Becky, Aric and Charlie who have put up with many days, weeks and months of me being less attentive whilst completing this book.

POINTS TO NOTE

Access to sites

Unless otherwise stated, all of the sites described or illustrated in this book should be assumed to lie on private land, to be visited only with the permission of the landowner and at the visitor's own risk. Details of sites which can be visited are given in Chapter 8, together with information about access and safety. Visitors should always strictly observe the Countryside Code (p. 252).

Dates

Most dates in this book are given in calendar years BC and AD, for the purposes of clarity. Where radiocarbon dates are described, the date ranges are given in calendar years without discussion of calibration issues and the underpinning percentage probabilities. Readers wishing to further explore the quoted dates should consult the published sources listed in the bibliography.

Royal Commission images

The images are Crown copyright and are reproduced with the permission of the Royal Commission on the Ancient and Historical Monuments of Wales (RCAHMW), under delegated authority from The Keeper of Public Records. The initials 'NPRN' in image captions refer to the site's unique National Primary Record Number which can be searched on www.coflein.gov.uk

∞ TIMELINE : IRON AGE & ROMAN WALES ∞

1150 – 800BC	**Late Bronze Age** Climate deteriorates; uplands depopulated. Earliest hillforts; coming together of larger communities. Deposition of rich metalwork & hoards of weaponry.
800 – 600BC	**The Earliest Iron Age / Llyn Fawr period** Climate recovers. Llyn fawr votive lake deposit. New metals technology; Halstatt weapons & artefacts.
600 – 50BC	**Early - Middle Iron Age** Expansion & development of hillforts & agriculture. European La Tène culture influences Welsh metalwork. Development of ironworking & mining.
50BC – AD43	**Late Iron Age & Roman conquest** Widespread clearance of lowlands for farming. Increasing complexity in hillforts and hutgroups. Wales not fully conquered by Romans until AD 80.
AD47/48 – 80	**Latest Iron Age / Roman campaigning period** Iron Age culture endures during conflict with Romans. Hoarding and burial of wealth reflects crisis in society.
AD43 – 410	**Roman Wales** Network of Roman forts built and occupied after AD 70s. Pacification of Romano-British Wales. Hillforts & farms continue in occupation using Roman pottery & tools.
AD410 – 1066	**Early medieval / post-Roman Wales** End of Roman rule in Britain AD 410. Age of Saints. New peoples arrive from Ireland & Europe. Re-occupation of old hillforts as new power centres.

1 Exploring the hillforts of Wales

Fig 1.1 (PREVIOUS PAGE)

An Iron Age 'village' of six to eight roundhouses, plus what may have been the village green in the right foreground, occupies a grassy saddle inside St David's Head or Penmaen Dewi coastal promontory fort, north Pembrokeshire. Excavation of the houses by Reverend Sabine Baring-Gould in 1898 revealed engraved spindle whorls, glass beads and pounding stones for everyday tasks. The rockscape of the headland provided a dramatic background to Iron Age life and may also have held a sacred importance. (T. Driver 2022)

1

Written history in Wales, with the exception of a few facts mentioned by Roman writers, does not go back much further than a thousand years; beyond that time we have little but tradition mixed up with romantic stories and legends. But where written history fails us, archaeology steps in and traces back the story of the human race in Wales for very many years.

Willoughby Gardner, in his 1926 Presidential address to the Cambrian Archaeological Association, on the subject of the hillforts of north Wales[1]

Of all the countries of the British Isles, Wales has a particularly rich legacy of Iron Age hillforts. Some of the largest are found here, from Penycloddiau in the Clwydian Range to Y Gaer fawr, Garn Goch in Carmarthenshire and Deer Park promontory fort on the coast of western Pembrokeshire. There are unique stone forts: there is nothing quite like Tre'r Ceiri on the Llŷn Peninsula anywhere in Britain. Where land was more marginal, particularly in the rocky uplands, communities clearly laboured hard to build smaller hillforts with a limited workforce, basic tools and technology. These family hillforts built 'on a budget' are part of what makes the Welsh Iron Age particularly special. They preserve many distinctive, smaller details lost at larger hillforts including visible repairs to stone wall faces, changes in direction of banks and ditches as decisions were taken during the build, or the construction of short sections of ramparts only where they were most needed; such details help us to 'decode' some of the reasons for how and why hillforts were built.

In upland country we can squeeze through small back doors – called 'postern' gates – which allowed people and animals to enter and leave the hillfort without using the main gates. We can marvel at deep rock-cut ditches which were dug by hand to defend and enclose remote mountain spurs and coastal promontories. In Pembrokeshire and Gwynedd we can walk through the doors of Iron Age roundhouses, crossing original threshold stones which have served visitors well for 2,500 years.

The hillforts were home to competitive, charismatic leaders; some may have used these walled villages as centres of redistribution of food and prestige goods which in turn yielded local or regional respect. Leaders of hillfort communities could be women or men; Roman authors remind us that the British made no distinction in the sex of their leaders. Whilst pitched battles were rare, feuding and raiding between neighbouring chiefdoms would have been commonplace. These raids bolstered the reputation of the leaders at home, exerted their authority in the wider territory and often resulted in real gains of stolen cattle and kidnapped men. Whilst there was poverty, hardship and hunger in the land of prehistoric Wales there was also wealth, prestige, feasting and ceremony. In recent decades some of the most fabulous Iron Age treasures known anywhere in prehistoric Europe have emerged from votive lakes and wetlands in Wales.

There is much we still do not know about the later prehistory of Wales. Many dark corners require illumination, or the spark of imagination, to piece together the lives of our Iron Age ancestors. Nor do we fully understand the details of the prolonged and brutal clashes with Rome in the first century AD which eventually saw Welsh tribes acquiesce to the new ways of Romano-British life. These uncertainties are precisely what make the study of Iron Age Wales still so vibrant and exciting. With each new excavation, each new archaeological find reported to the Portable Antiquities Scheme, each new idea put forward to reinterpret long-held beliefs, so our understanding of our prehistoric past develops and deepens. This book will shed light on many of these new insights which keep the subject of hillfort archaeology alive and constantly exciting.

Fig 1.2 Standing the test of time. Two-thousand-year-old rampart walling at the small upland hillfort of Craig y Dinas, Dyffryn Ardudwy, sited on a crag above the coastal plain of Gwynedd. In this section of wall alone the skills of Iron Age craftspeople can be appreciated and closely studied. The wall is artfully built of large, angular blocks but is finished with very small stone spalls inserted to fill spaces, known as 'snecks' among the wall builders of Scotland and northern England. It is remarkable that this human-scale snecking has survived to the present day. See also Fig 5.15 (T. Driver)

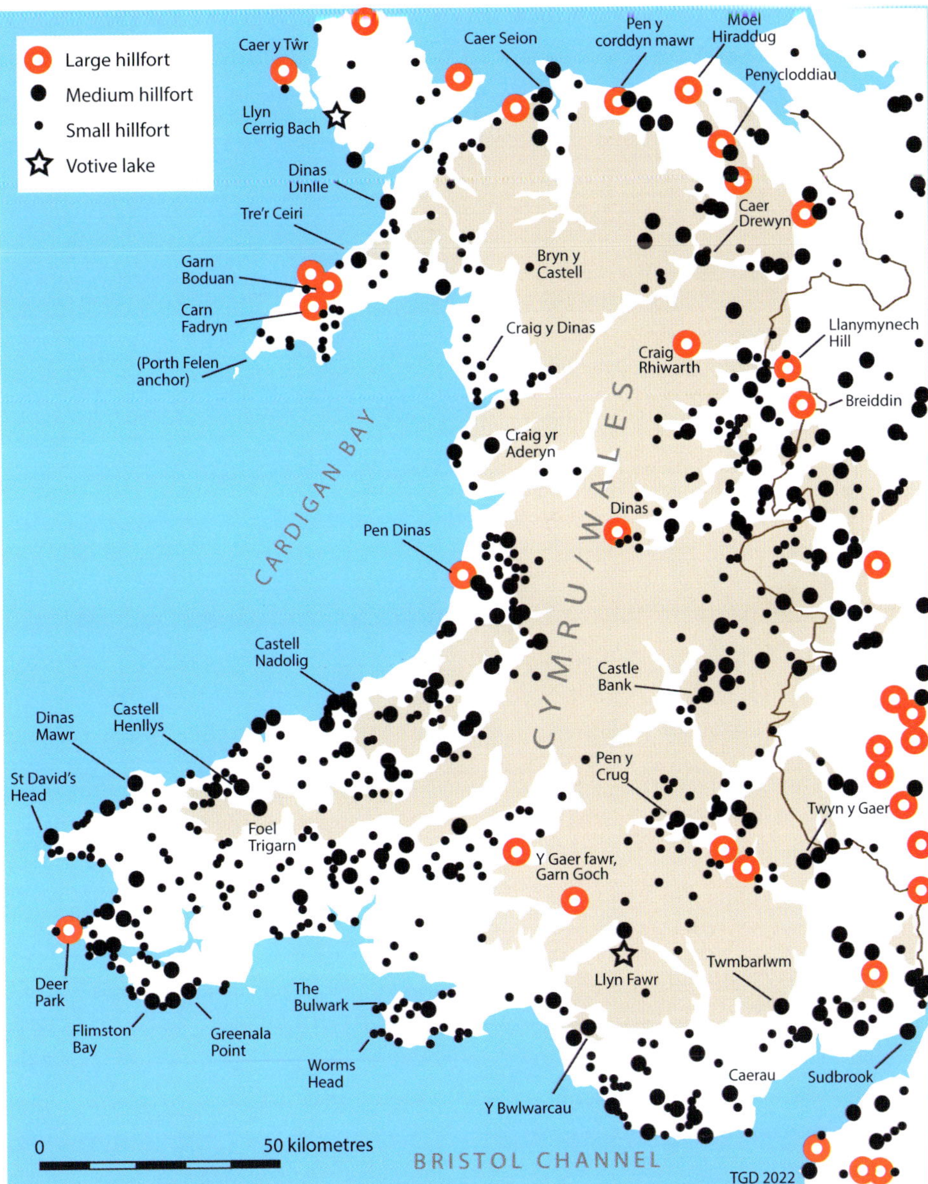

Fig 1.3 The hillforts and defended farmsteads of Wales. Map showing terrain over 200m (shaded) and the names of some of the key sites mentioned in the text. Note the Porth Felen prehistoric anchor find, labelled at the tip of the Llŷn Peninsula (T. Driver, sources various)[2]

Hillforts and defended farmsteads: a very brief introduction

Archaeologists use the term 'hillfort' to describe a range of Late Bronze Age (1200BC–600BC) or Iron Age (600BC–AD 80) hilltop enclosures which were built with substantial enclosing banks or ramparts, frequently – but not always – sited on commanding hills, cliffs, ridges or promontories. Whether these sites acted as defensive 'forts' as the name suggests, is the subject of much recent debate which will be introduced in later chapters. However, the term 'hillfort' remains a useful shorthand for describing a range of defended hilltop settlements, many of which continued in occupation throughout the Romano-British period (AD 43–AD 410) and into Early Medieval times (AD 410–AD 1066).

The publication of the nation-wide *Hillfort Atlas Project*[3] has brought new rigour and new standardised data to the study of the prehistoric fortifications of the British Isles. The *Hillfort Atlas* lists 3,354 confirmed hillforts across the British Isles including the Isle of Man, of which 626 are recorded in Wales. The *Atlas* specifically addressed hillforts, as opposed to smaller, less monumental defended farmsteads and non-hillfort settlements like hut groups; the actual number of Iron Age settlements in Wales is far greater. The *Atlas* can be read alongside the results of the Cadw-funded *Defended Enclosures Survey Project* which looked at all the defended settlements – large and small – of Iron Age Wales. This study, undertaken by the four Welsh Archaeological Trusts with Cadw and the Royal Commission, was published in 2018 as a set of open access authoritative papers in the online journal *Internet Archaeology*.[4] The results were incorporated into the regional Historic Environment Records for Wales, accessed via the online portal *Archwilio*. *Archwilio* presently lists 764 Iron Age hillforts for Wales, along with 1,191 prehistoric defended enclosures and 1,332 prehistoric hut groups – more than 500 in Gwynedd – giving a better idea of the population density of Iron Age and Romano-British Wales. In parts of Montgomeryshire and Pembrokeshire there is a prehistoric fort or farmstead for every modern farm, showing a level of sophistication towards land management and settlement in prehistoric Wales.

Over the years these majestic prehistoric settlements have been termed hillforts, ring forts, raths, small enclosures, defended enclosures and many other terms covering a range of site types across the regions of Wales. The Defended Enclosures Survey Project finally introduced some standardisation and made the distinction between three main types of later prehistoric settlements: **hillforts and promontory forts**, **small defended enclosures** and **hut groups and field systems**.[5]

Fig 1.4 Castell Henllys, Pembrokeshire. This splendid reconstruction perfectly evokes life in this small, long-lived Iron Age hillfort in the final centuries before the Roman Conquest. The fort was well defended with a complex gateway, complete with timber tower and walled recesses in the entrance passage. A shrine is imaginatively shown outside the fort alongside the river on the right. To build the fort and roundhouses the occupants would have drawn upon the resources of the surrounding landscape, including structural timber from managed woodland and reeds from wetlands for thatching (© Richard Allen. By kind permission of Pembrokeshire Coast National Park Authority)

In this book I will generally keep the terminology simple; the term '**hillforts**' describes substantially-built prehistoric defended settlements usually in prominent or commanding locations, on hilltops, ridges, plateaus or even atop lowland rises and knolls. It is generally the size and strength of the enclosing ramparts which define a hillfort, even those in lowland positions. The numbers of ramparts is described through vallation, from the Latin *vallum* for a bank or wall. Thus a hillfort with single or double lines of ramparts will be univallate or bivallate; with multiple banks it will be described as multivallate. Hillfort gateways, or weaker approaches, may be further defended by short lengths of banks called outworks. These may be angled at the gateway to form a protective hornwork or may enclose an outer space to create an annexe.

Coastal promontory forts are wave-washed Iron Age defended settlements which were often reoccupied in Romano-British and Early Medieval times. The term **defended farmsteads** is used for less substantially-defended smaller enclosures whose main function seems to have been farming or domestic settlement for one or more extended families. Many of these more lightly-defended sites have long since been ploughed away only to be rediscovered as **cropmarks** in summer droughts (see below). Alongside these hillforts and defended farmsteads were many roundhouse groups – commonly termed **hut groups** – particularly found in the Welsh uplands where scattered farming communities lived year-round or where they moved to only during summer months.

COASTAL PROMONTORY FORTS: LIFE AT THE EDGE

Promontory forts, as the name suggests, were prehistoric settlements with defences built to cut off the neck of a readily-defensible promontory or spur to enclose a space without the need to build ramparts on all sides. Such defended sites occur on inland promontories and also along the Welsh coast where there are at least 106.[6] A coastal promontory fort was a prehistoric or early historic coastal fort enclosed by timber, earth or stone defences, sited on an elevated promontory washed by the sea on at least one side.

Coastal promontory forts were very different places in the Iron Age landscape and are described separately in Chapter 7. The coast would always have offered a distinctive and different landscape in prehistoric Wales when compared with the woodland and farmland of the interior. There was danger inherent in the construction of permanent defended settlements on precipitous coastal promontories, as well as new opportunities offered by the proximity of coastal trade and the resources offered by the sea and shore.

There are other forts in set-back locations near to or overlooking the sea, which could be called 'coastal forts'. Such sites include major hillforts like Pen Dinas, Aberystwyth, Tre'r Ceiri, Llŷn and Caer y Tŵr, Holyhead, all of which lie adjacent to the coast or within a mile or so of the sea. They would have maintained visual command and contact across the sea and benefitted from a maritime economy. Some may even have acted as 'ports of trade', known locales for international coastal contact and exchange.

Fig 1.5 The enigmatic coastal promontory enclosure of Crocksydam or 'Moody Nose' in south Pembrokeshire is built around a prominent outcrop with a steep drop beyond. The enclosure is entirely hidden on all approaches and is reached by descending through a rocky canyon. It may have been a sacred or ceremonial site rather than a practical settlement. Crocksydam has been surveyed by archaeologists from the CHERISH Project and lies on the Castlemartin military training area with restricted access. (T. Driver)

A DIVERSE LANDSCAPE

These different terms – hillforts, promontory forts, defended farmsteads and hut groups – remain a useful way to describe the monuments we see, visit, study and excavate; but they conceal a huge variety of potential functions. Just as in medieval times a village may have contained a range of different buildings from a castle and a manor house to farmsteads, ordinary houses and places of worship, so we should recognise a similar range of site types in the Iron Age landscape.

Some Iron Age enclosures were truly defensive; others like a manor house were the ostentatious homesteads of wealthy communities who were keen to have an impressive 'front door' without any real intention of a military function. Among the scatter of other enclosures in the landscape were family farms, cattle-gathering corrals and ritual and sacred enclosures used for worship, burial and other non-settlement functions. It is not always easy to be sure of the original function, or range of functions, of a hillfort or defended farm without new investigation or excavation.

Beyond the built enclosures with their walls, ditches and gateways we must be mindful of the wider prehistoric landscape of fields, woodlands and reed-beds, early mines, fair and market sites and routes for trade and exchange. There were also significant locales in the natural landscape where Iron Age communities practised rituals and ceremonies. These included upland lakes, bogs and wetlands, springs, dangerous coastal promontories and dark caves, all of which were integral to the inseparable patterns of life and death in pre-Roman Wales. New prehistoric finds reported to the Portable Antiquities Scheme in Wales allow archaeologists to discover other inland votive or ceremonial sites which lay outside the ramparts of the hillforts. The Langstone tankard (Fig 3.2) from a wetland area in south-east Wales is just such an important recent find.

Fig 1.6 The Bulwark on Llanmadoc Hill, Gower. A defensively-sited hillfort which nonetheless incorporated a series of wide-spaced outer enclosures in its design, similar to a number of other sites in south Wales. These outer enclosures were probably used for the gathering in and management of livestock or cattle, the principal wealth of the community. Its position on a prominent hill on the far north-west tip of the Gower peninsula may have singled out The Bulwark as a place for seasonal markets or livestock fairs. (© Crown copyright: RCAHMW. NPRN 301327, AP_2012_0989)

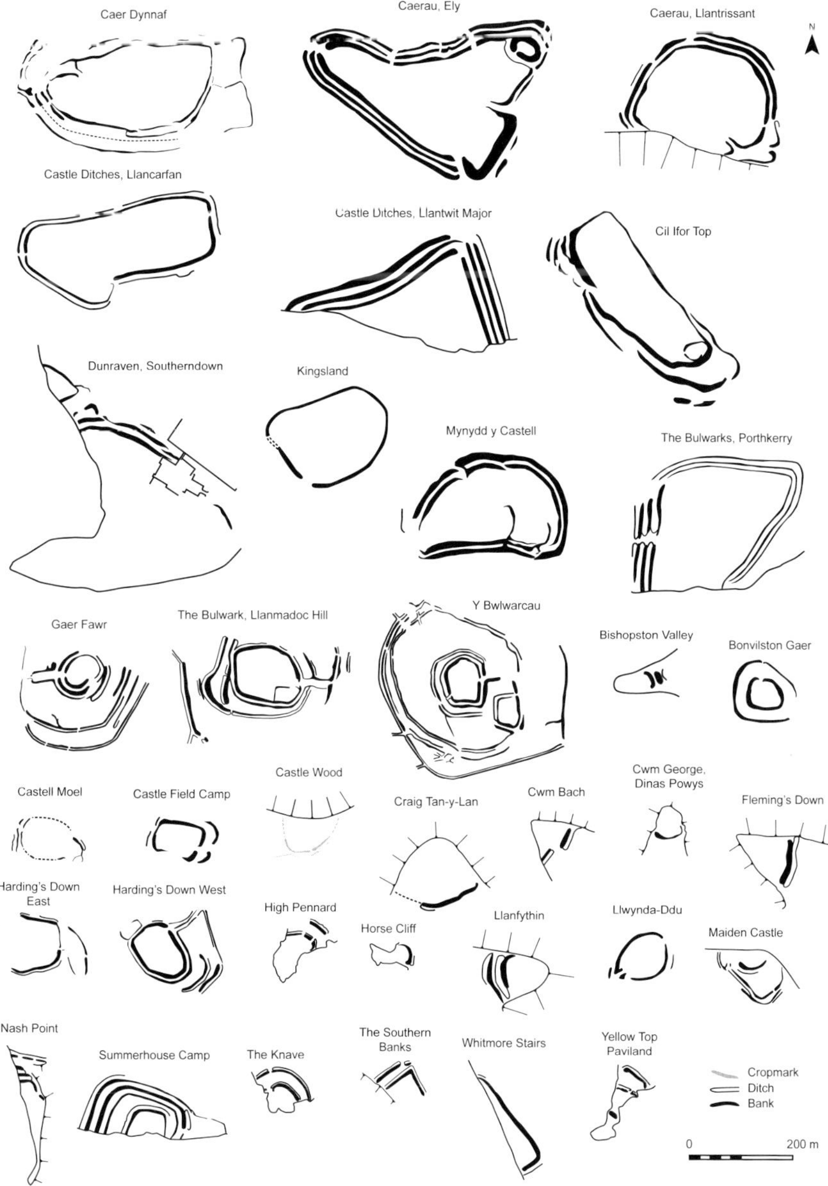

Fig 1.7 Many ways to build a hillfort. Oliver Davis at Cardiff University compiled this useful set of plans of selected hillforts and defended farmsteads in south Wales to better understand the context of major sites like Caerau, Ely (TOP CENTRE), focus of CAER Heritage. The comparison of plans displays a huge variety of sizes and styles, from the wide-space ramparts of Y Bwlwarcau (CENTRE) to smaller cropmarked defended enclosures and promontory forts at the bottom. Yet even at this scale one can see conformity and sharing of regional design traditions between hillforts. (After Davis & Sharples 2020, Figure 3; by kind permission of Dr Oliver Davis)

Fig 1.8 Understanding hillfort earthworks. When we visit hillforts today, we often enter via an old holloway at the entrance between two high banks or ramparts (**A**); prior to centuries of collapse this would have been a deep post-built or stone-lined gate passage into the fort beneath a crossing bridge or even a wooden gateway tower. Look out for prestige stone walling (**B**) and large boulders flanking the gateway which once made it appear more impressive. Ramparts often have outer ditches, now largely filled in, with counterscarp banks beyond (**C**) formed from episodic ditch cleaning. Quarry hollows from rampart-building may be visible behind the ramparts (**D**); some were re-used for sheltered house sites. Look out for levelled areas or shallow scoops (**E**) within the hillfort which mark the sites of roundhouses (**H**). Prominent boulders or outcrops within the fort (**F**) are usually unchanged since Iron Age times and once provided places to sit, work or carry out craft activities; they provide a tangible link to the past. Sometimes hillfort interiors have been ploughed (**G**) destroying older earthworks. Elevated 4- or 6-post buildings (**I**) were built alongside roundhouses to store the collected grain wealth of the hillfort, safe from damp and rodents. (T. Driver)

HILLFORTS AND MAPS

The variety of names given to archaeological monuments in gothic type on Ordnance Survey maps can often seem baffling. What is a 'homestead' and why is it different to a 'settlement'? What are 'settlements' meant to look like in the field, and how would one know what to look for when out on a walk? When I was younger and getting interested in archaeology, I found the term 'hut circle' on maps confusing. I once went out searching for a 'hut circle' on the hills below Moel Goedog hillfort above Harlech as a teenager on a family holiday, expecting to see a circle of huts arranged on the moorland. I now know that the term refers to the footings of a single roundhouse on moorland (Fig 1.9), and they can sometimes be very difficult to spot especially in high summer vegetation.

Hillforts, along with Later Bronze and Iron Age monuments, have a variety of names and terms on maps and in academic literature. On many occasions they mean the same thing, but differences arise in historical and regional naming traditions, and even in the changing policies of the Ordnance Survey Archaeology Section during the twentieth century.

On Ordnance Survey mapping, what would usually be described as a 'hillfort' or a 'defended settlement' will be depicted in gothic type and may be termed a 'fort', 'settlement', 'rath' or perhaps even 'homestead' for smaller defended sites; or it may bear its given name in gothic type, such as 'The Bulwark' hillfort on north-west Gower (Fig 1.6). For ambiguous defensive sites which have been difficult for surveyors to interpret, the ramparts may simply be labelled 'earthworks' or even more blandly, 'enclosure', a term also used for medieval and later monuments.

Fig 1.9 Footings of a Bronze or Iron Age roundhouse on open moorland amongst prehistoric fields on the slopes below Carn-ingli hillfort, Pembrokeshire. On a map this may be described as a 'hut circle' or 'settlement'. Archaeologists may call this an 'open settlement' if associated with other houses nearby and not enclosed within a wider wall, bank or rampart. (T. Driver)

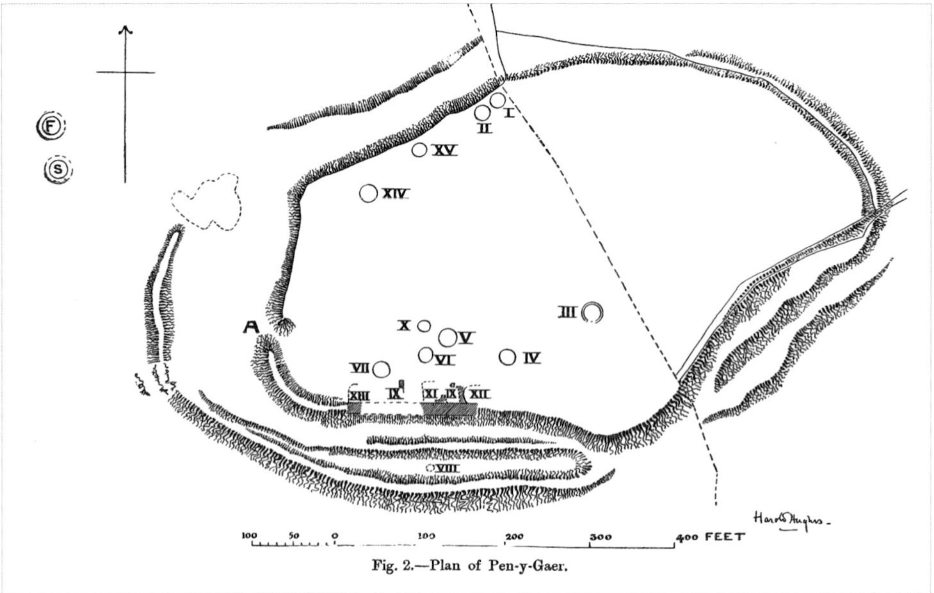

Fig 1.10 Early sketch survey of Pen y Gaer hillfort, Llanbedr-y-cennin, with hut sites numbered showing those excavated by Harold Hughes in September 1905. The quality of the plan is explained by Hughes: 'The whole of the day, from early morning till dusk, was fully occupied in supervising the excavations and noting the results. Although it is most desirable that a correct and detailed plan be made of the camp, it was quite out of the question in the limited time at our disposal.' (By kind permission of the Cambrian Archaeological Association)[7]

For much of the twentieth century in Wales, hillforts were labelled as 'fort' on Ordnance Survey maps reflecting their conventional interpretation as defended military sites. Confusion crept in later in the 1950s and 1960s with the rise of the 'New Archaeology' movement (see below) and the dismissal of earlier 'invasion theories' which led to a push to remove the implication that all hillforts were originally designed for defence. Therefore Iron Age hillforts clearly sited in a defensive position on the edge of a cliff or inland promontory retained the defensive term 'fort', whilst others sited on gentler slopes were renamed 'settlements', with a defensive role no longer implied by the name. This in itself raises problems. At the time of writing, perfectly acceptable small hillforts like Moel Goedog above Harlech are still termed 'settlement' on maps, a term at odds with their strategic hilltop positions.

RATH, GAER, DINAS AND CASTELL

Older traditional names for hillforts are common where Welsh remains in everyday use. One regional name still used in Pembrokeshire is 'rath', originally an Irish term. Today we may assume Pembrokeshire 'raths' to be broadly similar to other later prehistoric defended farmsteads in west Wales. However Irish archaeologist Michael J. O'Kelly, writing about Irish hillforts in 1970, which can be called ringforts or cashels (Fig 5.17), noted the very specific descriptive meaning behind the term 'rath':

> The Reverend Professor Shaw ... has made a study of the contexts of these words, ráth, lios, dún, etc., with interesting results. For instance the context of ráth shows that it was always dug. This must mean that a ditch was dug and the material from it was thrown up to form the bank. The word lios apparently meant the space enclosed by the ráth. The teach, that is the house, was a free-standing structure in the lios.[8]

Irish hillforts were generally built in the equivalent of our Bronze Age, and during the Early Medieval Period, rather than during the Iron Age as in Britain. Yet, the breakdown of these names reveals an interesting deeper meaning for the term 'rath' as a 'dug enclosure', as opposed to a rampart built as a free-standing wall or of scree, like Garn Goch hillfort in Carmarthenshire. The further terminology to describe the space enclosed by the rampart, the lios and the house within, the teach, are valuable distinctions showing how enclosure of living space was conceived in early Ireland. It shows that different names may have been applied to different types of defended enclosure in prehistoric Wales, each name perhaps describing subtleties of construction, siting and use.

The Welsh language gives us many names for hilltop enclosures and fortified prehistoric settlements and is equally rich in subtlety and description. Willoughby Gardner discussed some of these variations in his 1926 presidential address to the Cambrian Archaeological Association about the hillforts of north Wales:

> The names which these particular hill-forts doubtless once possessed have become entirely forgotten and lost. This itself marks them down as very ancient. Many others are known by the terms Caer and Dinas only – best translated, perhaps, as fort and walled town ... Dunum was the original Celtic name for a hill-fort, as found spread over ancient Gaul; in Ireland and in Scotland we have Dun, and in Wales Din, or, later, Dinas.[9]

Common names for hillforts include 'Caer' or 'Gaer' for a fort, 'Castell', literally 'castle' but often describing Iron Age forts, and 'Dinas' originally meaning 'walled settlement, fort or camp', now the modern Welsh word for city (this term is echoed in Scotland and Ireland through the use of 'dun' for a stronghold or fort, as Gardner relates). Individual site names can be highly descriptive of their particular topographic setting. For example Foel Trigarn hillfort in the Preseli hills of Pembrokeshire means '(The) three cairns on the bald/ bare summit'; Pen y Crug hillfort near Brecon means 'Mound (or a distinctly flat-topped mound or hillock) at the top or 'head of' the hill', and the famous hillfort of Penycloddiau high in the Clwydian hills of north-east Wales literally means 'The hill of many ditches' or 'At the top of the ditches', an apt description (see Fig 1.22).

Fig 1.11 Bilingual sign for Castell Henllys Iron Age village in Pembrokeshire. (T. Driver)

Other names for Welsh hillforts invoke distant legends: thus Dinas Dinlle coastal fort near Caernarfon, Gwynedd is associated in Early Medieval Welsh legends of the Mabinogi as the home of Lleu Llaw Gyffes, so the fort is literally named 'The fort ('din' in old Welsh meaning fort') of 'Lle' short for Lleu'. Some archaeologists have suggested the medieval storyteller may have fitted their narrative around a pre-existing site name. The splendid scree-built hillfort of Caer Drewyn, Corwen in north-east Wales is first named around AD 1600 where its construction is attributed to the hero or giant Drewyn Gawr (see Chapter 8).

In the past the name of the great stone hillfort at the northern end of the Llŷn peninsula, Tre'r Ceiri, was thought to have been derived from 'cewri', the plural of 'cawr' or giant in Welsh; thus it was boldly named 'Giant's Town' or 'The Town of the Giants' in the Royal Commission's 1960 Caernarvonshire Inventory. However, reinterpretation of the name in 2022 by Dr James January-McCann of the Royal Commission suggested it actually means 'Town of the Fortresses', with Ceiri being a variant plural form of Caerau, as originally used by Thomas Pennant in the eighteenth century.[10] This removes the notion of giants from the name and better reflects the appearance of multiple walls, gates and houses on this rocky summit, truly a place of many 'fortresses' (see Chapter 8).

WELSH PLACE-NAMES AND ARCHAEOLOGY

Welsh place-names are a great source of detailed topographic description and meaning, especially when it comes to the names of hillforts and archaeological sites. It is good to know the basics of Welsh place names, and how to correctly pronounce them, if you aim to research the archaeology of Wales further, if only to understand a little more about the nuances of the local landscape. Landowners around the country will also look kindly on visitors to their sites and monuments if they have managed to master some of the basic Welsh greetings before arrival.

Allt (or gallt)	hillside or wood
Bach/ fach	small
Banc	mound, bank or hillock
Bannau	peaks
Bedd	grave
Braich	literally 'arm', often 'promontory'
Bryn	hill
Bwlch	gap or pass
Caer (Gaer), Caerau	fort, forts (often mutated with a 'g')
Carreg, Cerrig	stone, stones
Carn, Carneddau	cairn, cairns
Castell	castle
Cefn	ridge
Clawdd	bank, hedge, ditch
Cnwch	small tump
Coch, goch	red
Craig	rock or crag
Crug	mound, cairn
Ddu	black
Dinas	fort or camp (now 'city')
Disgwylfa	watching place or 'lookout'
Esgair	mountain ridge
Fawr (mawr)	big
Foel (moel)	bare-topped hill
Hen	old
Mynydd	mountain
Nant	stream or small valley
Pant	hollow or valley
Pen	head of, or top
Tan	below
Tomen	mound

Emerging from a land of myth: from antiquarians to archaeologists

> *... the first real beginning was made in 1903, when Baring-Gould and Burnard, assisted by Mr. Harold Hughes, made extensive excavations in Tre'r Ceiri with good results.*
>
> Willoughby Gardner, 1926[11]

Hillforts have been attracting antiquarian attention since at least the seventeenth century when Edward Lhwyd (1669–1709) sent out questionnaires on Welsh antiquities, place-names and local geography to correspondents in parishes to compile his *Parochialia* – a summary of answers to parochial queries. Donald Moore quotes one of these early replies which described the hillfort of Castle Ditches in the parish of Llancarfan, Vale of Glamorgan, then of unknown date: 'Some old works or Bulwarks on ye fford farm ... call'd by ye name of Castle ditches wh. encircles 14 or 15 acres of land ... we have no account nor tradition for it'.[12] Lhwyd subsequently used the information he had gathered to revise the Welsh section of *Camden's Britannia* for the new 1695 edition, through which we have preserved some of these very early records of the great archaeological monuments of Wales, a number of which are no longer extant.

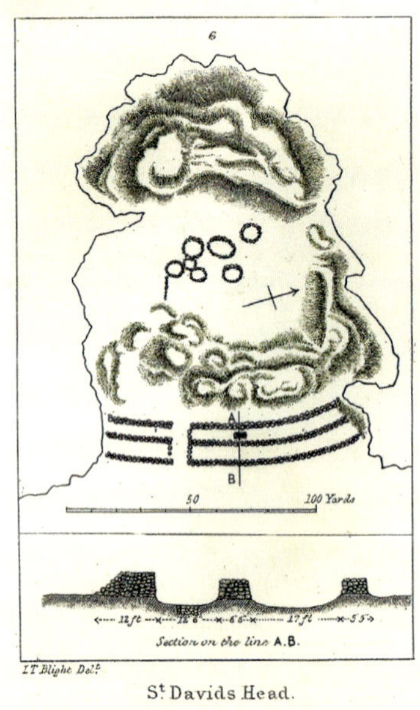

Fig 1.12 Survey of St David's Head coastal promontory fort, one of a number of new site plans to accompany Reverend Barnwell's overview of the site type in Pembrokeshire in 1875. (By kind permission of the Cambrian Archaeological Association)[14]

Many antiquarians and travel writers noted hillforts in the landscape, but few were as perceptive as Thomas Pennant (1726–98) who described many of the hillforts of Gwynedd and Clwyd in his *Tour in Wales* published in parts between 1778–84. These tours were illustrated with wash drawings and engravings of a number of key hillforts which form a valuable record today. Of Tre'r Ceiri on the Llŷn Peninsula he was amazed by what he saw: 'On the Eifl is the most perfect and magnificent, as well as the most artfully constructed British post I ever beheld'. He noted huts of 'various forms; round, oval, oblong, square' and noted similar cells on Garn Boduan hillfort nearby.[13]

Despite a growing body of evidence of a Roman or pre-Roman date for many of these ancient earthworks, fundamental questions remained at the end of the nineteenth century about the exact date and nature of occupation of the Welsh hillforts. In 1875 Reverend Barnwell was still debating the origins and dating of the coastal promontory forts of Pembrokeshire within the only frameworks available to him.[15] He rehearsed some familiar arguments which prevailed at the time: that the coastal promontory forts were built by Danish or Saxon pirates as 'temporary depositories of plunder ...' or that they were built by invading Irish who, '... would probably find it necessary to protect themselves against their Welsh neighbours by erecting these earthworks'.[16] Yet he cited new archaeological work then emerging on the very similar coastal forts of the Finistère coast, western Brittany, where evidence had been found of a 'Gaulish town' destroyed by the Romans. Finds from this French work included 'clay spindle-whorls' which Barnwell noted were exactly similar to those found in excavations on the Ty Mawr hut settlement near Holyhead, confirming what appeared to be a Late Iron Age, pre-Roman, date for these settlements.

Fig. 5.—Wall and Parapet, Treceiri.

Fig 1.13 In 1897 a Dr Christison spent a 'few hours' visiting Tre'r Ceiri hillfort, and recorded his thoughts and sketches in a published article. The main object of the article, he wrote, was to reproduce his drawings '... because there can be no question that the illustrations hitherto published are totally inadequate ... [my] drawings have no other merit than a certain rude faithfulness, but I trust they may stimulate others more skilled with the pencil, or still better ... the camera.' (By kind permission of the Cambrian Archaeological Association)[17]

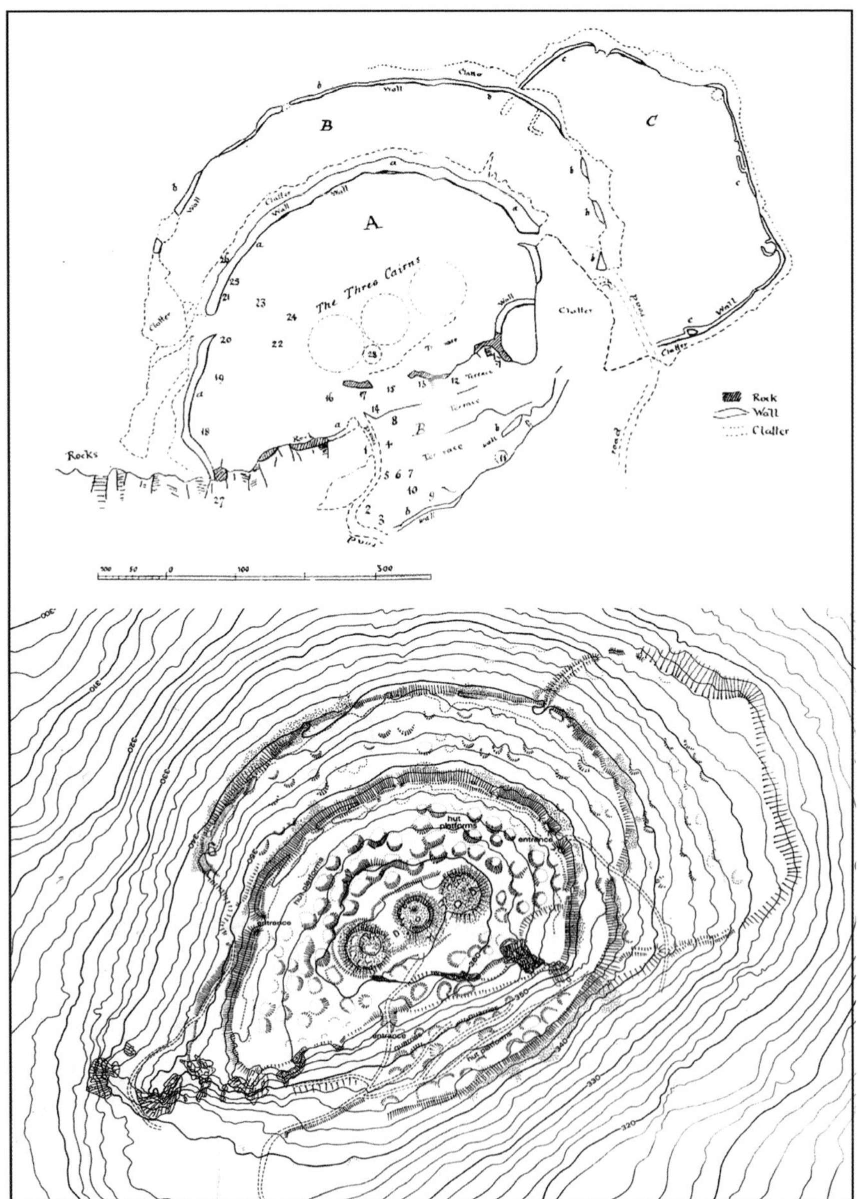

Fig 1.14 Striving for accuracy at Foel Trigarn hillfort, Pembrokeshire. The upper survey of the hillfort was made by Baring-Gould's team in 1899 during their excavations. The lower plan was made in 1988 by the Royal Commission and Portsmouth University by combining the results of photogrammetric aerial survey with a new ground survey. Despite nearly a century between them and a gulf in technology, Baring-Gould's survey still looks remarkably accurate for its day. (TOP: By kind permission of the Cambrian Archaeological Association; BOTTOM: © Crown copyright: RCAHMW. NPRN 94948. DI2006_0507)

In a bid for new scientific understanding and, crucially, a quest to employ better standards of archaeological fieldwork, several pioneering individuals began new projects at the turn of the century, surveying, mapping, excavating and publishing many hillforts for the first time. These included major Welsh hillforts like Foel Trigarn in the Preseli hills, St David's Head promontory fort, Pembrokeshire, Tre'r Ceiri on Llŷn and Caer Drewyn in north-east Wales. The energy and enthusiasm of these early antiquarian archaeologists is reflected in the fact that many of these famous sites have not been revisited by archaeologists in the intervening century. That said, the techniques of 1900, where relatively unskilled workmen would be set to clearing a roundhouse in a day or two with picks and shovels, is nothing compared to the demands of scientific excavation in the present day. Much was missed or poorly recorded and misunderstood in these early forays.

Towards the end of the nineteenth century, Reverend Sabine Baring-Gould, best known for writing the hymn 'Onward, Christian Soldiers', had travelled north from Devon with Robert Burnard and members of the Dartmoor Exploration Committee to bring their considerable expertise in prehistoric remains to bear on the question of Welsh hillforts. In July 1898 he and his team commenced excavations and survey work on St David's Head promontory fort in Pembrokeshire and he describes the method of excavation in the published report:

> The manner of digging was as follows: the turf was first skimmed off the surface and placed on the walls to be re-laid when the hut was finished. ... Each section was trenched to at least 2 ft; the soil was then sifted and replaced ... at a later period ... [the workmen] became so expert that nothing escaped them.[18]

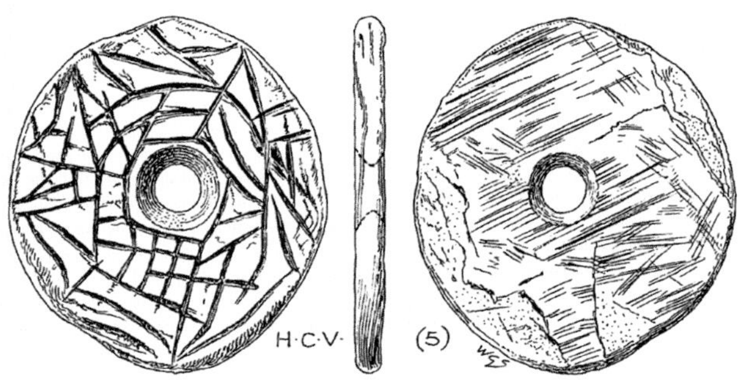

(By kind permission of the Cambrian Archaeological Association)

Fig 1.15 Personal objects: a decorated spindle whorl discovered during the 1898 excavations of roundhouse 5 at St David's Head promontory fort. Sabine Baring-Gould noted: 'It is highly ornamented on one side with deep incisions, forming curves, angles and squares.'[19]

Despite these excavations, chronological uncertainties remained. When discussing the St David's Head work, Baring-Gould noted: '... the remains may appertain even to the late Celtic period, but before this can be stated with any degree of certainty further exploration in similar camps with stone ramparts, as, for example, Carn Fawr and Moel Trigarn [now Foel Trigarn], should be undertaken'.[20]

A year later in June 1899 he returned to direct a new excavation on another north Pembrokeshire hillfort, Foel Trigarn in the Preseli hills.[21] His motives for clarity on chronological and cultural questions were clear from the start:

> Whether erected by the natives as strongholds and look-out places against invaders, or whether thrown up by a people who had landed on this coast, and had obtained a footing, and were resolved on permanent occupation cannot as yet be determined.[22]

Baring-Gould's full report on his excavations at Foel Trigarn makes fascinating reading. He was at pains to note the care that his excavation team took during their work, under the strictest supervision:

> [The team] ... devoted fourteen working days mainly to the examination of the hut-sites; and during nearly the whole of this time six men were busily occupied ... the rule that the workmen should do nothing except under close supervision, from the time they commenced in the morning until they ceased work in the evening, was strictly adhered to.[23]

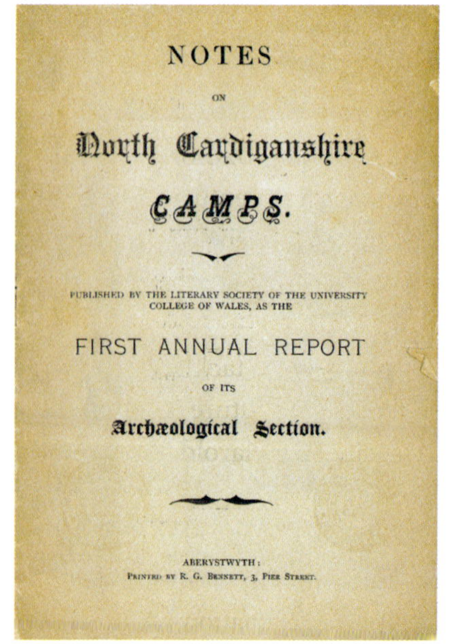

NOTES

ON

North Cardiganshire

CAMPS.

PUBLISHED BY THE LITERARY SOCIETY OF THE UNIVERSITY COLLEGE OF WALES, AS THE

FIRST ANNUAL REPORT

OF ITS

Archæological Section.

ABERYSTWYTH:
PRINTED BY R. G. BENNETT, 3, PIER STREET.

Fig 1.16 Early aspirations evident in a 1900 pamphlet of the Archaeology Section of the Literary Society of the University College of Wales, Aberystwyth, setting out its plans to investigate the local hillforts; imminent parallel reports on the flora and fauna of the district were also promised by the Scientific Society. (T. Driver, with thanks to Gerald Morgan)

Fig 1.17 The ambition of the 1930s. The 1934 excavations of Pen Dinas hillfort, Aberystwyth, directed by a young and ambitious Professor Daryll Forde – then Gregynog Professor of Geography and Anthropology at Aberystwyth University. The project took place in the Depression era, providing valuable seasonal work for local labourers. This view shows an array of intersecting trenches designed to investigate the isthmus gateway, and also groups of onlookers. In 2023, the Dyfed Archaeological Trust reinvestigated Forde's trenches here with new community excavations. (© Crown copyright: RCAHMW. NPRN 92236. DI2015_0403)

THE HILLFORT DECADES: 1900–39

The twentieth century saw archaeological work in Britain rapidly develop from a pastime to a science with a flurry of new projects in the early decades. A number of Welsh hillforts were explored. Baring-Gould and Robert Burnard progressed from their Pembrokeshire investigations to excavate at Tre'r Ceiri hillfort on Llŷn in 1903,[24] tackling 32 'cytiau' or roundhouses with gusto and leaving the defences for a future investigation. Three years later the Cambrian Archaeological Association's Harold Hughes returned to carry out further excavations at this great stone hillfort,[25] setting a pattern for revisits and study at this particular site over the twentieth century.

The 1920s and 1930s saw a considerable expansion in hillfort surveys and excavations as a fascination with these ancient fortifications gripped Britain. During the

1920s a number of projects commenced including Harold Hughes' investigations at the now destroyed stone hillfort at Braich y Dinas, Penmaenmawr, and Willoughby Gardner's survey at Caer Drewyn (see Chapter 8). In 1926 Willoughby Gardner delivered a seminal and wide-ranging Presidential Address to the Cambrians on the state of research on the 'Native Hill-forts' of north Wales,[26] which remains an insightful paper describing the advances in thought and study up until that point.

The beginnings of 'modern' Iron Age research owe much to the publication of an important paper in 1931 by Christopher Hawkes. In the years before precise dating was available, Hawkes introduced a classificatory scheme for the British Iron Age into A, B and C, describing a sequence of invasion, assimilation and 'immigrant cultures' which he proposed were responsible for introducing hillforts to the British Isles. This spurred archaeologists on to mount new excavations on hillforts, and to focus on oft-rebuilt sections of the defences like gateways, to gain evidence for invasion events and to help develop regional cultural sequences.

Against the background of Sir Mortimer Wheeler's and Tessa Verney Wheeler's 1930s campaigns at Maiden Castle in Dorset, various new excavations with a more scientific focus on trench design, stratigraphy and finds recovery were started. Prior to the hiatus of the Second World War, there were a number of new hillfort excavations including that at Pen Dinas hillfort in Aberystwyth under Professor Daryll Forde between 1933–37, at The Knave coastal promontory fort on Gower in 1938 directed by Audrey Williams[27] and campaigns at Llanmelin Camp in 1930–2 and Sudbrook promontory fort on the Severn Estuary in 1934–6, both directed by V.E. Nash-Williams. Nash-Williams employed what archaeologist Graeme Guilbert termed 'extreme trenching': laying out very narrow trenches on an almost military scale seemingly regardless of terrain or the scale of the hillfort ramparts.[28] This was the prevailing fashion of the time; yet, while sections could be obtained across entire defensive schemes, there was often too little space inside the trench to accurately see or understand the complex archaeology being cut through.

Several of these projects adopted the latest technology; Nash-Williams included pioneering aerial photographs in his Sudbrook report whilst Daryll Forde appears to have had his Aberystwyth excavations specially flown by the Royal Air Force in 1933 and 1934, perhaps as a training exercise.[29] More encouraging was the rebalancing of gender in the previously male-dominated world of Welsh archaeology. Not only was Audrey Williams directing an excavation in south Wales but Nash-Williams prominently thanked a number of women who worked on key tasks for his Sudbrook project.

Fig 1.18 Llanmelin Wood hillfort in south-east Wales was surveyed by Mortimer Wheeler in 1923 and extensively trenched in early excavations by V.E. Nash-Williams in 1930–32. The narrow trenches revealed little about the development of the fort but recovered many datable finds including rare inhumation burials from the unusual boxed-annexe which adjoins the main camp. The hillfort saw new excavations by Cadw in 2012 and was re-surveyed in 2015 by the Royal Commission. The combination of burials with an unusual hillfort annexe structure has led some archaeologists to suggest Llanmelin may have had a role as a centre of ceremony, burial or for the excarnation of bodies in the Iron Age. (© Crown copyright: RCAHMW. NPRN 301559. AP_2015_1081)

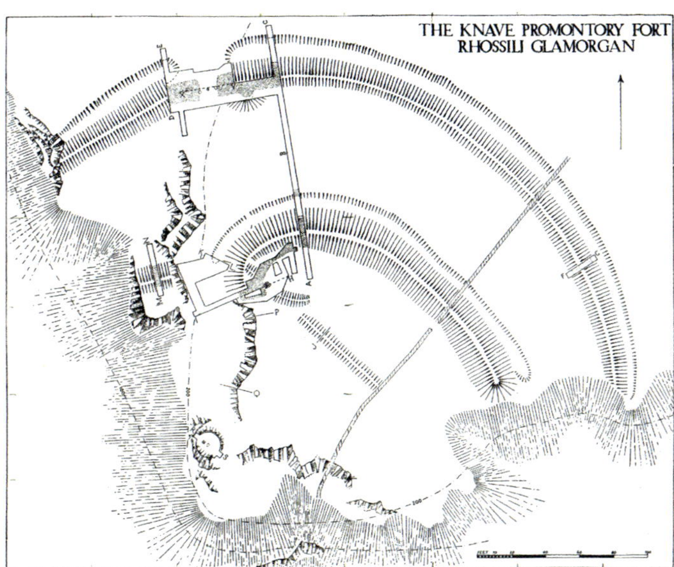

Fig 1.19 Site plan from Audrey Williams' 1938 excavations of The Knave on Gower, showing a developing technique to excavation in the 1930s. Running section trenches were cut to study relative phasing of features, whilst wider area trenches were opened where structures needed to be examined in plan, as with the gateway to the north. (By kind permission of the Cambrian Archaeological Association)[29]

A NEW QUEST FOR PROCESS AND PRECISION

By the end of the 1950s a wealth of new excavated evidence and new thought began to weaken the influence of Christopher Hawkes' invasion theories. This previously robust argument, citing waves of immigrant settlement to British shores from the continent, was undermined by new evidence for greater regional differences across the British Isles which could not be easily explained by one simple theoretical model. There were also questions of how far continental invaders had actually shaped the Iron Age of Britain, with new evidence emerging for the indigenous, early development of our own monuments in the Late Bronze Age. Coupled with these changes there was a quest for the deeper integration of process and analysis into archaeology, influenced by the 'New Geography' movement. Archaeologists following this 'processual' approach termed the 'New Archaeology', began to study hillforts and settlements at a landscape scale, using statistics to break hillfort groups into zones of influence with market centres and emphasising the economic and social power of hillforts as 'central places' with a role in the redistribution of goods. While these developments undoubtedly brought new scientific direction to the study of Iron Age Britain they have also been seen by some, with hindsight, to have had a rather dehumanising effect to the study of the past, reducing people and places to systems and statistics.[31]

Hillfort studies in Wales continued to develop from the 1960s to the 1990s. New Inventories of ancient monuments were compiled and published by the Royal Commission on the Ancient and Historical Monuments of Wales for several counties of Wales, giving researchers standardised accounts and surveys of buildings and monuments. The key inventories of modern times are those for Caernarvonshire (1960), Glamorgan (1976) and Brecknock (1986); for many monuments the surveys have not been bettered. Archaeology in Wales was put on a more solid footing from the mid-1970s with the formation of the network of regional Welsh Archaeological Trusts in Gwynedd, Dyfed, Clwyd-Powys and Glamorgan-Gwent between 1974–76. This network was instigated by the Ancient Monuments Branch of the Department of the Environment, partly based on the success of the Rescue Archaeology Group (RAG) formed in 1970.[32] The formation of the Trusts was followed a decade later by the founding of the new state body for heritage, Cadw, in 1984 to manage guardianship monuments, to legislate and to fund new programmes of threat-led research. Throughout the 1980s and 1990s many programmes of excavation and survey were funded around the country through the work of the Welsh Archaeological Trusts, including ground-breaking

Fig 1.20 Threat-related excavations were carried out at the Collfryn defended enclosure near Welshpool in Montgomeryshire in 1980–82 by the Clwyd-Powys Archaeological Trust. The third century BC defended farming settlement was discovered in pasture in 1976 but began to be ploughed shortly after. This aerial photograph was taken in 1981, when the unexcavated half of the enclosure was showing as a cropmark. Excavations revealed evidence for metalworking, animal husbandry and a complex development of houses within the multiple-ditched enclosure. The ditches may have been one way that prehistoric and Roman occupants coped with waterlogging across this low-lying, clay-bound site. (Clwyd-Powys Archaeological Trust. © CPAT Photo Number: 81-007-0034)

threat-related excavations of a small group of hillforts at Llawhaden in Pembrokeshire (Fig 5.28)[33] and at the lowland cropmark enclosure at Collfryn, near Welshpool in Montgomeryshire (Fig 1.20).[34]

The early 1990s saw something of a shift in British Iron Age studies as younger researchers began to react against what they saw as a stagnation of critical thought. In 1989, archaeologist J.D. Hill published a groundbreaking paper for Britain entitled 'Re-thinking the Iron Age', which signalled a shift away from established opinion. It sought to focus more attention on the strange, complex and 'other' aspects of Iron Age society.[35] In his opening statement he was blunt: 'The Iron Age is boring, particularly when compared to earlier periods of prehistory, which seem stimulating and exciting'. He was concerned that the 'Celtic' narrative of a 'familiar' Iron Age past of villages, farms, cooking and crafts did not adequately explain evidence for many more unusual and strange rituals that were commonly unearthed during excavations of Iron Age sites in southern England. He proposed 'A Different Iron Age' founded in a deeper appreciation of the complexities of

Fig 1.21 New ways of digging. Community excavations by DigVentures on the National Trust and Pembrokeshire Coast National Park-owned Caerfai promontory fort, Pembrokeshire, September 2022, where professional archaeologists worked alongside members of the local community and students. The excavations continued a project initiated by the CHERISH Project in 2021, designed to study the eroding interior of this previously unexcavated site before more is lost to the sea. (T. Driver)

ethnography and an enhanced theoretical approach to the material culture – where and how finds including pottery and bones were discovered around a site. Following this influential paper there was a push to rebalance Iron Age studies away from a 'familiar' Celtic past and towards new and challenging interpretations of the settlement evidence. Previously hard lines between religious/ ritual and practical/ domestic spheres were effectively removed, acknowledging the strangeness of life and monuments in Iron Age Britain.[36]

Understanding hillforts in twenty-first century Wales

The study of Welsh hillforts, and the Welsh Iron Age, has enjoyed something of a resurgence in the last 20 years since the turn of the millennium. In 2001 leading archaeologists published a Research Agenda for the British Iron Age[37] which set out five priority themes for research: (1) chronological frameworks, (2) settlement patterns, (3) material culture, (4) regionality and (5) socio-economic changes. There was a drive towards the better recovery of finds (or 'material culture') from Iron Age sites in the hope that this could shed better light on how hillforts, enclosures, homes and villages were peopled and used. There was also a reinvigoration in the way hillforts and defended settlements were researched with a greater recognition of regional differences in the British Iron Age, and the non-defensive aspects behind monumental ramparts and ditches – themes explored later in this book. The process

Fig 1.22 Large-scale research excavations in progress on the north-east gateway and ramparts of Penycloddiau hillfort, Clwyd, by Liverpool University in July 2015. Compare with Fig 5.18. (© Crown copyright: RCAHMW. NPRN 500539. AP_2015_2650)

for a Research Framework for the Archaeology of Wales began in the same year and has grown and strengthened with each new revision and iteration, in particular bringing new questions to the study of Later Bronze Age and Iron Age monuments and landscapes. At a British scale, the *Hillfort Atlas Project*, described above, saw important new baseline work by Oxford and Edinburgh Universities, arriving at an updated and standardised database of the hillforts of Britain and Ireland.

Alongside these advances there has been a new drive to make hillforts the centrepiece of community and heritage projects. In 2007 Denbighshire County Council were successful in receiving funding for the three-year Lottery-funded 'Heather and Hillforts' Landscape Partnership Scheme which embraced six of Wales' most important hillforts which command the heather-clad moorland of the Clwydian Range: Penycloddiau, Moel Arthur, Moel y Gaer, Llanbedr, Moel Fenlli, Moel y Gaer, Llantysilio and Caer Drewyn. The legacy of this project can still be seen in visitor signage, car parking and erosion-resistant stone-and-timber pathways which guide visitors up to the hillforts. In south Wales CAER Heritage, established in 2011, raised the profile of one of south Wales's largest hillforts in the heart of Cardiff by embracing the community which lives around it. Caerau hillfort was an unexcavated and overgrown hillfort rising above the deprived community of Ely, Cardiff. Despite commanding a prominent plateau it had almost been entirely forgotten by generations of archaeologists. The project began with a

Fig 1.23 Building new communities through hillfort research: the CAER Heritage Community Centre, Cardiff, in 2022. The community building can be seen just beyond the hillfort-themed gateway into a play area at the heart of Ely community. Waymarked paths from this community centre lead visitors up to the multivallate hillfort. (T. Driver)

visit from the Time Team in 2012 who mapped the interior with geophysics and made the first tentative excavations. With subsequent funding work has grown with the involvement of Cardiff University, local schools, community groups and others, culminating in the construction of a new hillfort-themed community centre.[38] CAER Heritage is a flagship for what could be possible at other Welsh and British hillforts, revitalising both neglected Iron Age archaeology and challenged communities in a single long-running initiative.

As this book was being written there were a number of hillfort and promontory fort excavations taking place right across Wales, all involving professional archaeologists working alongside members of the community, volunteers and students. The last decade alone has seen many major projects carried out on Welsh hillforts including, but not limited to: Penycloddiau and Moel y Gaer, Bodfari, hillforts in the Clwydian Range by Liverpool and Oxford universities respectively; at Moel Fodig hillfort, Clwyd and the Mellionydd defended enclosure, Llŷn, by Bangor University; at Llanmelin Wood hillfort by Cadw and the Royal Commission; at Beacon Ring hillfort, Powys, by the Clwyd-Powys Archaeological Trust; at Dinas Dinlle hillfort, Gwynedd, by the CHERISH Project, Cadw, The National Trust and Gwynedd Archaeological Trust; and at Porth y Rhaw promontory fort, Pembrokeshire and Pen Dinas hillfort, Aberystwyth, by the Dyfed Archaeological Trust.

A range of other non-hillfort projects have also shed new light on the prehistoric landscapes of Wales, including the Five Mile Lane landscape investigation in south Wales by Rubicon Heritage Services Ltd, the Skomer Island Project by the Royal Commission, Cardiff, Aberystwyth and Sheffield Universities, the discovery and excavation (2018) of the Pembrokeshire chariot burial by National Museum Wales, Dyfed Archaeological Trust and Cadw, and the continuing work of the

Portable Antiquities Scheme across Wales, which seeks to investigate the findspots of newly-discovered artefacts and Treasure cases as they arise.

FINDING HILLFORTS: ADVANCES IN SURVEY AND PROSPECTION

Our ways of discovering, mapping and understanding Iron Age and Roman sites in Wales have developed considerably in the last 20 years. There have been major advances in 'remote sensing' and prospection technologies; techniques which allow us to see and discover more about prehistoric sites in Wales without actually breaking the ground. These form part of a wider 'toolkit' approach for investigating the archaeological landscape. One of the best ways to survey many tens of kilometres of the archaeological landscape is by using **airborne remote sensing**, a term which encompasses a range of techniques from traditional aerial survey, to airborne laser scanning and drone or Uncrewed Aerial Vehicle (UAV) survey.

Aerial survey or aerial photography has a long history, with the first archaeological aerial photographs taken in Britain of Stonehenge using a tethered army war-balloon in 1906. As aircraft technology developed during the 1920s and 1930s so did the work of pioneering aerial photographers like Major George Allen who recorded ancient monuments across southern England and Wales from 1933 until 1939. The technique proved particularly effective as – from an elevated perspective – complex patterns of earthwork ditches and banks resolved themselves into clear overviews of henge monuments, hillforts and prehistoric field systems. Even more remarkable were the effects seen in summer droughts, when crops under stress grew taller and greener over plough-levelled ditches, or withered and turned yellow over stony buried remains like old walls and roads. These colour differences, known as **cropmarks**, were found to reveal sites which were completely invisible from the air at all other times of year. Conversely, low winter light was found to reveal **shadow sites** as differences in light and shade, picking out faint traces of almost ploughed-out prehistoric monuments and medieval settlements.

Today archaeological aerial reconnaissance using a light aircraft or helicopter is still relied upon as a standard method of national survey across Britain and Europe, to discover previously unknown monuments and to closely monitor the condition of known sites. Many sites can be surveyed in an hour with a light aircraft travelling around 130 knots, regardless of terrain or access. In record drought summers, which are happening more frequently as an effect of human-induced climate change, hundreds of nationally important archaeological sites may be discovered as cropmarks in the spring and summer months.

Fig 1.24 How cropmarks can reveal lost archaeological sites from the air:

TOP: Iron Age defended farmstead around 100BC with a deep outer ditch dug through the subsoil, and a rampart of earth and stone

MIDDLE: The same site in the 1970s. The prehistoric farm has collapsed to form low earthworks, or 'lumps and bumps' in the field, and the farmer is ploughing the pasture to plant crops

BOTTOM: The field today. While the ground surface is ploughed flat and all traces of the prehistoric site have vanished, drought summers place the ripening crop under stress. The crop grows taller and greener over buried ditches with their deeper soil but turns ripe and yellow over stony material. These differences are best seen from above

(© Crown copyright: RCAHMW. DI2006_1443C)

Aerial survey in all its forms has been expanded in the last 20 years by the magic that is **Airborne Laser Scanning** or **LiDAR** (Light Detection And Ranging) and the ready availability of **drone** or **UAV surveys**. LiDAR technology was originally developed by the military but has been employed over the last 20 years and more for the accurate mapping of terrain, particularly for flood risk management. A large survey aircraft flies over the required area with a scanning laser sweeping the ground thousands of times a second. Data is stored by computers which then cancel out the pitch, roll and yaw effects of the aircraft in flight through reference

Fig 1.25 (LEFT) Extracting hidden information from aerial photographs. Rebalancing the colour bands hidden within digital aerial photographs can highlight new information, particularly for parchmarks in grassland. The pictures show Cilifor Top hillfort on north Gower in the drought summer of 2018. (RIGHT) The rebalanced (now monochrome) image shows new structural details of the defences invisible on the colour image, including a great curving ditch crossing the interior: possibly an early phase promontory-edge enclosure. New ditches are also revealed in the foreground of the image, in the area of the south-eastern annexe of the hillfort. There is no public access to the hillfort. (© Crown copyright: RCAHMW. NPRN 301311. AP_2018_5077)

to ground survey stations and orbiting satellites. The result is a 3D model of the ground surface accurate to 25cm and better, showing every subtle change in height and terrain (Fig 1.26).

The real power of LiDAR data for archaeology is threefold. Firstly it can be used to map large or remote areas to a high degree of accuracy, often providing data more accurately than rural Ordnance Survey base mapping allows. Secondly it can be used to 'magically' remove trees and vegetation from wooded or overgrown landscapes, frequently revealing entirely hidden archaeological monuments for the first time (Fig 1.26). The first laser points which strike the top of trees, buildings and other vegetation are deleted from the 3D model, leaving only the last points to hit the ground. This produces a model of the 'bare' land surface below woodland canopies, revealing hidden archaeology as a Digital Terrain Model. The third strength of LiDAR is the ability to light the 3D computer model in any way one wishes, effectively producing strong shadow-marks from any sun angle; even multiple sun angles and other effects can be used. This is one of the best ways to reveal and analyse earthwork archaeology in Welsh landscapes.

Fig 1.26 Revealing Caerau hillfort, Ely, Cardiff with airborne laser scanning or LiDAR

TOP: Caerau is heavily wooded and the ramparts have always remained hidden

MIDDLE AND BOTTOM: New LiDAR data flown for the Royal Commission and Cardiff University by the Environment Agency was analysed using specialist computer software, allowing archaeologists to 'strip away' the woodland canopy, leaving only those laser points which had hit the ground below the trees

The results were spectacular and helped to illustrate the 'hidden hillfort' for the first time to the community who live around it

(© Crown copyright: RCAHMW. Ibase ID: 180743 - LD2012_01_01. NPRN 94517)

The ultimate new technology which has benefitted archaeological aerial survey in recent years has been the use of **drones** or **UAVs** (**uncrewed aerial vehicles**). Developments have been so rapid that each year brings ever more capable drones for surveying, with new gadgets and abilities. Most archaeological companies in Britain are now equipped with at least one drone. Whilst the drone has immediate strengths in being rapidly launched to take high aerial views or videos of archaeological sites, it can also be programmed to carry out photogrammetric surveys. Here, hundreds

Fig 1.27 Using drone photogrammetry to accurately map the eroding coastal hillfort of Dinas Dinlle, Gwynedd. TOP: pre-programmed flight lines used to survey the fort for photogrammetry by CHERISH Project archaeologists. Lines of blue squares represent hundreds of overlapping aerial photos. BOTTOM: The resulting 3D digital model, capturing the eroding coast edge of this hillfort at a moment in time in incredible detail. (Visualisations by Dan Hunt for the CHERISH Project. © Crown: CHERISH PROJECT 2022. Produced with EU funds through the Ireland Wales Co-operation Programme 2014-2023. All material made freely available through the Open Government Licence.)

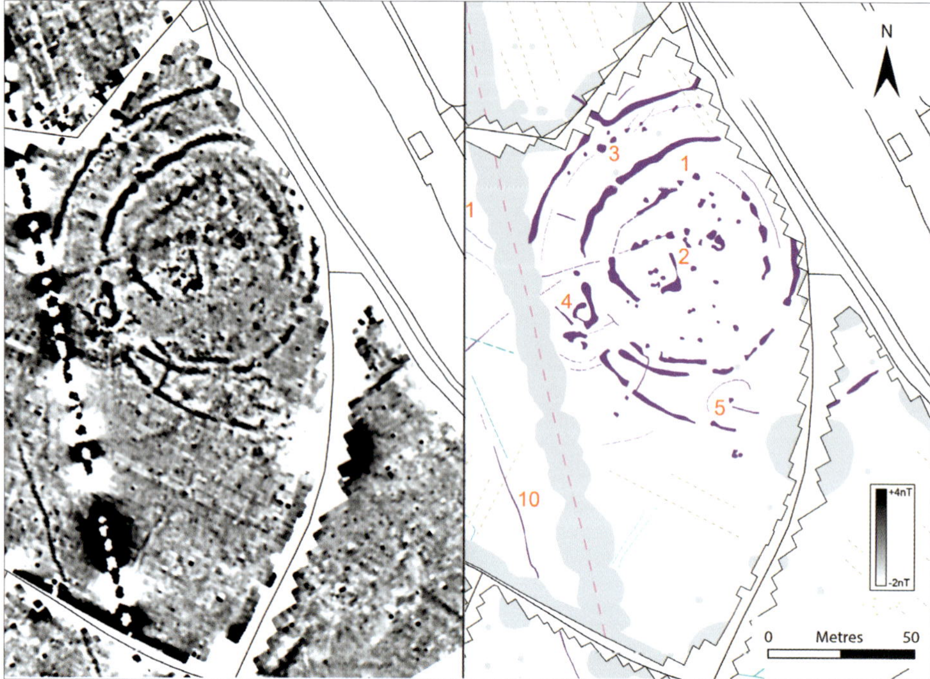

Fig 1.28 Geophysical survey (magnetometry) commissioned by the CHERISH Project to investigate a cropmark enclosure discovered during aerial survey in the 2018 drought summer at Abersoch, Gwynedd. Whilst cropmark evidence suggested it was a possible coastal Roman watchtower, the geophysics results suggested instead a later prehistoric date for the defended enclosure. The multiple enclosures measure 115m across. (© Crown: CHERISH PROJECT 2022. Produced with EU funds through the Ireland Wales Co-operation Programme 2014-2023. All material made freely available through the Open Government Licence. NPRN 423304)

of overlapping photographs are automatically taken in parallel lines over the survey area; these are then processed in powerful computer software which can 'pop up' highly detailed 3D models of the site. The drone complements regional or country-wide aerial survey in a light aircraft by providing an intermediate aerial survey and photography platform for local landscapes and individual sites.

To look more closely at archaeological sites one can use ground-based remote sensing or **geophysical prospection**. This is an essential tool to investigate unexcavated sites, or the buried components of larger archaeological monuments. The technique uses hand-held or cart-based electrical probes to pass currents through the ground surface. Onboard computers then measure and plot tiny disturbances in the earth's magnetic field to reveal hidden archaeological sites. Techniques like **magnetometry** can be very effective for plotting large areas of buried archaeology,

Fig 1.29 High resolution geophysical survey of the environs of Darren Camp hillfort, Ceredigion, by Wessex Archaeology for the Royal Commission in 2020. The metal-free geophysical cart is mounted with six Bartington gradiometer probes set at half-metre intervals, allowing rapid and accurate survey of almost any terrain. (T. Driver)

for example the interior of a hillfort, as the probes only have to be rapidly passed over the ground surface to take a reading. Magnetic differences include areas of burning or heated soil beneath the ground, such as hearths or furnaces, but also the fillings of ditches and postholes. Where one is seeking to discover buried stonework or lost buildings, **resistivity** can be a better technique but is slower. Here, electrical probes need to make contact with the ground to take an accurate measurement, meaning smaller survey areas are usually selected for this approach.

Ground Penetrating Radar or **GPR** is perhaps the ultimate technological solution to ground-based remote sensing. A transmitter and receiver are passed over an archaeological site, usually mounted on a quad bike or cart, whilst radio waves beam down below the soil. Wherever they are interrupted by buried archaeological features like stony surfaces or stone-built features, a response is produced. The great strength of GPR is its ability to 'time-slice' buried archaeology, producing very accurate depth-maps of what lies under the soil. One of the most recent GPR applications in Wales was a survey of the sandy interior of Dinas Dinlle coastal fort in Gwynedd by the company SUMO Survey for the CHERISH Project in 2019. Here the GPR survey produced a map of the hillfort interior, showing several buried stone roundhouses and yards connected by a series of cobbled roadways running in from the main gate. Where ground conditions are just right, advanced survey techniques like this can transform our understanding of buried or unexplored Iron Age sites in Wales.

THE FUTURE OF WELSH HILLFORTS

What will the future hold for Iron Age studies in Wales? Better technology provides archaeologists – and non-specialists – with ever more inventive ways to survey and analyse archaeological sites and landscapes. One can browse LiDAR, aerial imagery, historic maps and heritage databases online without leaving the house, discovering sites in one's own local landscape – and around the world. The paths to study archaeology are open to all nowadays via university courses, community excavations and endless online resources. However, costs to participate in field projects, excavations and taught courses have inevitably risen.

To advance the study of the Iron Age in Wales we should continue to ask new questions of old sites, particularly those excavated a century or more ago. New PhDs and new research projects show how far we have come since the days of the antiquarian archaeologists of the nineteenth century. Yet, as this book will show, there are still major gaps in our knowledge of Welsh prehistory. Important hillforts remain unexcavated and undated. Big questions also remain unanswered and uncertainty surrounds some of the significant changes in society and settlement that we see in the Welsh landscape between 1000BC and AD 500.

Some of the paths to answering these questions will begin in schools, with the next generation. The archaeology of the 'Celts and Romans' is an essential part of the story of how Wales developed as a nation and could be elevated out of primary schools, to be taught more at high school level. Better funding for our regional and national museums could also allow our very best prehistoric and Roman artefacts to be exhibited and housed in dedicated galleries with engaging, world-class displays. Access to hillforts in the countryside is improving every year with new waymarked paths and on-site interpretation opening up some of our best sites; but more can always be done to improve access and information at hundreds more field monuments. Only by sharing the results of archaeological research more widely, by engaging the wider public and the next generation of archaeologists and by recognising the role of the Iron Age in the wider story of Wales, will we significantly advance our understanding of the country's prehistory through the twenty-first century and beyond.

Fig 1.30 The 'Toolkit' approach to archaeological survey developed by the EU-funded Ireland-Wales CHERISH Project, an optimum way to document the past landscape which incorporates geographical approaches. Ideally, no one archaeological survey technique should be thought superior to the others. They are all part of the wider 'toolkit' of techniques that archaeologists deploy to properly survey past landscapes. The toolkit approach illustrated includes LiDAR (**1**), aircraft (**4**) and drone (**2**) aerial survey, terrestrial ground survey using GPS (**7**) and laser scanning (**9**), paleoenvironmental coring of wetland deposits (**6**), geophysical survey (**5**), excavation (**10**) and even marine survey (**11**) and underwater archaeology (**12**). Eroding coastal sites can also be explored using rope-access (**8**). Only using this combined approach, with each technique or a combination of techniques deployed as appropriate, can we advance an understanding of the archaeological past. (© Carys Tait/Carys-ink.com. Image created for the EU-funded CHERISH Project. © Crown: CHERISH PROJECT 2022. Produced with EU funds through the Ireland Wales Co-operation Programme 2014-2023. All material made freely available through the Open Government Licence)

Fig 1.31 New ways to map a hillfort: drone photogrammetry of Pen Dinas hillfort, Penparcau, Aberystwyth, flown in March 2023 by the Royal Commission for the Pendinas Hillfort Community Project. The centimetre-accurate rendered 3D model (TOP), mapped against surveyed ground 'control', is also shown as a Digital Surface Model (DSM) in the bottom image. (© Crown Copyright: RCAHMW NPRN 92236)

2 Iron Age Wales and the wider world

Fig 2.1 (PREVIOUS PAGE)
Trwyn Porth Dinllaen coastal promontory fort juts into the western seaways of Wales off the Llŷn Peninsula, Gwynedd, enclosing a sheltered anchorage in its eastern arm. It is a good candidate for a port of coastal trade during the Iron Age. An anchor from a first century BC Mediterranean ship was found offshore just 20km to the south-west, at Porth Felen, suggesting contact from distant lands (see Fig 2.15). (© Crown: CHERISH PROJECT 2022. Produced with EU funds through the Ireland Wales Co-operation Programme 2014-2023. All material made freely available through the Open Government Licence. CHE 3 May – Flight 1-218. NPRN 402783)

2

Most of the island is flat and overgrown with forests, although many of its districts are hilly. It bears grain, cattle, gold, silver, and iron ...

Strabo (Greek geographer) on Britain, *c*.7 BC,
in his *Geographica* (Geography), Book IV, Chapter V

WHAT glimpses do we have of the people and places of pre-Roman Wales? In the popular imagination prehistoric Britain was an untamed, forested wilderness before the Romans arrived to 'civilise' the country and its population. We now know that this is an outdated and inaccurate view. Prehistoric Wales in the later first millennium BC was a complex and diverse mosaic of different groups of people who presided over a well settled, farmed and owned landscape. The population traded far and wide and were well connected to international maritime trade routes along the west coast and inland river systems. They travelled overland to neighbouring regions of Britain to trade pottery, salt and fine goods and also to exchange ideas and cultural influences.

By definition, *pre-history* is the time before written records. While we have no written history of Iron Age Britain from its inhabitants, we do have vivid records of its land and people from early Greek and Roman writers. These include sketchy descriptions of the 'first contacts' of Greek mariners with Middle to Late Iron Age peoples of Wales, which, while necessarily brief, provide a tantalising record of western Britain three centuries before the Roman invasion. Even more enlightening, and thoroughly gripping for a modern reader, are the writings of the Roman historian Tacitus who documented the first century AD clashes between Romans and the native Iron Age British, describing the hillfort builders on the cusp of overwhelming change. Within the writings of Tacitus, there are the very first descriptions of the people of prehistoric Wales.

THE CELTIC QUESTION

The commonly-used term 'Celtic' to describe the Iron Age people of Wales, and Britain, is problematic. 'Celtic' has specific meanings but is commonly used to imply that the varied languages, cultures, peoples, artistic creations and religions of north-west Europe during the Iron Age were broadly similar, if not basically the same. It is a term often used to describe the hillforts, and hillfort builders, of Iron Age Wales.

Fig 2.2 A noble Iron Age face from Wales adorns a Late Iron Age decorative scabbard chape for a sword, probably dating to the first century AD. It was found near Talgarth in the Black Mountains and was recorded through the Portable Antiquities Scheme (PAS). For such a small object the detail is impressive. The PAS description notes: 'The faces are somewhat naturalistic but have long, raised oval eyes, defined by adjacent grooves and with raised brow ridges. The nose begins slender but expands to a raised tricorne, flanked by faceted cheeks. A linear, pointed oval groove depicts the mouth.' (Creator: PAS. Unique ID: NMGW-E6F3B0. Cropped, reorientated. This work is licensed under a Creative Commons Attribution 4.0 International License)

The problems with the term originated in the scholarship of the nineteenth and early twentieth centuries, which suggested Celtic culture emerged from the 'Celtic Cradle' of Austria and Switzerland, spreading outwards towards the peripheries of Europe. At the time it was thought that this culture, and the notion of hillforts, arrived via successive waves of invasion and settlement to the shores of Late Iron Age Britain, in turn 'civilising' the native population. This now outdated view suggested Celts were 'immigrant invaders' to Britain, whereas now we understand that many of our hillforts were 'homegrown' innovations from the Later Bronze Age onwards. When we ascribe the hillforts of Wales to the 'Celts', we take something away from the local and regional peoples who actually built them.

From the evidence we have it does not seem likely that the Iron Age people of the British Isles actually thought of themselves as 'Celts'. Archaeologists like Professor John Collis[1] who have studied the classical sources demolish the myth of the 'British Celt'. Both Greek and Roman writers consistently commented that the inhabitants of Britain were *like* Celts but were *not* Celts. Collis cites Caesar's writings on Gaul, ancient France, where Caesar noted that the Celts were a people occupying part of Gaul along with the Belgae and the Aquitani and were also found

Fig 2.3 The great stone rampart of Caer y Tŵr hillfort, Holy Island, Anglesey, commands wide views over the western seaways of north Wales. This image shows the view east over the modern ferry terminal of Holyhead with the Iron Age rampart in the foreground. (T. Driver)

in northern Italy. Three other groups of people were mentioned: the Germani who were separated from the Gauls by the Rhine, the Cantabri of northern Spain who were separated from Gaul by the Pyrenees, and the Britanni, or inhabitants of Britain. Collis writes:

> Thirdly there were the Britanni, the people who lived on the other side of the Channel. Caesar and other classical authors ... were clear that these people were not Celts or Gauls. According to Caesar they were similar to the Gauls ... and it was those who lived in the south-east of the island who most resembled the Gauls. No ancient author ever refers to the inhabitants of Britain as being Gauls or Celts.

The Greek geographer Strabo, quoting Pytheas, (see below) also noted that the people of Britain were 'like the Celti', but were not Celti. Yet, classical authors do acknowledge some similarities between Britons and Celts including a similarity of language. On the matter of linguistics Dr Simon Rodway[2] notes: 'The only language for which we have evidence in pre-Roman Britain belongs to what modern linguists call the Celtic language-family, and was evidently very similar to, and indeed virtually indistinguishable from, Gaulish'. This Celtic language, which linguists today call Brittonic or British Celtic, was the direct ancestor of modern Welsh, Cornish and Breton. Rodway notes that movements of population need not have been large to spread the Celtic language to Britons, and fashions may have begun to change through the visits of even a small number of high-status Celtic-speakers to Britain.

The Iron Age communities of formative Wales were certainly exposed to, and welcoming of, wider European artistic, cultural and linguistic traditions. Characteristic design trends in metalwork and material culture which reached British shores from central Europe are commonly referred to as 'Celtic'. Ornate metalwork from the period, often manufactured in Wales, typically blends various artistic devices synonymous with the La Tène culture of central Europe, including complex interlinked spirals – often with the triple interlinked 'triskele' device (see Fig 4.6) – flowing, sinuous patterns based on vines and vegetation, fantastic mythical animals and beasts, among them boars and bulls, and characteristic Celtic faces with oval eyes, grim-set mouths and well-combed hair (Fig 2.6). La Tène design elements permeated the art and culture of Iron Age Wales.

Fig 2.4 Cutaway of one of the rectangular Late Iron Age buildings at Din Lligwy hut group on Anglesey, showing skilled blacksmiths at work. The metals of Wales – copper, iron, lead, silver and gold – were well known across the wider classical world and were in demand before and after the Roman Conquest. (Menter Môn with funding from the Heritage Lottery Fund, Cadw and Welsh Assembly Government; illustration by Brian Byron)

The metalworkers, smiths and artisans of later prehistoric Britain clearly wished to incorporate the latest and most fashionable ideas – 'Celtic' motifs – into their work. But while they employed Celtic design traditions, and spoke Celtic languages, the identities and culture of the peoples of the island of Britannia remained distinctive and different from those of mainland Europe until the arrival of the Romans in the first century AD.

FIRST CONTACT: BRITAIN THROUGH GREEK AND ROMAN EYES

Some of the earliest written records of prehistoric Britain and Wales on the eve of the Roman conquest come indirectly from the extraordinary Greek mariner Pytheas, whose words are preserved in the works of several subsequent and more famous classical writers. Knowledge of Pytheas today, and the significance of his voyage from Marseille to the British Isles, seems to have fallen out of fashion. Yet in the 1953 popular book of British history for school children, Odham's Press *British History in Strip Pictures*, the story of Pytheas in comic-book form is there as an essential step in British prehistory between the Iron Age and Julius Caesar's invasion of Britain. Who was Pytheas and why is his ancient record of Britain so important when we come to reconstruct the past?

What little we know of Pytheas is gleaned from the work of later writers and historians. He was a geographer and explorer from the Greek colony of *Massalia*, modern Marseille, in southern France. More recently his story has been told again by the archaeologist Professor Barry Cunliffe.[3] Around 340BC he set off from the *Massalia* on a journey north which took him past *Gaul* (France) and its north-west peninsula of *Armorica* across the channel to Cornwall and Lands End, his *Belerion*, thence north along the Irish Sea, passing Pembrokeshire, the Llŷn peninsula and Anglesey (*Mona*) before making for the Isle of Man (*Monopia*) and onwards north.

His major book *On the Ocean*, published around 320BC on his return from a sea voyage to northern Europe, does not survive. Cunliffe[4] speculates about the fate of this elusive, yet hugely significant book:

> How many copies of *On the Ocean* were ever made? No doubt the Massaliots had one and there must have been at least one in Athens. Copies would also have been produced for the great libraries of Pergamum and Alexandria, but all have disappeared – destroyed in acts of violence or dispersed to monasteries to lie forgotten and crumble away.

Thankfully tracts of his great work were preserved by later Greek and Roman writers who quoted from him. Their opinions of his work were not always kind, and in their day Pytheas was often accused of fantasy in his talk of a land of tin at the far north of the world. Yet it is from these writings of later authors that we learn of Pytheas' incredible voyage and his early observations of the land and people of Britain.

It is likely that Pytheas first made landfall on the Cornish coast, called by Greeks *Belerion* which means 'bright, shining one'. We learn from Pytheas that the inhabitants of Britain called themselves the *Pretani,* the 'painted' or 'tattooed' ones, and that the mainland was called *Albion*, although later Greek writers like Siculus also called it *Pretannia*. Albion is a very early name indeed for the British Isles and, when first mentioned by Avienius before Pytheas as INSULA ALBIONUM, it referred to the people too, thus: 'island of the Albiones'.[5] Of the name Pretannia, Cunliffe[6] further notes:

> ... although in standard Latin the B-form became common ['Britannia'], the original Celtic pronunciation still persisted, and in Welsh the ethnic name *Pritani* eventually became the name of the island Prydain (Britain).

It is remarkable that an ancient Greek word from the first documented contact between the classical world and ancient Britain is still in everyday use by the people of Wales today: Prydain is the Welsh word for Britain.

Fig 2.5 A rugged face from the Iron Age. Reconstruction of a warrior in the Museum of the Iron Age, Andover, guarding a section of reconstructed hillfort gateway. His helmet and torc are decorated with La Tène-inspired ornament. See also Fig 4.2. (By kind permission of Dr Miles Russell, Bournemouth University)

Pliny the Elder wrote in the first century AD that the British landmass with its various offshore islands was called, collectively, 'the Britannias'; mainland Britain was thus 'Britannia Island'. Cornwall was a prime source of tin to prehistoric traders and it is worth quoting from the *Historica* of Diodorus Siculus, a Greek historian of 60–30BC, who probably paraphrased Pytheas' first-hand observations:

> The inhabitants of Britain who live on the promontory called *Belerion* [Cornwall] are especially friendly to strangers ... because of their interaction with traders and other people ... they work the tin ... and convey it to an island which lies off Britain, called *Ictis* ... On the island of *Ictis* the merchants buy the tin from the natives and carry it from there ...

It has long been speculated that *Ictis* was St Michael's Mount near Penzance, a dramatic rocky islet rising from the sea and separated from the mainland by a tidal causeway.

We have further glimpses of the Britain that Pytheas encountered from the later writings of Strabo in his *Geographica*,[7] published around 7BC. The description, thought to have been derived from Pytheas and the time he spent onshore among the communities of the *Pretani*, is worth quoting at length. Note how the description distinguishes the 'people of Britain' from those he calls the '*Celti*' of mainland Europe:

> Most of the island is flat and overgrown with forests, although many of its districts are hilly. It bears grain, cattle, gold, silver, and iron. These things, accordingly, are exported from the island, as also hides, and slaves, and dogs that are ... suited to the purposes of the chase; the *Celti*, however, use both these and the native dogs for the purposes of war too. The men of Britain are taller than the *Celti*. ... Their habits are in part like those of the *Celti*, but in part more simple and barbaric. ... And they have powerful chieftains in their country. For the purpose of war they use chariots for the most part, just as some of the *Celti* do.[8]

Once again, even the Greeks noted that the 'men of Britain' were different to 'the *Celti*'. The Roman historian Tacitus makes a similar observation in introducing the people of Britain to Roman readers, continuing the descriptions of Caesar on Gaul.

A CLASH OF CULTURES: TACITUS ON WALES

In our quest for a more detailed historical narrative of the people and customs of Late Iron Age Wales we turn next to the Romans. Although the Romans clashed with the people and cultures of Late Iron Age Wales they nonetheless left us with a valuable, fragmentary, written record of the country as it stood 2,000 years ago. The key historian we rely on for the narrative of the conquest of Britannia is Senator P. Cornelius Tacitus (AD 55–*c*.AD 120). A career politician, he married the daughter of Gnaeus Julius Agricola, a Roman general who commanded the final conquest of Wales and the north of Britain between AD 77–83 as consul and governor of Britannia.

Fig 2.6 Portrait of a muscular Late Iron Age warrior, possibly of the Durotriges people, modelled on a copper alloy pommel of a sword or dagger from Taunton Deane, Somerset, recorded through the Portable Antiquities Scheme (PAS). The PAS description notes the thick neck, slightly smiling mouth and almond-shaped eyes and the lack of knot or hairband in the neatly-combed hair. This combed hairstyle is paralleled on the heads which adorn metal plaques found as part of the Tal-y-llyn hoard, Gwynedd. Size: face 2cm wide. (Creator: PAS. Unique ID: DEV-5965A6. This work is licensed under a Creative Commons Attribution 4.0 International License)

Tacitus wrote his *Histories* and *Annals* of the Roman Empire broadly covering the years AD 68–96, and AD 104–118. His works cannot be considered thoroughly accurate and dispassionate in the modern sense; they were written to be 'declaimed' or spoken aloud by the victorious to celebrate the conquest of un-Roman people and they contain much propaganda. They are peppered with wit and irony to impart maximum impact to the listening audience. His major work, the *Agricola and Germania,* written between AD 97–8, was a biography of his father-in-law but also a eulogy to celebrate Agricola's great legacy.[9] This is the testament of a conquering force, laden with political propaganda. Yet, it is the only record we have of the 'Welsh' peoples of western Britain and the hilly terrain they called home, during the four decades it took for the Romans to sweep west and finally take control of Wales.

In his *Agricola* (11), Tacitus introduces the reader to the British:

> Who the first inhabitants of Britain were ... remains obscure; one must remember we are dealing with barbarians ... The reddish hair and large limbs of the Caledonians proclaim a German origin, the swarthy faces of the Silures [the people of south-east Wales], the tendency of their hair to curl and the fact that Spain lies opposite, all lead one to believe that Spaniards crossed in ancient times and occupied the land.

Within his text are tales of chieftains and legions, battles and campaigns, set against the mountains and plains of prehistoric Wales. Despite deficiencies in detail, the text of *Agricola* still provides us with the memories of a Roman general less than 20 years after he led active campaigns against the last surviving peoples of Late Iron Age Wales. This is perhaps the only 'eye witness' account we have of Wales as it endured the onslaught of Roman Conquest. Aspects of the Roman Conquest of Wales are further discussed in Chapter 4.

Fig 2.7 Drumanagh coastal promontory fort north of Dublin is an Iron Age and Roman-period settlement which may have been used for coastal trading across the Irish Sea. Its defensive architecture, with a pair of relatively straight ramparts cutting off an expansive interior, shares similarities with Welsh coastal forts at Deer Park and Bosherston Camp (Fig 7.12) in south Pembrokeshire, both postulated as later prehistoric coastal trading hubs. (© Crown: CHERISH PROJECT 2022. Produced with EU funds through the Ireland Wales Co-operation Programme 2014-2023. All material made freely available through the Open Government Licence. CH_2019_0405)

THE PEOPLES AND TOPOGRAPHY OF PREHISTORIC WALES

In his *Agricola*, Tacitus summarises the land of Britannia in a description that would probably be recognisable for many parts of Wales today (12):

> The climate is objectionable, with its frequent rains and mists, but there is no extreme cold ... The soil can bear all produce, except the olive, the vine, and other natives of warmer climes, and it is fertile. Crops are slow to ripen, but quick to grow ... Britain yields gold, silver and other metals, to make it worth conquering ...

While the Romans conquered the peoples of formative Wales, and largely swept away its indigenous identities, we do have the Greek geographer and mathematician Ptolemy to thank for a record of these regional groups of people on the eve of conquest.

Ptolemy's map suggests five main regional groups of people in Wales and the borders: the Demetae in south-west Wales, principally Carmarthenshire and the Tywi valley but possibly also reaching parts of Pembrokeshire. An interpretation of the Demetae's name has suggested its meaning as 'the supreme cutters-down', hinting at a special proficiency with swords and the ostentatious use of weaponry.[10] The Silures, oft-mentioned by the Romans during the first century AD, occupied the south and south-east of Wales, approximately modern Glamorgan and Monmouthshire although some authorities suggest their power extended north to the Brecon Beacons. Ptolemy names particular rivers within the territories of the Silures, specifically the Loughor in the western border, the Ewenny which marks the western end of the Vale of Glamorgan at Bridgend, the Usk which is a major regional river draining from Crickhowell and Abergavenny south of the Black Mountains to Caerleon and Newport in the south, and the Severn which defines the southern edge of modern Wales. It seems likely that the deep natural boundary of the Wye Gorge at Chepstow may have marked the eastern extent of their territory. The Ordovices, whose name suggests the 'hammer fighters', have been variously placed in mid and north-west Wales, but may principally have occupied the central Severn Valley, north-west to Eryri (Snowdonia). It was once suggested that the hillfort of Dinas Dinorwig, close to the Menai Strait and the crossing to Anglesey, was their capital but the interpretation of the place-name as 'Fort of the Ordovices' is now not generally accepted.

In the north-east of Wales were the Deceangli, occupying modern Denbighshire, to whom the impressive hillforts of the Clwydian Range can be credited. The name of the Deceangli survives on contemporary artefacts, chiefly Roman lead pigs or ingots produced from local heartlands. Differences in the spelling of these inscriptions with the writings of Tacitus have led some previous archaeologists to suggest two adjacent groups of peoples: the Deceangli in Flintshire and the Decangi in Herefordshire, but this has not won wide support.[11] Two of the lead pigs bearing their name are on display in the Newstead Gallery of the Grosvenor Museum, Chester, having been found in and around the city in the nineteenth century. The one from the Roodee, Chester (Fig 2.5) dates to AD 74 and is marked 'DECEANGL', showing imperial extraction had commenced under the Emperor Vespasian (AD 69–79) and during the campaigns of Sextus Julius Frontinus, Governor of Britannia (AD 74–77), before north Wales was fully pacified under Agricola's later campaigns. Another found in 1771 along the line of Watling Street at Hints Common, Staffordshire, is on display in the British Museum. It is stamped 'DECEANG' and dates to AD 76.[12] Even earlier extraction of Welsh lead by the Romans in north-east Wales was recently proven, in 2019, with the discovery of the Rossett lead pig, found just north of Wrexham. This bears the inscription of Marcus Trebellius Maximus, the governor of Britannia between AD 63–69, and analysis shows the lead is from a north-east Wales source, conceivably Ffrith or Minera. The lead pig is on display in Wrexham Museum.

Fig 2.8 The spoils of war. The Deceangli people of north-east Wales, who were responsible for building the great hillforts of the Clwydian Range, were conquered early on by Ostorius Scapula in his campaigns of AD 48. By AD 74, when this 76cm-long Roman lead pig was stamped with their name, their treasured mines were under Roman control. The inscription reads: IMP.VESP.AVG.V.T.IMP.III. [CO]S DECEANGL which translates as: '(Cast) while the Emperor Vespasian Augustus was consul for the fifth time Titus, acclaimed imperator, consul for the third time: Deceanglic (lead).' The lead pig was found buried in 1886 on the Roodee, Chester. (Image: CHEGM 1999_6_197. © West Cheshire Museums, courtesy of the Grosvenor Museum, Chester)

Fig 2.9 A power on the north Wales coast. Moel Hiraddug hillfort with its stony ramparts running the length of a ridge, sits at the northern end of Deceangli territory. It is one of a string of large hillforts on the Clwydian Range which includes one of the largest hillforts in Britain – Penycloddiau. Moel Hiraddug commands views over the Vale of Clwyd and the coast of Liverpool Bay. Road building for the quarry on the northern (RIGHT-HAND) tip of the ridge in 1872 discovered rare shield fittings (Fig 4.3), decorated metalwork and parts of a sword. (© Crown copyright: RCAHMW. AP_2015_2940, NPRN 34002)

What is now Wales was bounded by the wider peoples of the English borders. The Dobunni were a major group occupying parts of Wales east of the Usk, together with parts of Avon and Somerset and no doubt had strong cultural and trading links with the peoples of south Wales. The Cornovii or 'horn people' occupied the north-eastern borders of Wales including the Cheshire and Shropshire plains. After the Roman Conquest, the seat of government for their tribal authority was based at *Viroconium*/ Wroxeter Roman city, built in the shadow of the Wrekin – home to one of the great regional hillforts.

These great, regional names of the peoples of western Britain, bequeathed to us by Ptolemy on the eve of the Roman conquest, no doubt give a false impression of regional unity. They mask the many smaller, un named groups who surely existed but who remain anonymous. Tacitus (*Annals* XIV 26–30) described Anglesey as 'thickly populated ... [and having given] sanctuary to many refugees', but no actual name has ever been associated with the people of this distinctive island. On the west coast of Wales the county of Ceredigion, bounded by the estuaries of the Dyfi to the north and the Teifi to the south, was well occupied in the Iron Age but similarly we have no record of the name of the peoples who lived here. The author's research based on the settlement pattern in Iron Age Ceredigion suggests at least three distinct 'pockets' of population with territories of around 15–30km across; a group in the north of the county around the Rheidol and Ystwyth rivers, a group in the central eastern part around Lampeter on the Teifi, and in the south-west around Cardigan bounded by the Teifi estuary. The late Roman or early medieval 'Corbalengi' stone at Penbryn, Ceredigion, is inscribed 'Corbalengi Iacit/ Ordovs', an inscription which translates as '(The body) of Corbalengi lies here, an Ordovician' (Fig 2.10). The phrase he was 'an Ordovician' not only preserves a pre-Roman tribal name in post-Roman Wales but suggests he was an incomer to the region. Some indication of the lost mosaic of smaller groups of people in Wales comes from the record of the Roman name of the Gangani/ Ganganoi occupying the Llŷn Peninsula, a region with a distinct tradition of stone-built hillforts.

Fig 2.10 The Corbalengi stone near Penbryn in Ceredigion vividly preserves the name of the Ordovices people. It is inscribed 'Corbalengi Iacit/ Ordovs', an inscription which translates as: '(The body) of Corbalengi lies here, an Ordovician'. The post-Roman inscription repurposes what may have been a prehistoric standing stone set on a low mound. A Roman cremation burial with silver coins was found at its foot in the nineteenth century,[13] and some authorities have even suggested the inscription may be of Roman date. (© Crown copyright: RCAHMW. NPRN 304135. DI2010_1418)

IRON AGE WALES ON THE EVE OF THE ROMAN CONQUEST

In our modern world the western coast of Wales can seem very distant from the vibrant 'hubs' of Cardiff and London, and a difficult and remote place to travel to. Modern perceptions can affect the ways we think about the west in prehistoric times. **Figure 2.11** dispenses with traditional map conventions, with north usually at the top, allowing us to visualise prehistoric Wales and the Atlantic coastline of western Britain differently. With this new map, which turns Wales on its head, the western coasts are shown at the core of the Atlantic and Irish Sea maritime region with all its trading contacts and cultural influences, rather than appearing peripheral and distant to south-east England.

Fig 2.11 Map of the western seaways of Wales on the eve of the Roman Conquest, with the names of regional groups and topographic features recorded by classical authors. (T. Driver)

The map shows place-names left to us by the Ancient Greeks and Romans. From these classical sources we understand the people of Britain identified themselves as the *Pretani*. The Greeks referred to the land as *Pretannia*, which was changed later either deliberately or accidentally to a 'B' for *Britannia*. Pytheas and the Greeks also documented certain coastal and island names: *Belerion* for Cornwall, *Mona* for Anglesey and *Hieriyo* for Ireland. The name '*Octapitarum Promontorium*' for St David's Head may refer to 'eight dangers' or maritime hazards off the north Pembrokeshire coast.

From the Greek geographer and mathematician Ptolemy we have the names of the Iron Age peoples of Britain. These are generally thought not to represent the original local 'mosaic' of smaller groups and communities that may have existed before the invasion, but a drawing together of people into larger regional groupings in the face of the Roman threat in the early first century AD. The main names of these people can be mapped to broad regions across Wales and the borderlands. What is less clear is whether distinctive smaller groups, similar to the *Gangani* recorded for the Llŷn Peninsula, also occupied smaller 'local' territories such as south Pembrokeshire, Gower, Ceredigion and Anglesey for which no names have survived.

Fig 2.12 The identity of a regional people recorded in stone: the Paulinus stone, a Roman civic inscription, was excavated at the Roman city of Venta Silurum/ 'The Market Town of the Silures', modern Caerwent in south Wales, in 1903. It now stands in the porch of the village church, accessible to visitors. The inscription dates to around AD 220 and is dedicated to imperial governor Tiberius Claudius Paulinus. In abbreviated Latin the inscription reads: '... the Canton of the Silurians [set this up]'. Professor Ray Howell notes that, by implication, the inscription records the resilience of tribal tradition in the new Romanised settlement. (T. Driver)[14]

Cultural connections: the maritime landscapes of Wales

The ... ships were built and rigged in a different way ... Their keels were somewhat flatter, so they could cope more easily with the shoals and shallows when the tide was ebbing. Their prows were unusually high and so were their sterns, designed to stand up to great waves and violent storms. They used sails made of hides or soft leather ...

Caesar describing the ships of the Veneti people encountered along the Amorican coast. *De Bello Gallico* 3.13[15]

The country that is now Wales was always a distinct territory on the western rim of mainland Britain. The distinctiveness of Wales begins along the hilly borderlands of present-day Herefordshire and Shropshire and continues west across the valleys of the Severn and Wye to the uplands of central and north Wales. Across the western seas lies Ireland. While the land was often challenging to traverse, rivers and the sea were always natural corridors for trade and contact.

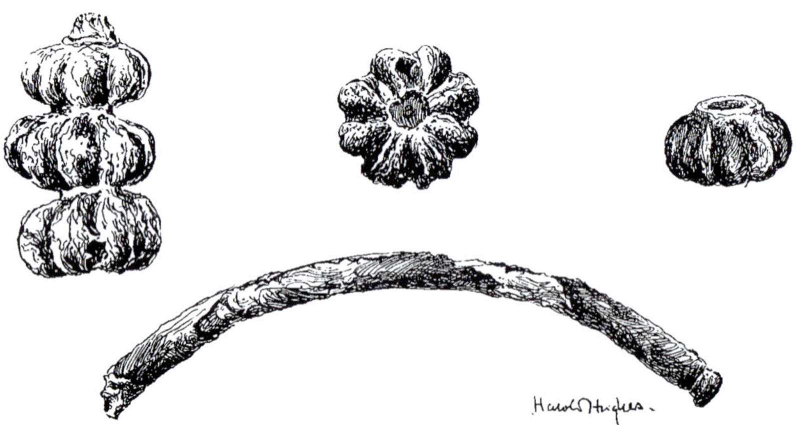

Fig 2.13 'Portions of a bronze torque or armlet (gold-plated)' excavated from hut 41 at Tre'r Ceiri by Harold Hughes' team in 1906.[16] This unusual La Tène bronze beaded collar featured a curved bronze bar, of which only a corroded fragment survived, onto which the solid bronze beads were threaded. It is significant in that a very similar collar was found in a burial on Lambay Island in Dublin Bay, dated by the National Museum of Ireland to the second half of the first century AD.[17] These two closely-related finds, separated by the Irish Sea, speak of a tradition of trade and contact between the hillfort communities of Wales and Ireland in the Late Iron Age and early Roman period. The collar is now in the National Museum Wales. The curved bronze bar is 8.5cm long. (By kind permission of the Cambrian Archaeological Association)

Today a visitor to Wales standing anywhere along the western Welsh seaboard from Anglesey and the Llŷn Peninsula to Aberystwyth or St Davids may feel, perhaps with some justification, that they are comparatively remote from the major market towns and cities of south Wales and England. That, after a long car or train journey, they are at the western 'periphery' of Britain and far from the busy 'hubs' of London and the south-east. In actual fact they are standing at the edge of what was, from the Neolithic until perhaps the early decades of the twentieth century, one of the busiest international sea lanes in north-west Europe. These seaways brought trade, contact, people, ideas and cultures from Scandinavia, the Low Countries and the Mediterranean right into the small ports, creeks and inlets of western Britain and Ireland. It is only in recent decades that we have lost this almost daily reliance on the sea for opening Wales to the influences of the wider world.

Fig 2.14 The contorted coastal headland of Worms Head on western Gower, with its natural arch and blow hole, is home to a small coastal promontory enclosure on the Inner Head as well as a cave at its far end. It would have been an ideal location for a later prehistoric port of trade, separated from the mainland at high tide and marked by a prominent natural rock 'tower', the Outer Head, at the far end; an Iron Age jewellery mould was found near the Outer Head some decades ago (Fig 7.13). Worm's Head may have functioned in tandem with Burry Holms island, 5km to the north across Rhossili Bay, which also has a promontory fort. This is a locale made more extraordinary by the Scandinavian reference to a 'worm' or sea serpent in its name, a place where coastal settlement, sea trade and deep mythology may have combined to heighten its significance. (By kind permission of Dr Adelle Bricking)

In an era of dwindling local fishing fleets and accessible foreign air travel, it is hard to imagine even the early years of the twentieth century when a great deal of trade and travel along the west coast of Wales was still by sea. Children raised in apparently isolated villages along the western coast of Wales would have begun working on coastal 'lighters', unpowered sailing boats or cargo vessels, by early adulthood. This life brought travel to distant ports far from home, and not without hardship along the way. Limestone for farmland, coal for heating and industry and other heavy goods could be moved efficiently by sea when land transport was still arduous and unreliable.

Fig 2.15 A rare prehistoric anchor stock from Welsh waters. Our only archaeological evidence for pre-Roman shipping off the Welsh coast is this 1974 find by sport divers of a Roman lead anchor stock from the second or first century BC. It was discovered by chance in a submerged rock crevice below the coastal cliffs of Porth Felen off the Llŷn Peninsula, the headland opposite Bardsey Island. There were no signs of a wreck. The anchor may have come from a relatively small Mediterranean ship of the first century BC travelling to and from Anglesey, where copper was being mined, or scouting north Wales for gold, showing '... clear evidence of trade between Wales and the Mediterranean in the late Iron Age'.[18] The four lumps on the side show a lucky throw in the game of knucklebones played by sailors. Evan Chapman notes it is the best throw in the game, representing a 'tacit prayer' to ensure the anchor gains the best hold on the seabed. (© National Museum Wales. Item no. 75.27H)

Our landward perspective has a significant bearing on how we visualise the country of Wales. We tend to think intuitively of 'south Wales' as being distinct from 'south-western England, Devon and Cornwall', but by reversing the usual orientation of the map (Fig 2.11) the Severn Estuary becomes not the 'southern end of Wales' but one great estuary dividing two peninsulas and two very similar landscapes. The Land's End peninsula and the Scilly Isles match very well the western Pembrokeshire headlands and the offshore islands of Skokholm, Skomer and Ramsey. In prehistory hide bound boats navigated by hardy sailors would have hopped from the Cornish peninsula to the indented coastline and islands of Pembrokeshire across St George's Channel. These twin promontories flanking the entrance to the Bristol Channel may have once been viewed as part of the same coastal archipelago of the Celtic Sea by opportunistic mariners and traders of the Iron Age. The great estuary of the Severn allowed shipping to continue far inland from the sea. These themes are further explored in Chapter 7.

Fig 2.16 Looking out from the north Pembrokeshire promontory of St David's Head across to Ramsey Island and the Bishops and Clerks islands. The promontory is named as *Octopitarum Promontorium* on Ptolemy's record of the Welsh coast which appeared in his *Geography* (AD 140–150).[19] Rivet and Smith,[20] note the 'figure of eight' in the name may refer to the group of offshore islets known collectively as the Bishops and Clerks, or the wider treacherous seaways around Ramsey Island. Archaeologist and sailor Heather James agrees: 'The key location of St David's Head, marking the transition from the Bristol Channel to the Irish Sea and its eight dangers (as well as its tidal constraints) would be well known.' Indeed, western Pembrokeshire is beset with wider offshore hazards including the Smalls Reef, which was finally graced with a stone lighthouse in 1858. (T. Driver)

3 People, land and territory

Fig 3.1 (PREVIOUS PAGE)
Farming the land in the shadow of a hillfort. An evocative reconstruction painting by Ivan Lapper based on Old Oswestry hillfort in the Welsh borderlands. Cattle were a major source of wealth and prestige in Iron Age society and are frequently shown in the art and religious symbolism from the period. Oxen (male bovines) were also the main animal used for traction, and would have been required to haul timber to hillforts during construction as well as for agricultural uses. (© Historic England Archive; IC073/004, Ivan Lapper)

3

How was the land of prehistoric Wales perceived, farmed and owned by the hillfort builders and by those who came before them? Prehistoric Wales was a sum of its regions, each divided by mountains, upland moors, valleys and estuaries. This regional character may well have influenced the types of society which developed in this part of western Britain during later prehistory. Roman historians, from a conqueror's perspective, documented kings, chiefs and tribes in Britannia and also recorded the particular identities of groups of people in formative Wales including the Silures and Ordovices. Yet terms such as 'chief', 'tribe' and 'clan' have particular meanings in the ethnographic study of different peoples around the world. Where possible in this book therefore I will refer instead to 'leaders', 'groups' and 'communities' of Iron Age peoples, to avoid attaching modern values to the complex regional mosaic of people who inhabited prehistoric Wales.

This chapter explores some of the different ways that archaeologists have interpreted Iron Age society and explores what we know about the ways that land and territory may have been organised and owned. It also looks at how the positioning of hillforts was influenced by the natural terrain, and other factors, and how resources were obtained or controlled. Opinions amongst archaeologists still differ about how leadership was organised and how hierarchical Iron Age society really was.

Hillforts and hillfort communities: changing ideas

What type of woman or man became the leader of their hillfort community? Certainly the task would have demanded a person with charisma; one who embodied those rare qualities of 'leadership' and someone who could strike allegiances and win confidences as necessary. We know from the Roman historian Tacitus that, contrary to biased modern assumptions, both women and men could rise to be leaders. He wrote '... Britons make no distinction of sex in their leaders'[1] and this is borne out by our knowledge of strong female leaders like Boudicca of the Iceni and Cartimandua, queen of the Brigantes.

Tacitus discussed the character of the Britons on the eve of the Roman Conquest. In his *Agricola* (12), a record of Roman Britain in the late AD 70s, Tacitus noted the factionalism and in-fighting of tribal politics, strongly echoing Dodgshon's study (see below) of the constantly feuding and competitive Highland chiefdoms of early modern Scotland:

> Once they owed obedience to kings; now they are distracted between the jarring factions of rival chiefs. Indeed, nothing has helped us more ... than their inability to cooperate. It is but seldom that two or three states unite to repel a common danger ...

Despite accusations of factionalism by Tacitus, no doubt seen through the conqueror's eye, it appears the bond among these people was strong. In his description of the last stand of the native 'king' Caratacus in AD 51 (*Annals*, XII. 33), Tacitus described the local leaders mustering support and bolstering the confidence of their warriors; it appears they may have had 'tribal oaths' to bolster them as they entered battle:

> The British chieftains went round their men, encouraging and heartening them to be unafraid and optimistic ... Then every man swore by his tribal oath that no enemy weapons would make them yield ...

We can gain some insight into what made a leader in the pre-modern world from a study of the Kiowas, a small First Nations tribe of the southern plains of early nineteenth-century North America.[2] With the passing of one chief, another had to be selected. This was done by members of the tribal council. We are told that the council dwelt at length on the requirements for the office of principal chief and on the qualities desired in the man named to fulfil it:

> [The future chief] ... must possess a compelling personality that would draw others to him and inspire their loyalty and respect. Indeed ... to be truly effective he must be a man of great wealth – the owner of many horses

> obtained by leading raids. Moreover, he must have demonstrated his generosity by giving feasts ... he must be energetic, equable of temper, receptive to the opinions of others, deliberate in reaching judgements and gifted with an eloquent tongue. These traits would be indispensable in carrying out his primary duties: ... mediating factional and personal disputes within the tribe, and at all times encouraging the unity of his people.

This is a good description of the qualities required by any leader; mention of the need to mediate factional disputes within the tribe accords with Tacitus' description of British peoples. Showing generosity towards those less fortunate than oneself would have cemented strong bonds of loyalty between the people and their new leader, which could then be called upon in times of strife. Such bonds of debt and obligation, referred to as the 'potlatch' system of gift and exchange across many tribes of the world, very likely prevailed in Iron Age Wales. Whereas the ownership of horses was greatly valued as a symbol of mobile wealth and raiding prowess by the Kiowas, it was cattle which held the same crucial social role for much of the Iron Age. Only during the Roman campaigning era of the early first century AD do we really see the emergence of horse-gear as a showy symbol of status (Fig 4.11).

Fig 3.2 Raising a pint, or four: a Late Iron Age or Early Roman tankard embodies the prevailing culture of feasting and communal drinking of mead, ale or berry juice rather than wine.[3] This well-preserved example was discovered in a votive wetland deposit at Langstone, south Wales in 2007, and still preserves its wooden staves. It is similar in style and in the nature of its burial to the famous Trawsfynydd tankard found in a Snowdonia bog around 1850, equidistant between the ironworking settlements of Crawcwellt and Bryn y Castell. When full, the Langstone tankard held nearly 4 pints (2.2 litres); our modern challenge – the yard of ale – is only 2.5 pints (1.4 litres). (© National Museum Wales. Item no. 2008. 15H)

Fig 3.3 Still commanding the capital: Boudica in London. This great statue of 'Boadicea' by Thomas Thornycroft was erected at Westminster Bridge in 1902. Whilst dated in some aspects, it is still an effective rendering of the warrior queen of the Iceni, wife of the slain king Prasutagus, who took revenge on the Romans sacking both Colchester and London. Tacitus[4] wrote: 'Boudica drove round all the tribes in a chariot with her daughters in front of her. "We British are used to women commanders in war," she cried ... "I am fighting as an ordinary person for my lost freedom, my bruised body, and my outraged daughters ... the gods will grant us the vengeance we deserve!"' (T. Driver)

CELTIC HIERARCHIES

The idea of a wealthy, stratified 'Celtic' society ruling the population from great hillforts has always been an attractive one for those studying Iron Age Britain. A particularly influential model for interpreting hillforts and their communities was developed following the long-term excavation of Danebury hillfort, Hampshire, by Professor Barry Cunliffe, which commenced in 1968. His long-running excavations there, published in several volumes, argued that the hillfort was a great redistributive centre during the Early and Middle Iron Age, with no break in occupation between 550BC and 100BC. The model he developed based on his work, termed *Celtic Clientship,* dominated archaeology in the 1970s and 1980s but was principally based on the great hillforts of southern England. This way of interpreting hillfort communities drew upon classical, Irish and early Welsh texts.

Professor Cunliffe suggested Danebury was ruled by a king, linked by oaths of allegiance to both higher and lower kings. The king was supported by noble

Fig 3.4 Slavery in the Welsh Iron Age. Fragments of two wrought iron gang chains were discovered in the Llyn Cerrig Bach votive lake deposit on Anglesey, shedding light on a grim side of Iron Age society. The most complete chain, seen here in use, had five neck rings. Author Philip Steele reminds us that Strabo listed slaves among the 'products' offered by Britannia and notes this chain may have been used '... in punishing criminals, in securing prisoners-of-war, or in forced labour ...'. Upon its discovery in 1942 during construction of an American air base, the well-engineered prehistoric gang chain was briefly used by a tractor to pull lorries out of the mud. (National Museum Wales)[5]

warriors and skilled men, of high status. Below these sat the ordinary freeman or farmers. Danebury and other 'paramount' hillforts were suggested by Cunliffe[6] as the settlements of tribal kings and their entourages, with their nobles either residing in the main hillfort or in surrounding small 'vassal' hillforts. The king's residence served as a high-status centre for the collection of taxation or tribute and its subsequent distribution or exchange. The farming surplus of the surrounding countryside would have been brought to the hillfort as tribute and stored conspicuously in raised granary structures or in one of many hundreds of deep storage pits dug in the chalk.[7] Cunliffe was aware that this model was only one way to interpret the available evidence from years of excavation and concluded the Danebury report by modestly stating the following:

> The writer is aware that much in this section is purely speculative and that alternative explanations have not been fully explored, but the intention has been to parade some of the broader implications of the Danebury evidence. Rather than serve as a conclusion let it be the opening salvo of a continuing debate.[8]

The Danebury model of Celtic Clientship had its supporters. Archaeologists George Williams and Harold Mytum, writing up the 1980–84 excavations of a series of small hillforts at Llawhaden in central Pembrokeshire, referred to this model of high status 'consumer' sites occupied by a Celtic elite, supported by low status 'producer' sites or farms. There was some evidence to support the interpretation. The small hillforts of Woodside and Dan-y-coed (see Fig 5.28) were indeed elaborate settlements with large banks and ditches, complex gateways and interiors packed with roundhouses; yet there was barely any room inside the ramparts for a working farmyard, suggesting food was brought to the residents rather than being processed and stored on site in four-post granaries. Other excavated Pembrokeshire hillforts like Walesland Rath had central groups of roundhouses surrounded by groups of four-post storage granaries around the peripheries of the interiors. Smaller defended farmsteads with weaker defences and large yard areas in the nearby hills were seen to be the lower-status 'producer' sites.

Fig 3.5 A once-treasured, decorated Late Iron Age (50BC – AD 80) or Early Roman bronze neck collar found along with two bronze bracelets in a disturbed burial near Llantwit Major in south Glamorgan in 2005. Prompt reporting of the metal detector find allowed archaeological investigation of the findspot by staff from the National Museum Wales. The small 14cm-diameter collar was inlaid with blue and red enamel, which would have appeared fresh and bright against the shining gold of the original polished bronze. On display in the 'Life Is' gallery at St Fagans Museum. (© National Museum Wales. Item no. 2007.19H/1)

COMMUNITIES OF HILLFORT BUILDERS

There were robust challenges to this idealised Celtic model of hillforts and their hierarchies right from the start. One of the main problems with a fixed model of a hierarchical society was expecting it to be the same across the whole of Iron Age Britain, with little allowance for regional variation. A particularly influential paper was published by archaeologist J.D. Hill in 1995, called *How Should We*

Understand Iron Age Societies and Hillforts?.[9] Hill argued that the old model of Celtic society was fraught with assumptions and generalisations, particularly assuming a single model for society for a prehistoric landscape full of hillforts and larger family farms. He proposed instead that the strength of the individual households was paramount, with property held by the lineage or clan. Water and grazing land were communal resources shared by the community. In this more egalitarian approach to the Iron Age he also challenged the idea that hillfort defences were purely military in function, suggesting instead most were largely symbolic in their form and outward appearance.

Certainly the defences of many of the hillforts of Wales were never designed to be impenetrable barriers capable of withstanding sustained military assault. At most sites, great ramparts protect the main approaches to the gate while leaving the 'back doors' spectacularly undefended. It seems more likely that the *appearance* of strength was more potent in terms of warding off a potential attack. Ramparts which *looked* strong effectively conveyed the might and status of the hillfort community. Archaeologists call this appearance of strength 'monumentality', which is more fully examined in Chapter 5.

There is another way to consider 'leadership' of hillforts with no elite in place: that the communities themselves came together willingly to help build hillforts on a reciprocal model of 'gift and exchange'. Archaeologist Oliver Davis likens the building of hillforts to that of large Amish barns of eighteenth- and nineteenth-century North America, raised communally. As each Amish barn was more than a single family could build themselves, the community came together to work on it with everyone contributing something to the build. Each family knew that, in turn, they would reciprocate with their own labour if and when needed. In many ways this idea of mass communal labour and working for everyone's benefit is repeated throughout history, including the rural tradition of gathering in the harvest.

Projecting back to the Iron Age, this idea suggests that the construction of a hillfort by a great workforce need not have been a coercive act on the part of a powerful leader. Instead people from miles around would have arrived to help raise the ramparts, possibly against a festival atmosphere with the offer of food, feasting and beer and a chance to forge new friendships during the build. Through their 'gift' of labour to the hillfort's community, people in turn received protection, food and a stronger sense of group identity. When the time came to build their own more modest defended family farms they could call on a wider network to help with materials and labour.

Fig 3.6 The hillfort community. Reconstruction of Foel Trigarn hillfort in the Preseli hills, Pembrokeshire, shows the main west gate (FOREGROUND) and crowded interior. Foel Trigarn has around 227 house platforms within its ramparts, but it is unlikely all were occupied at the same time. The drawing shows many abandoned terraces in between other roundhouses. The platforms in the outer enclosure are shown, speculatively, to hold raised granaries; such a visible display of stored grain wealth at the edges of the interior is seen at other hillforts. There is earthwork evidence that the large burial cairns on the summit may originally have been fenced off from the rest of the hillfort. This may have been to acknowledge the sacred space or to prevent access to those outside the hillfort community. (T. Driver)

THE PETTY CHIEFDOMS AND LEADERS OF PREHISTORIC WALES

> *The social hierarchy of chiefs and followers was cemented by the distribution of favours and hospitality; consequently equipment for feasting looms large in the archaeological record ...*
>
> Jeffrey Davies and Frances Lynch discussing Iron Age society in Wales[10]

There is an alternative model of Iron Age society in Wales that this author prefers, which strikes a path between the idea of structured Celtic hierarchies, and more recent thoughts on egalitarian hillfort communities building for mutual benefit.

Professor Robert Dodgshon made a useful study of the historic chiefdoms of the Western Isles of Scotland prior to 1745, as a way of reconstructing the potential shape of the Celtic chiefdoms of prehistory.

In his study Dodgshon noted that the Highland chiefdoms secured themselves and their powerbase in two distinct ways: through strong social networks of kinship and alliance and as controllers of land and its resources. Land and territory were pivotal to the success or otherwise of the chief. Those chiefs with the most fertile land, producing the best crops and meat, were well placed to strike favourable alliances with neighbouring chiefdoms. These Highland chiefs were also 'cultivating men as well as land' on their territory, a crucial idea that reminds us that the people of the community, particularly young warriors, were as much of a valued resource as the crops, timber and animals[11] and could be snatched in lightning raids by rival groups.

Fig 3.7 The stored wealth and food security of the hillfort on display. Reconstructed raised Iron Age granary at Castell Henllys hillfort, Pembrokeshire. This 'four-post' structure protected stored foodstuffs from damp and rodents. Kate Waddington noted '... the importance of food storage and its central role in facilitating gift exchange and fertility ceremonies ... Some granaries were truly monumental and were designed for display'.[12] At Moel y Gaer hillfort, Rhosesmor, four-posters were arranged in rows behind the rampart to ensure they were visible. (T. Driver)

The Highland chiefdoms practiced redistributive exchange, namely a trade in staples like food and cloth but also in prestige items like weaponry. There was power to be gained in controlling the flow of goods between regions, and this role brought status. There was also status to be gained through the storage of food, both receiving food in tribute from farmers in the surrounding landscape but also storing produce as an insurance against times of scarcity or starvation. Such a model provides a good explanation for the large numbers of raised storage granaries, set on four or six posts, which stood inside most Welsh hillforts and hut groups. These served the dual function of being a practical method of storing the community's food surplus, but also standing as a conspicuous display of 'food wealth' (and by implication control of the surrounding land) to all who visited the hillfort or viewed its interior from afar. Food storage and the Highland chiefdoms are further discussed by Professor Andrew Fleming:

> The power of chiefs was based on the uplifting, storage and distribution of food, which they used to maintain and reward retinues of fighting men ... designed to instil loyalty, respect, fear and subservience ... The chief's power depended on the regular exercise of violence ... in an atmosphere drenched in machismo.[13]

These very real historic chiefdoms fall short of the idealised model of a wealthy Celtic elite. Dodgshon noted that these 'petty chiefdoms' were always prone to collapse. Jostling for power was a constant feature of life in these highly competitive societies, with '... each chief trying to maximise the ... advantage to be gained from the productivity of both land and kin, from favourable marriage alliances, feasting, and feuding'.[14]

These Highland lives, where wealth and status were built on land, trade and food and where the chief's position was bolstered by violence, raiding and competition, seem to provide a vivid model for the way at least some Iron Age leaders may have ruled their territory and people in pre-Roman Wales. Iron Age Wales was strongly regional, a fact reflected in the huge disparities in building styles and hillforts across western Britain. Therefore we must acknowledge that ways of life and leadership which may have been worked among the numerous smaller, strongly defended hillforts of south-west and north-west Wales may not have been favoured elsewhere.

Creating special places: hilltops before the Iron Age

Many of the great hillforts of Wales occupy striking natural locations; the most prominent ridges, the most visible hills, the best strategic positions at valley junctions. What long-held memories or folk traditions haunted these hills before the first Iron Age ramparts were raised? These are interesting questions to consider and explore.

From earliest times, hills were good places for people to meet. Before hillforts became features of the Welsh landscape hilltops had already been well-used by earlier peoples as recognisable, iconic places which were easy to navigate to in local and regional landscapes.

Fig 3.8 A display of strength. Reproduction double-edged iron sword based on an example from the Late Iron Age votive lake of Llyn Cerrig Bach on Anglesey. The weapon, along with many others, was consigned to the dark lake waters in a ceremony to appease the gods of the underworld. (By permission of Oriel Môn; photography by Ian Jones)

As far back as the Neolithic, 3000–4000BC, archaeological finds tell us that people were using prominent hills for meetings, trade and festivals even without constructing early enclosures. In his excellent 2006 book *The Tomb Builders*, Steve Burrow discusses the '… hill tops, river confluences and lakes that people could return to year after year. These landscape features might have been sufficiently well-known in their own right, without the added definition of a bank and ditch'.[15] Scatters of prehistoric flints and larger tools like stone axes can be indicators of long-lived meeting places. Such finds beneath later hillforts at the Breiddin and Ffridd Faldwyn, Montgomeryshire, at Pen Dinas hillfort, Aberystwyth and at many of the coastal promontory forts of Pembrokeshire, indicate an importance for these prominent locations at least two millennia before they became hillforts.

Causewayed enclosures are early Neolithic hilltop meeting places, characterised by non-defensive banks and ditches with frequent gateways and gaps – the 'causeways' of the name. These are still rare in Wales but a handful have been discovered since the 1990s in east and south Wales, mostly through aerial survey by the Royal Commission but also through excavation. One of the few upstanding causewayed enclosures in Wales crowns a level summit at Banc Du, on the western arm of the Preseli hills above New Inn, Pembrokeshire. The ditch of this special enclosure has been radiocarbon dated to 3650BC, contemporary with the first phase of construction at Stonehenge.

At Caerau hillfort in Cardiff, an unexpected causewayed enclosure was discovered on this high triangular plateau on the Ely river beneath a long-lived Iron Age hillfort, during major recent excavations by Cardiff University for CAER Heritage. Its discovery shows what we may still be missing beneath other unexcavated hillforts. It now seems that the main eastern entrance to the Neolithic enclosure aligns on one of the later gateways of the hillfort (Fig 3.10). It is likely that the causewayed enclosure remained as a visible earthwork while Iron Age people began work on their far larger defended settlement.

Fig 3.9 Stowe's Pound, Bodmin Moor, Cornwall. A Neolithic 'tor enclosure' in south-west England, a landscape readily navigable from southern Wales in prehistory. The broad stony enclosing rampart has similarities to unusual prehistoric enclosures in Wales, such as Garn Goch and Carn-ingli, and we can learn much by studying these Cornish sites. At Stowe's Pound, dramatic other-worldly granite tors are captured within the Neolithic ramparts, the tops of which are engraved with mysterious cupmarks and stone basins. These enclosures suggest potential Neolithic or Bronze Age origins for some Welsh 'tor enclosures'. (T. Driver)

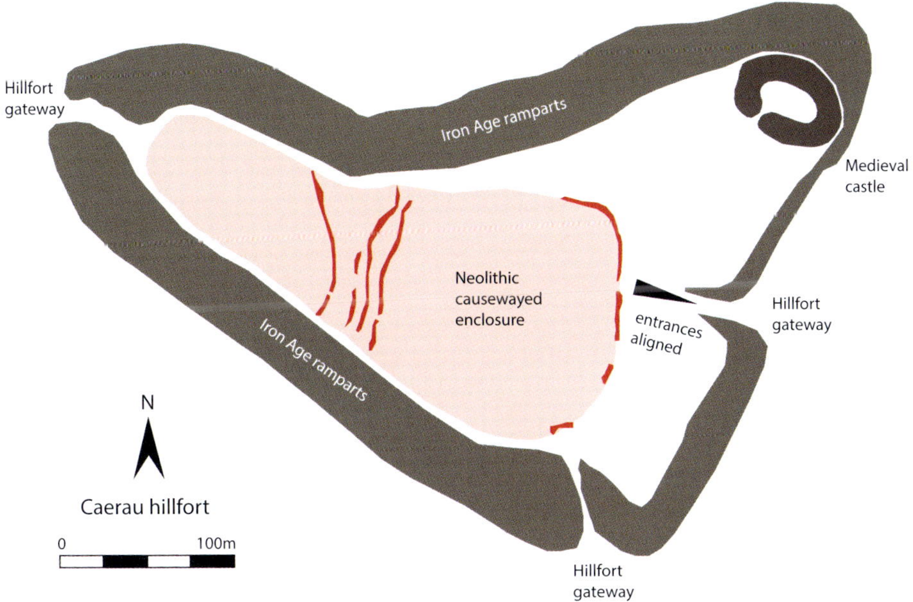

Fig 3.10 Caerau hillfort in Ely, Cardiff, commands a large triangular plateau above the River Ely. Thousands of years before the Iron Age, a Neolithic causewayed enclosure dominated the plateau. This rare early enclosure was only discovered during recent geophysical surveys and excavations by CAER Heritage. The major eastern gateway of the hillfort aligns with the far earlier entrance into the Neolithic enclosure, suggesting parts of it remained visible into the Iron Age. (T. Driver, after Oliver Davis/ CAER Heritage)

Neolithic burial mounds, known as long barrows or long cairns, are virtually unknown within the hillforts of Wales. One notable exception is the prominent stone long cairn within the unusual Carmarthenshire hillfort of Y Gaer fawr, Garn Goch (Fig 8.33). Although opinions differ on the date of this unexcavated long mound, it would be readily classed as a Neolithic long cairn if encountered anywhere else in Wales. It speaks of a long use of this high moorland ridge, overlooking the great valley corridor of the Tywi, for meetings, trade and burial which continued into the Iron Age and Roman periods. There is a comparable hilltop site at Knocknashee in south Sligo, Ireland, where a plateau-top Late Bronze Age hillfort encloses two great Neolithic cairns.

We may be missing other unusual Neolithic or Bronze Age hilltop enclosures in Wales, simply because they have never been excavated or dated. Great straggling summit 'forts' which incorporate rocky outcrops, particularly Carn-ingli in Pembrokeshire or Garn Goch have both been mooted as long-lived defended settlements originating in the Neolithic. Only at Clegyr Boia walled outcrop to the west of St Davids in Pembrokeshire have excavations from the first half of the twentieth century produced sherds of Neolithic round-bottomed pottery, confirming its early date. Garn Goch, more fully discussed in Chapter 8, is a very large hillfort enclosing 16.6ha with at least eight entrances, yet the interior is devoid of obvious houses or other structures. The gateways, too, resemble other Late Bronze or Iron Age examples. It has similarities to the much larger hillfort at Penycloddiau in the Clwydian Range which encloses some 21ha and where recent excavations by Rachel Pope have demonstrated a Bronze Age, rather than Iron Age, rampart sequence at the main north-east gate.

Carn-ingli hillfort has similarities to Neolithic 'tor enclosures' from south-western Britain like Carn Brea, Redruth and Stowe's Pound, Bodmin (Fig 3.9). Both these Cornish examples enclose spectacular granite tors which may well have had ritual or spiritual associations; one of the outcrops inside Stowe's Pound is covered in magical rock art, scatters of cup marks, and basins to capture water. Carn-ingli hillfort is also an interesting and mysterious site (Fig 3.11). It is long-lived and was built and rebuilt over generations with walls and enclosures clinging to outcrops at different levels. Parts of the rocky summit form secluded chasms and spaces which exclude external noise. Perhaps this was, at times, a ceremonial site for special gatherings and seasonal festivals.

Fig 3.11 Carn-ingli hillfort, Newport, Pembrokeshire. Built ramparts (LEFT) of the lower northern enclosure ran below large outcrops which dominated the interior of this complex, multi-period hilltop fort. (T. Driver)

Early Bronze Age burial mounds, recognisable as large circular mounds of earth ('barrows') or mounds of stone ('cairns') occur across Wales in huge numbers and can be found on valley floors, in upland valleys and sometimes in great 'cemeteries' in high mountain or moorland positions. They are frequently found enclosed within later hillforts. That such cairns and barrows survived untouched amongst roundhouses and ramparts – all of which consumed earth and stone for building – is the most potent expression of their continuing importance or reverence in Iron Age society. Kate Waddington[16] notes that many cairns stand in open areas, avoided by roundhouses, as seen in Tre'r Ceiri and the destroyed north Wales hillfort of Braich y Dinas; an upstanding barrow occupies a prominent position within Moel Fenlli hillfort in the Clwydian Range. The three great stone burial cairns inside Foel Trigarn hillfort in Pembrokeshire command the fort's summit, yet are surrounded by a low bank. This was possibly the footing for a palisade fence closing the mounds off from the densely occupied hillfort interior (Fig 3.6).

Early Bronze Age burial mounds can be seen within many other Iron Age hillforts: at the highest points of Pen y Gaer, Llanbedr-y-cennin on the Conwy Valley, within Penycloddiau and Foel Fenlli hillforts on the Clwydian Range, at the highest point of Ysgyryd Fawr (the Skirrid hillfort) in Monmouthshire and Caer y Tŵr on Holyhead Mountain.

Fig 3.12 The three monumental Bronze Age burial cairns on the summit of Foel Trigarn hillfort which give the site its name. The hillfort builders may have seen these great stone mounds as the seats of old ancestral power. The fact that they remained untouched despite intense house building all around them in the Iron Age suggests they retained relevance and importance throughout the life of the hillfort, and may even have been reused for burial. (T. Driver)

There may have been old knowledge, or at least recognition, of the function of these mounds as places of ritual and burial. The 2018 discovery of the Pembrokeshire Iron Age chariot burial beneath a similar circular mound on the approach to an inland promontory fort suggests indeed that such mounds were specifically associated with high status burials into the Iron Age. There is also archaeological evidence that Iron Age communities chose to bury their dead within or close to pre-existing Bronze Age burial monuments. At Plas Gogerddan, Aberystwyth, Iron Age cremation burials were placed in the ditches of a conjoined Early Bronze Age double ring ditch, with further Iron Age boulder-packed burials interred close by. Clearly, Iron Age people revered and respected earlier places of burial and ritual.

A CHANGING SOCIETY: FROM FARMSTEADS TO HILLFORTS

It is difficult to be sure why Middle to Later Bronze Age communities, between around 1300BC to 800BC, began to move from living on open family farms of roundhouses, to more crowded living conditions within early hillforts. Indeed a number of archaeologists are still grappling with this most interesting issue.

A long-standing explanation for the rise of Late Bronze Age hillforts in the borderlands of Wales is the widespread deterioration of the climate which occurred between around 1000BC and 500BC, characterised by higher rainfall and lower summer temperatures. This climatic downturn to cooler, wetter conditions saw the widespread, renewed formation of upland peatbogs in the uplands of Wales on a scale not previously evidenced. It is thought that families living in the hill-fringe and upland zones of Wales in roundhouse settlements would have experienced successive seasons of failed crops. It may even have been that hill farming became untenable[17] as Jeffrey Davies and Frances Lynch note:

> ... this climatic deterioration is the most crucial factor in bringing about major changes in landscape and settlement pattern ... These changes may have included a fall in population in the Later Bronze Age and subsequent recovery during the Iron Age. Wales ... was severely affected, palaeoenvironmental evidence indicating far-reaching changes in land-use, ranging from the abandonment of much of the uplands and coastal regions for permanent settlement until about 500 cal BC [a calibrated radiocarbon date] or later.[18]

Fig 3.13 Iconic hills. The long-lived Breiddin hillfort crowned the flatter left-hand summit of the Breiddin hills, which rise from the lowlands of the Severn Valley in Montgomeryshire. This historic view shows the 'three peaks' of the volcanic Breiddin hills, of which Moel y Golfa (RIGHT) rises to 403m. These peaks still form an iconic silhouette in the Welsh borderlands and would have made the hillfort instantly recognisable and easy to navigate towards. (© Crown copyright: RCAHMW. NPRN 141162. CMC_PA_714_02)

Some writers suggest that the coastal and lowland areas of Wales, including the Welsh borderlands, would have seen an influx of displaced populations from central and upland Wales who were forced to move and resettle into new areas. In the south the high concentration of burial cairns and cairnfields along the uplands of the South Wales Valleys, but noticeable lack of upland hillforts, has been suggested as showing a wholesale movement of the Bronze Age people down to the lowlands of the Vale of Glamorgan.[19] Yet, the Valleys may always have been a distinctive landscape in prehistory and used differently from other regions. Although there is a lack of hillforts, there is the votive focus of Llyn Fawr lake at Rhigos (Fig 3.18), and a number of more unusual (for south Wales) hut group settlements like the Rhondda 'ancient village'. Further to the south there is evidence that Middle Bronze Age settlements on the estuarine edge of the Severn had to be abandoned around 1200BC when large areas of the Severn Levels began to be inundated by the sea,[20] no doubt pushing the displaced population inland.

Fig 3.14 The dramatic silhouette of Carn Alw hillfort in the Preseli hills, Pembrokeshire, seen on the northern approaches. The fortified outcrop (CENTRE) is surrounded by field lynchets and substantial boundary earthworks – visible here as horizontal terraces – attesting to millennia of settlement from at least the Bronze Age to medieval times (see also Fig. 5.35). (T. Driver)[21]

Along the Welsh border, it is the clustering of Later Bronze Age hillforts, including those at the Breiddin on the Severn and Llwyn Bryn Dinas on the Tanat valley, which have encouraged the theory. It is against this background of new tensions over land and the movement of people that some archaeologists have seen the natural rise of hillforts; a radical shift in living which reflected the desire of lowland communities to defend their territory against new settlers. Britnell and Silvester,[22] discussing prehistoric settlement of the Welsh border, argue:

> ... the change to a cooler, wetter climate towards the end of the second millennium BC, resulted in ... competition for resources that would have been particularly acute at pressure points around the fringes of the uplands. These crises were the likely catalyst for the proliferation of weapons and the emergence of defended settlements in the region at this period.

There are spectacular Later Bronze Age hoards from the region which show the availability of wealth and weaponry during the period. One of the most famous metalwork hoards in Wales is the Guilsfield hoard. In 1862, labourers digging a drain below Crowther's Camp near Guilsfield, 3km south-east of Gaer fawr, unearthed 120 pieces of Late Bronze Age (1150–800BC) metalwork including palstaves, socketed axes, spearheads, swords and chapes (fittings for sword scabbards). Dating of several artefact types suggests it was deposited around 700BC during the Earliest Iron Age, but as a scrap hoard.[23] This hoard, and several other similar hoards from this region of the same date, shows the extraordinary metalworking prowess of the region in the Later Bronze Age, along with the availability of wealth and weapons among the leaders, no doubt linked to displays of aggression. The fact that these fine objects were eventually buried as scrap perhaps shows the true impact of the Later Bronze Age climatic crisis, and the changing value of old weapons being repurposed and buried to reinforce new ideas about territory and identity as Wales entered the Earliest Iron Age.

Fig 3.15 How were the high mountains and summits of Eryri (Snowdonia) perceived in the Bronze and Iron Ages? It is very likely these remote and dangerous places were considered sacred. A famous Late Iron Age bronze bowl, whose handle bears the likeness of a cat's face in red enamel, was found by chance in scree below Crib Goch ridge on the slopes of Yr Wyddfa (Snowdon) in 1974; it is a likely votive offering fallen from the ridge above. A rare Late Bronze Age shield was also found in a bog below nearby Moel Siabod in the nineteenth century. This view shows the spectacular Castell y Gwynt or Castle of the Winds high on the Glyders range of Eryri. This natural outcrop with a strongly architectural appearance may well have been interpreted as a long-abandoned fortress by prehistoric communities. What secrets do its crevices and gullies hold? Note hikers for scale. (T. Driver)

The theory of climatic deterioration spurring on radical changes in later prehistoric society is well established but may not yet explain all the reasons why hillforts rose to such dominance. Some archaeologists have challenged the climatic explanation as being far too simplistic: would a long-held family farm be willingly abandoned just because of a spate of hard winters and failed harvests? Another problem with the environmental theory is that it is based on a limited number of Later Bronze Age hillforts excavations. Between the 1960s and the 1980s, very few upland hillforts in the heartlands of Wales had been excavated. A higher number of hillforts had been excavated on the Welsh border, due in part to there being plenty of 'rescue' excavations in the same period, giving us a greater proportion of dated hillforts for that region. It is only in recent decades that more excavations on inland, upland hillforts along with new surveys and reappraisals of characteristically early, remote defended settlements have begun to suggest Later Bronze Age beginnings are more common even among these high hillforts. And indeed, the number of excavated hillforts in Wales as a whole is still very low. We need more robust scientific dates from a range of our hillforts and defended farms, across a range of landscapes, before we can begin to better understand the 'creation of hillforts'.

LEARNING TO LIVE AS A COMMUNITY

Other more complex social factors may have been in play in the initial construction of massive hillforts at the end of the Late Bronze Age and the start of the Early Iron Age. Hillforts were the 'new technology' of the Early Iron Age in most parts of Wales, although a number of Later Bronze Age forts are known. These massive new monuments required a harnessing of communal effort and also created a new place in the landscape where people and leaders would reside. Previously most families had lived in more dispersed rural communities. Hillfort construction also required and consumed a huge amount of resources from across a wide area.

Oliver Davis and Professor Niall Sharples have excavated sections of the large hillfort at Caerau on the outskirts of Cardiff, whilst at the same time studying the significant prehistoric sites of the surrounding landscape. The lowlands of the River Ely are dotted with Late Bronze Age metalwork hoards, which the authors describe (2020, 175) '... may have possessed considerable symbolic value as a means to develop and maintain social relationships between communities'. Davis and Sharples note that this trade, hoarding and deposition of bronze suddenly ceased around 600BC across south Wales, perhaps with the rise of the new material – iron.

Fig 3.16 Three closely-spaced roundhouses reconstructed in their original positions inside Castell Henllys, Pembrokeshire. (T. Driver)

The excavators wonder if the cessation of gift exchange and hoarding, and the sudden creation of hillforts, were related. Whatever the reason for the demise of bronze hoarding, they note that '... groups sought new ways to build relationships'. Here they see the creation of a hillfort as providing that new function in society:

> The initial boundary enclosing Caerau [hillfort] was a timber fence. This would have required considerable felling, preparation and transportation of timber, along with significant resources of food to sustain the construction team ... [this] provided a means for creating new relationships and alliances between groups through the acquisition and control of the timber and ... resources, and the provision of labour.[24]

The careful excavation and scientific analysis of Caerau hillfort by researchers from Cardiff University is showing a new way to understand the 'reasons' behind the rise of hillforts across Wales.

How comfortable people were with living within the defences of a hillfort, cheek by jowl with their neighbours, is open to question. At a number of Welsh hillforts, roundhouses and platforms for houses 'spill out' beyond the ramparts, implying that – at least during some periods – the hillfort was not always a confined community and homes did not always need to be 'protected' by ramparts. At Carn Fadryn on Llŷn, roundhouses of 'open' settlements are scattered to the north, north-east and south of the main hillfort. At its near neighbour, Tre'r Ceiri, houses were also found outside the southern gate. Similar roundhouse settlements are found outside lesser stone hillforts of Gwynedd like Craig y Dinas, Ardudwy. At Foel Trigarn, Pembrokeshire, house platforms from this crowded hillfort are also found outside the ramparts on the north-east hillslopes (Fig 3.6).

Excavations by Professor Gary Lock at Moel y Gaer, Bodfari, in north-east Wales suggest that it may not have been permanently occupied. A reappraisal of the great Breiddin hillfort also suggests it was not intensively settled during the Iron Age. Bill Britnell and Bob Silvester write:

> reconsideration of the environmental evidence from the Breiddin ... radically alters our interpretation of the settlement geography of the region ... This suggests that despite the structural and artefactual evidence the Breiddin was neither densely nor permanently occupied during the Iron Age. This clearly undermines the case for envisaging the hillfort as a proto-urban centre and suggests instead an association with seasonal activities such as the exploitation of upland pastures.[25]

The power of place: hillfort siting

We have seen that hilltops had their own roles and significance throughout prehistory, long before the serious construction of hilltop forts began across Wales and western Britain sometime around 1200BC. The later enclosure of pre-existing Bronze Age or Neolithic burial mounds may have heightened the sacred and ideological power of a hillfort, its leader and its community. But perhaps nothing was more significant than the 'power of place'.

The choice to build on a given hill incorporated many decisions, not least ownership of or access to the hill in question, the availability of resources ranging from water and agricultural land to the availability of exotics: metal ores, coastal trade or imports from overland. Vitally important too was the regional power balance and the complex social arrangements which may have existed between the builders of the new hillfort and neighbouring peoples. What follows are some of the reasons that hillforts may have been built in the locations we find them today.

Fig 3.17 Garn Goch hillfort in Carmarthenshire is virtually devoid of houses or hut platforms. It is one of the largest hillforts in Wales: the 2.4km of stony ramparts enclose 16.6ha, and the summit is accessed by numerous gateways. Yet there is no good evidence, as yet, that the interior was densely settled. Was this instead a large gathering place in the regional landscape where cattle were traded and where disparate communities gathered to rekindle the bonds of kinship and identity? The site is fully described in Chapter 8. (© Crown copyright: RCAHMW. AP_2012_1579. NPRN 100866)

SACRED LANDSCAPES OF THE IRON AGE

Fig 3.18 Llyn Fawr lake, Rhigos, south Wales. (T. Driver)

> *The repeated deposition of prestigious goods in watery contexts undoubtedly reflects highly ritualized action associated, perhaps, with the episodic renewal of allegiance to the spirit-powers perceived as residing in remote, liminal, dangerous and inaccessible places such as bogs and pools.*
>
> Professors Miranda Green and Ray Howell[26]

The Iron Age landscape was alive with places of religious and sacred significance. The hoarding of prestige metalwork including swords, weapons and valuable metalworker's scrap, had been taking place since the Bronze Age. Later Bronze Age hoards may have been deposited for safekeeping in times of strife or during climatic catastrophe, but were also likely to have been associated with conspicuous rituals by leaders who sought to reinforce their identity and ownership of particular territories. Into the Iron Age across Britain, Ireland and wider continental Europe, the conspicuous deposition of metalwork became ever more associated with watery places: the bends of major rivers, natural springs, the dark waters of upland lakes and the dangerous pools of mist-shrouded bogs. Professor Barry Cunliffe writes: 'the implication is that such locations were perceived to be the liminal spaces through which it was possible for our world to communicate with the world below'.[27] Springs, bogs and lakes were thought to be where waters from the underworld rose to flow into the land of the humans.

Two Iron Age votive lakes are currently known in Wales, at Llyn Fawr near Rhigos in the south Wales Valleys and Llyn Cerrig Bach near Valley Airport on western Anglesey. Both were discovered by chance in the early decades of the twentieth century through intrusive construction works. In 1909 the 12-acre Llyn Fawr lake was chosen for conversion to a reservoir due to a growing population in the Valleys. The digging out and deepening of the lake discovered 21 bronze and iron objects including two spectacular large cauldrons, one of which could hold 50 litres of stew – enough to feed over 100 people – a spearhead and sword, horse harness equipment and other tools. Many other artefacts were probably lost in the construction work. The Llyn Fawr finds date from the very earliest Iron Age in Britain, 800–600BC. Llyn Fawr is a striking landscape feature to visit today (**Fig 3.18**). The cauldron-like setting of the lake faces out from the northernmost escarpment of the Valleys, looking north to the mountains and moors of Bannau Brycheiniog (the Brecon Beacons). It is clear the lake sat at a critical interface between territories. Rock ridges overlooking the lake may have made good vantage points for onlookers at ceremonies of deposition.

Fig 3.19 The clear, deep waters of Llyn Cau upland lake, on the southern flanks of Cader Idris, Gwynedd, may have been a votive focus in the Late Iron Age. The Tal-y-llyn hoard of shields and metalwork (Fig 4.7, chapter frontispiece) was discovered close by, concealed in a rock chamber alongside the same mountain path used to reach the lake today. (T. Driver)

The other votive lake we know about is Llyn Cerrig Bach on Anglesey, discovered during airfield construction in 1942, when peat was mechanically dragged out of the wetland to stabilise coastal sand dunes around the newly-built runways. A large hoard of metalwork dating to the last three centuries before the Roman Conquest included swords, spears, shield and chariot fittings (see Chapter 4). The location of the finds suggests that they were thrown into the dark waters from a rock platform on the lake edge.[28] The position of the lake, very close to the western seaways off Anglesey, may suggest that this intensely-used sacred location was known far and wide to seafaring visitors. Archaeologists Miranda Green and Ray Howell note:

> Despite the differences between Llyn Fawr and Llyn Cerrig ... the essential similarities are very clear: both were watery sites in antiquity; each site would have been relatively remote; the metalwork in both included valuable high-status material that would not have been discarded as rubbish ... both assemblages are best understood as ritual deposits in watery contexts ... never intended to be recovered.[29]

Welsh bogs have also produced finds, some of which may have been deliberate ritual deposits. These include the Langstone and Trawsfynydd Iron Age tankards (**Fig 3.2**) and the Capel Garmon wrought iron fire-dog (**Fig 6.21**). More rare are finds of wooden heads and figures, but where are the other votive lakes of prehistoric Wales? Llyn Fawr and Llyn Cerrig Bach are surely not the only ones. There are clues in strong legends attached to particular lakes, like Llyn y Fan Fach in the Black Mountains of Carmarthenshire, or hoards of metalwork discovered close to isolated mountain lakes, like the Tal-y-llyn hoard (**Fig 4.7**, Chapter 4 frontispiece) discovered on a mountain path up to Llyn Cau lake below Cader Idris in Gwynedd. Further research work may well discover new votive lakes and bogs which were held sacred by the Iron Age people of Wales, and offer opportunities for new scientific excavation of the findspots than the chance discoveries at Llyn Fawr and Llyn Cerrig Bach allowed.

STRATEGIC COMMAND OF HILLS AND VALLEYS

Hilltops gave the occupants power. From the highest summits, such as the striking Breiddin which rises in a sheer massif 365m from the floor of the Severn Valley, one could survey 100km of the surrounding countryside on a clear day including the lands of the Cornovii to the east (Fig 3.13). The builders of these high forts literally acquired a 'map of the known world' laid out below them, an important source of knowledge for the hillfort community. Trade routes could be observed, approaching visitors monitored, livestock and grazing herds checked and approaching storms prepared for. Occupied settlements and even distant hillforts could be picked out from their rising smoke.

Hillforts within sight of the sea could observe international traffic and the world beyond our shores: Moel Hiraddug in north Wales (Fig 2.9) looks out across Liverpool Bay, with a vista taking in the Great Orme in the west to the Dee estuary in the east and beyond to the Isle of Man. From Pen Dinas hillfort on the coast at Aberystwyth on a clear day, one can see the characteristic silhouette of Carn Fadryn hillfort on its angled summit on the Llŷn Peninsula, 70km to the north-west. The hillforts of south Pembrokeshire, Gower and south Wales have clear views of south-west England across the Severn Estuary, the former lands of the Dumnonni in modern-day Devon and Cornwall.

Hillforts may also have acted as controlling entities in the wider landscape, exerting authority or a binding sense of community whilst also acting as a 'hub' where different communities met for festivals, feasting, markets and to forge new alliances. As archaeologist Kate Waddington noted, hillforts acted as focal points in the prehistoric landscape, providing '... conspicuous stages for the periodic gathering of groups from different geographic zones, forming new arenas for social competition'.[30]

Much is made about the role of 'intervisibility' between neighbouring hillforts. Indeed, complex geographical maps are sometimes constructed in order to show the mathematical linkages between hillforts, with higher numbers of intervisible forts somehow implying closer social relations between those sites. Unfortunately Iron Age people did not have modern maps to pore over and work out the effectiveness of such mathematical equations when siting their forts. The hillfort specialist A.H.A. Hogg succinctly dealt with this question of intervisibility in his 1975 *Hill-forts of Britain*:[31]

> Claims have often been made that forts form deliberately planned strategic systems, but these hypotheses are not necessary to account for the distributions of the sites. Similarly ... several writers made a great point of the intervisibility of hill-forts; but hill tops can usually be seen from other hill tops ...

Rivers no doubt always acted as significant through-routes for communication, and potentially also as territorial boundaries. The command of valley-junctions and overland trading routes through the Welsh hills was as important in the Iron Age as to later Roman tacticians who sited their forts to command and control well-used lowland corridors. Reflecting this, a number of hillforts exerted visual command over key valley junctions and lowland plains, including Caer Drewyn at Corwen and Pen y Crug at Brecon. Other smaller hillforts were sited on hills overlooking key bends of great river valleys and lowland vales, so as to command views in both directions. Good examples can be seen along the River Teifi in west Wales, including – from south to north – Pencoed-y-foel at Llandysul, Pen y Gaer at Llanybydder and Castell at Tregaron.

It may be that the *direction* of the strongest defences at some hillforts implied the key areas of land over which the hillfort maintained visual command. It is entirely likely that hillfort communities commanded particular local territories; these may even have been hereditary 'estates' – indications of family rather than community ownership – mentioned during the Roman Conquest. In the harsh treatment of Boudicca and the suppression of the Iceni peoples of the east of Britannia,[32] we learn from Roman historian Tacitus that: 'The Icenian chiefs were deprived of their hereditary estates as if the Romans had been given the whole country'.

The hillforts of Twyn y Gaer and Pentwyn Camp in the Black Mountains and Pen y Crug (Fig 8.28), to the west near Brecon, all show their strongest defences towards the higher upland territories to their north rather than directing all their monumental prowess south towards lower lying valleys and farmland. At Pentwyn Camp the largest rampart is built at its 'rear', well away from the main south-east gateway and facing north towards hill country and visitors descending from the Black Mountains. Such 'directional defences' may have been designed to look out over upland sheep or cattle grazing hill pasture, implying the main source of each hillfort's wealth. It may even be that the repeated strengthening of the northward defences of all these forts is an archaeological imprint of the northern edge of Silurian territory, a landscape boundary which perhaps required visual reinforcement in the early years of the Roman campaigns.

Fig 3.20 The most prominent defences of Twyn y Gaer hillfort, Cwmyoy, face northwards towards the higher hill country of the Black Mountains, perhaps implying visual control over this hill grazing. (T. Driver; photograph by Alice Thorne)

Fig 3.21 Pentwyn Camp above Cwmyoy on the southern borderland spur of the Black Mountains presents its monumental 4m-high ramparts towards the north, effectively at the 'rear' of the hillfort. This monumental symbolism appears to have been designed to greet visitors descending from the higher ground to the north. Along with Twyn y Gaer and Pen y Crug hillforts which share similar northward-facing ramparts, we may be seeing the monumentalising of the northern boundary of Silurian territory. (T Driver)

COMMAND OF ICONIC LOCATIONS

A number of Wales's best-known hillforts occupy prominent, spectacular or iconic locations, enclosing and utilising extraordinary landscape features. These locations were often renowned even before the Iron Age, being marked by chambered tombs, burial cairns and stray finds or offerings. Ownership and enclosure of a particularly striking landscape feature would undoubtedly have conveyed status and power upon the leader and their hillfort community. In these cases it can be argued that the hillfort builders saw visibility, and visual command of the surrounding landscape, as important politically and culturally. Kate Waddington notes that '... some hills were undoubtedly attractive for ideological reasons'.[33] Ian Armit, in studying

Fig 3.22 The power of place: Craig yr Aderyn or Birds' Rock crowns a high domed crag overlooking the Dysynni valley in Gwynedd. There are few more visually striking hillforts in north-west Wales. The fort is more fully discussed in Chapter 8. (T. Driver)

the Atlantic roundhouses or brochs of western Scotland[34] described the consistent selection of highly dominant settings, on highly visible sites, as an attempt to imprint the household on the landscape. Of broch settings he wrote:

> It served as a symbol to outsiders of the control of the household over the surrounding land ... their centrality within the landscape which supported them, and of their isolation and independence from other households.[34a]

Good examples of Welsh hillforts built in iconic locations include the ramparts which enclose the Ysgyryd Fawr (the Skirrid ridge) in Monmouthshire, which rises some 350m like a shark's fin from the surrounding lowlands; also Twmbarlwm hillfort and later castle which commands a supremely strong 419m-high ridge at the south-eastern edge of the South Wales Valleys. The high hillforts of Gwynedd including Conwy Mountain, and the now destroyed Braich y Dinas above Penmaenmawr, would have been visible from miles around. Craig yr Aderyn or Birds' Rock inland promontory fort in southern Gwynedd clings to an iconic and highly recognisable leaning crag which rises from the valley floor of the Dysynni (Figs 3.22 and 8.25), no doubt adding to the mystery and power which surrounded the fort in prehistoric

Fig 3.23 Approaching Tre'r Ceiri hillfort from the south-west, showing the col or valley on the north-west (LEFT) side of the fort. The hillfort crowns a scree-covered summit with a distinctive 'mottled' appearance arising from the heather growing amongst the stone. When augmented with timber defences and roofed roundhouses, the fort would have appeared as a commanding mountain citadel. Prehistoric burials on the external south-west approaches would have reminded visitors of the presence of powerful ancestors. Although often illustrated through aerial photographs and plans, we must remember that such modern views are a very artificial way to perceive these prehistoric settlements. (T. Driver)

times. Flimston Bay coastal promontory fort encloses a great, deep chasm known as 'the Cauldron' (Fig 7.23), a dominating feature of the interior which may have had ceremonial or ritual importance as a 'portal' to otherworlds. Both Craig yr Aderyn and Flimston bay are further described in Chapter 8.

Many hillforts occupy highly conspicuous locations, either heightening their visibility with extensive artificial defences or utilising, and 'borrowing', the pre-existing natural strength and visibility of outcrops to make their mark. At Darren Camp hillfort in Ceredigion (Fig 3.24), a great ridge of outcropping rock below the fort may have been interpreted by the hillfort builders as an ancient line of defence. It appears to have been co-opted as a forward defence for the new hillfort built in the fourth century BC. Gaer fawr hillfort near Guilsfield in the Welsh borderlands was a towering structure built on a prominent ridge (Fig 8.21). Outside the south-western gate are a series of natural ridges, valleys and slopes which appear to continue the shapes of the artificial defences. It may be that the hillfort builders assumed, from the unusual landforms, that they were reoccupying an earlier fortress and thus acquiring its ancient power. Outcrops form structural elements within a number of hillforts including Garn Boduan, Tre'r Ceiri, Crug Hywel, Craig yr Aderyn and Foel Trigarn.

CONTROLLING METAL RESOURCES

Metal ores were a novel resource for prehistoric communities across Europe from the Early Bronze Age onwards. Wales had its own rich copper mines on Anglesey (Fig 7.15), on the Great Orme and in significant metal lodes across north Ceredigion. Copper was a soft metal which could be used on its own for some functions but which became far harder and more useful when alloyed with around 12% Cornish tin to produce bronze. Gold, both alluvial and mined, was also a valued metal resource for Bronze and Iron Age communities and the Dolgellau goldfields may well have become renowned in prehistory as a rare source for this precious metal. As demands for metals changed into the Later Bronze and Iron Ages so iron ore sourced from bogs became essential for metal-working communities in upland Eryri (Snowdonia) (see Chapter 6) and northern Montgomeryshire. As the Romans pushed west to conquer Wales they sought out lead in the hills of Ceredigion and Clwyd (Fig 2.8) and

Fig 3.24 Darren Camp hillfort in the coastal hills of Ceredigion is enclosed with an oval rampart and packed with house platforms. Its main rampart, seen here, is fronted by a series of lower outworks (marked by grazing sheep) which controlled access to the main gate (RIGHT OF CENTRE). These outworks were disturbed by medieval and later mining opencasts which pursued copper, silver and lead ores around the fort. Evidence from excavation suggests the hillfort builders intercepted these ores when digging the ditches of the fort. Wooden spades of Late Iron Age character were also discovered, then lost, by nineteenth-century miners. The strip of opencast mines also left a gap of unexcavated ground in front of the hillfort gate, suggesting they originated in prehistory. On balance it seems likely that Darren Camp was principally built to exploit and control local metal resources in the Iron Age. The hillfort lies on private land. (T. Driver)

opened new industrial enterprises to mine gold in Carmarthenshire at Dolaucothi and iron ore in south Wales at Mathern, as well as several other key locations.

Pre-Roman peoples sought to command these mining sites by building strong hillforts close to them or even straddling the ore veins. The access up from the coast to the Great Orme copper mines on the summit of the steep limestone plateau was overlooked by the strongly-sited Pen-y-Dinas promontory fort, the only recorded Iron Age defended site on the entire Orme. Nineteenth-century investigations of a house site yielded little apart from a characteristic sherd of early Roman 'Samian' pottery.[35] A modern excavation here may shed useful light on the degree to which this promontory fort commanded an Iron Age trade in copper.

By contrast we now understand more about how the lead and copper mines of Ceredigion in mid Wales may have been controlled in the Iron Age, thanks to investigations at local hillforts by the Early Mines Research Group. The strong outworks defending the approaches to Darren Camp hillfort, inland of Aberystwyth, are crossed by deep opencast mines yielding lead, silver and copper ores (Fig 3.24). Finds of early oak spades here in the nineteenth century (see Fig 5.5) suggested that the mines were worked in the Iron Age or Roman times, and this was confirmed by excavations in 2005 by the Early Mines Research Group. They found that an outer ditch of the hillfort intercepted the copper ore in the bedrock; the huge opencast mines also stop at either side of the main approach to the hillfort's gateway, clearly respecting it. This suggests the mines were first properly exploited in the Iron Age and were contemporary with the main gateway to the fort.

Findings at Darren Camp help us to interpret the landscape settings of other Ceredigion hillforts which command later mine sites, like Castell Grogwynion on the Ystwyth valley or Dinas hillfort at Ponterwyd whose rear defences are tilted north towards the metal resources of the Pumlumon hills. Copper resources may also have been exploited, and protected, around the Pembrokeshire coast, a region rich in copper ores and historic mines and also dotted with nearly 60 coastal promontory forts. Within the prehistoric coastal promontory fort of St David's Head is the mysterious, undated Ogof Geifr or Goats Cave (Fig 7.17). It resembles an early copper mine and its presence suggests ore was present on this defended promontory. Further medieval or post medieval coastal copper mines are known along the southern cliff lines of north Pembrokeshire between St Davids and Solva. Excavations at Caerfai promontory fort at St Davids in 2021 by DigVentures for the CHERISH Project uncovered Iron Age bronze slag, suggesting processing and production of locally-available ores.

HILLFORTS AND WATER SUPPLY

Fig 3.25 The infilled northern ditch of Pen y Crug hillfort, Brecon, still damp and boggy from subterranean springs even in periods of drought. (T. Driver)

One of the most common questions about hillforts today concerns water supply. How, one wonders, did the inhabitants live, cook and maintain their livestock so far from obvious supplies of water? In fact many hillforts were, and still are, well-served by supplies of spring water even if perched on high hills. Climbing to the summit of the Breiddin hillfort (see Chapter 8) in the winter months, every rock face runs with water issuing from below the ground; springs and pools are in abundance on this rocky summit as they are inside Garn Boduan hillfort on Llŷn. Elsewhere, inside Penycloddiau hillfort in Clwyd or Castell Nadolig in Ceredigion, there are generous pools or ponds. At many others there are streams, bogs and pools close by. The low-lying defended farmstead at Collfryn near Welshpool (**Fig 1.20**) occupied such a waterlogged location that bunds were left in place in the ditches to hold back water during construction. Where ground water was unavailable one would have needed to gather and store water from the roofs of buildings during rainstorms, no doubt a frequent event in prehistoric Wales.

One problem with access to water which is often raised is that of siege warfare, whereby the hillfort inhabitants may have been prevented from leaving their settlement to seek water. This was discussed by Baring-Gould and Burnard as a problem at Tre'r Ceiri hillfort back in 1904:

> The only water procurable within the walls of the fortress is ... but a meagre supply, quite inadequate for the needs of any considerable number of men and animals ... If these meagre supplies were seized and held by a hostile force, the supply of surface water within the fortress would soon be exhausted.[36]

Although raids and attacks may have periodically interrupted a community's access to water, siege warfare was a tactic introduced to Britain by the Romans. It would not have been a common method of resolving disputes in the Iron Age.

In truth, we have grown accustomed to ready access to fresh drinking water throughout the day in our modern world. Such a luxury would have been unthinkable in rural Wales, or even in many towns, a century ago when one relied on communal pumps, springs or even river water. Willoughby Gardner, in his masterful presidential address to the Cambrian Archaeological Association in 1926 on the hillforts of north Wales, dealt with the question of water and hillforts succinctly. All that was required to supply a hillfort's inhabitants with water was some hard work and initiative. He supported his case with reference to a contemporary analogy of developing countries:

> Water supply was, of course, a *sine quâ non* [something that must be done or achieved before anything else] for a hill-fort. The natives naturally preferred a hill with a good spring near its summit; but this was not often available, and they ... had to content themselves with springs round the base of the hill or even with a stream nearby. In this event water had to be carried up by the inhabitants every day, just as it is by the women and children of many a hill-village in India and Africa at the present time.[37]

Figure 3.25 shows the infilled ditch of the rear, northern ramparts of Pen y Crug hillfort near Brecon. When the author visited during an unseasonably dry April in 2022, the start of a major drought, the ground underfoot was still boggy; one can see the hoof-marks of grazing horses pressed into the soft ground. The enclosure of this spring, now infilled, within the hillfort ramparts may have further guarded the source for daily use even during times of strife.

A WEALTH OF RESOURCES

Land and territory provided meaning to the leader of a hillfort and their community; the greater the range of resources within the ownership of that community, the greater their kudos and social standing.

Access to mixed resource zones for agriculture, livestock and building materials would have been of prime importance. A number of hillforts were sited in the hill-fringe zones of Wales, allowing access to a range of upland and lowland resources. The Royal Commission's 1986 study of the Brecknock hillforts found that they were largely sited '... on hilltops ... all within easy reach of good or medium-quality land and adequate water' while 'Enclosures ... on hill-slopes, appear to be sited at the transition between the open uplands and the more wooded valley slopes, indicating a mixed economic strategy'.[38] In north-west Wales and the marginal lands of Pembrokeshire the hill-fringe zone is crowded with long-used prehistoric field systems, roundhouse groups and hillforts. A similar positioning of hillforts in relation to mixed resource zones of the uplands and lowland has been noted in the Yorkshire Wolds landscape.[39]

Conversely some of the most remote hilltop enclosures such as Castell Rhyfel in the high Ceredigion moorlands above Tregaron or the Cefn Cil-Sanws scree enclosure high on a bare limestone ridge overlooking Merthyr Tydfil in southern Bannau Brycheiniog (the Brecon Beacons), both sited far away from good agricultural land, may have been only occasionally used for refuge by herders or for seasonal meetings and ceremonies at the junction of remote mountain territories.

Access to mixed agricultural resources made sound economic sense but their value may have resonated more deeply than this, actually underpinning the hierarchies of Iron Age society. Professor Robert Dodgshon,[40] discussed above, noted that Highland chiefdoms secured themselves both as controllers of '... social networks of kinship and alliance and ... as controllers of land and its resources'. He notes that Highland clans drew *meaning* and *relevance* from being rooted in particular areas and became 'broken clans' without land.

The more land a leader and their community owned or controlled around the hillfort the wider the range of food they could access, from bread and beef from the lowland pastures and freshwater fish from river valleys to wildfowl and game from the high moorlands; possessions may also have included ownership of metal ores and mining sites. When hosting visitors and great feasts at the hillfort for neighbouring communities and families, the range and scale of the leader's feast would have demonstrated the range and wealth of their landholdings, the more

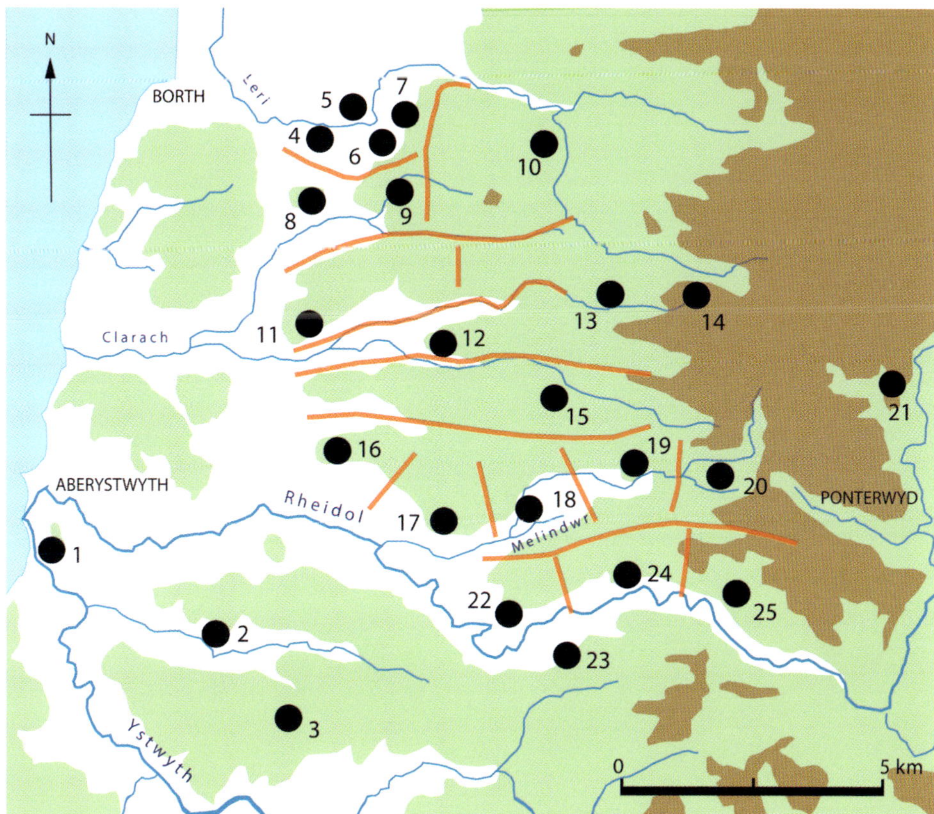

Fig 3.26 A study by the author of hillforts in the coastal valleys north of Aberystwyth in Ceredigion, west Wales, revealed an interesting distribution. The largest hillfort in the region, Pen Dinas at Aberystwyth (**site 1**), occupies a crucial position at the confluence of the region's two arterial rivers, the Rheidol and Ystwyth. It may have controlled the resources of both these rivers, as well as those of the coast; no other coastal hillfort is recorded nearby. Inland, key hillforts like Hen Gaer (**site 11**) and Darren Camp (**site 15**) appear to have had sole ownership of long east–west ridges linking the uplands with the lowlands, thus commanding a range of resources. Larger forts like Pen Dinas Elerch (**site 10**) on its own upland plateau, appear to occupy exclusive territories far removed from neighbouring forts. The uplands here were rich in metal ores, as well as food resources. (T. Driver)[41]

exotic the better. In parts of Wales, certain hillforts appear to have been the sole occupiers of long ridges linking the high moorlands to the lowland valleys, evidence of extensive territories designed to capture a range of resources (Fig 3.26).

Coastal resources may have been more tightly controlled. The sea shore offered exotic resources from fish and shellfish to seaweed and salt, and indeed access to trade. Yet while the hillforts of Gower, for example, showed evidence for the exploitation of intertidal resources like shellfish, there is little evidence of fishing which may have remained taboo, or controlled by particular hillforts. Some Welsh coastal forts, among them Pen Dinas in Ceredigion and Greenala, Pembrokeshire, occupy great 'exclusion zones' on the coast where neighbouring hillforts are notably absent for several kilometres in each direction. These coastal forts may have exerted particular controls over access to the shore. Some hillforts within sight of the sea, like Mynydd Carn-ingli in Pembrokeshire or Caer y Tŵr, Holyhead, very likely oversaw and controlled aspects of coastal trade from their exceptional vantage points. The subject of ports of trade is examined in more detail in Chapter 7.

Fig 3.27 Grinding the daily bread. On a routine Royal Commission site visit to a scheduled hillfort in Ceredigion in 2021, the author and archaeologist Louise Barker noted an unusual stone lying among boulders at the field edge. This turned out to be a broken saddle quern of Middle Iron Age date (400–50BC), used to grind corn into flour before the advent of the Roman-style rotary quern. It would have sat at the heart of the home. It is the first such example recorded in south-west Wales and has now been placed in Amgueddfa Ceredigion Museum with the permission of the landowner. (T. Driver)

4 Weaponry and conflict

Fig 4.7 (PREVIOUS PAGE)

Museum reconstruction of one of a pair of La Tène-style Late Iron Age shields, found above Tal-y-llyn on the slopes of Cader Idris in southern Gwynedd in 1963. The fragmentary remains of the original shield fittings and central boss are decorated with protective triple triskele designs; only the central and right-hand triskeles can be clearly seen in this photograph. This shield can be seen on display at the Gweithdy gallery at St Fagans Museum. (© National Museum Wales. Item no. 63.419/6)

4

There is no great difference in language, and there is the same hardihood in challenging danger, the same subsequent cowardice in shirking it. But the Britons show more spirit; they have not yet been softened by protracted peace ...

Tacitus, *Agricola*, 11. Comparing the peoples of *Britannia* to Gaul

WE have seen in the previous chapter that the precarious positions of rival Iron Age leaders in formative Wales were bolstered by violence, inter-clan rivalry and conspicuous displays of wealth. The hillforts of Wales and the borderlands were largely built to withstand or repel acts of competitive raiding and aggressive rivalry. Such raids set out to disrupt, damage and steal property, including people and animals. Yet warfare and conflict in prehistoric societies took many different forms, from bloody attacks and running skirmishes between groups to more symbolic raiding and inter-clan clashes designed to boost the prowess of warriors. In recent history, the Plains Indians of North America launched raids and shows of bravery on rival groups which did not end in violence or death. Instead, activities such as

Fig 4.1 The howl of a war horn: a carnyx being played by a re-enactor at Castell Henllys hillfort, Pembrokeshire, illustrating how dramatic this type of instrument would have been when played, bellowing eerie sounds out over the heads of assembled crowds. (T. Driver 2022; with thanks to Pembrokeshire Coast National Park Authority)

horse-stealing and 'counting coup' by young warriors were focussed on *touching* your enemy with your hand or a weapon during a lightning raid, but not killing them; this was seen as the ultimate show of daring and bravado.

In this chapter we look at the weapons of Iron Age Wales which, once again, embodied not only practical necessity but also enormous symbolism and spiritual motifs to protect the user in battle. While evidence for individualised combat is quite rare during the Early to Middle Iron Age in Wales, we do see the emergence of a warrior identity in the Late Iron Age, particularly during the Roman campaigning period of the first century AD. During this later period finds of exquisite chariot fittings and elaborate horse-gear, shields and swords conveyed the aspirations of an 'equestrian elite' among the wealthier communities, particularly across southern Wales. These elaborate artefacts projected the values of leaders and hillfort communities out into the wider landscape, inspiring awe and wonder from the ordinary farming population as young warriors rode past on ponies and chariots. The only certainty is that these prehistoric attitudes to defence, warfare, bluster and bravado were roundly tested by the arrival of thousands of Roman soldiers into western *Britannia* from the mid first century AD. Iron Age Wales suddenly faced a well-armed professional army and shocking new tactics like siege warfare; after a protracted struggle they eventually lost.

Fig 4.2 Andover Museum's Iron Age warrior is one of the few realistic reconstructions to be seen in England and Wales. Although he is dated in some respects, and his clothes and weapons are an eclectic mix of different finds, he allows us to imagine our Iron Age ancestors who lived in the Welsh hills. While his splendid neck torc and long sword may have been beyond the reach of many lesser leaders, Wales has produced boar-shaped helmet mounts, from Guilsfield and Gower, and the shield and spear are paralleled by authentic Welsh finds. See also Fig 2.5. (By kind permission of Dr Miles Russell, Bournemouth University)

SWORDS AND SPEARS

How were the warriors of Late Iron Age Wales armed? The country has not produced large quantities of Iron Age weaponry, in contrast to the high numbers of weapons discovered in major hoards from the Later Bronze Age. However, the finds we do have are instructive and allow us to piece together something of what was available to Welsh peoples arming themselves in the later Iron Age. One of the key hoards of weapons and related objects, spanning a 300-year period towards the end of the Iron Age, comes from the Llyn Cerrig Bach votive lake on Anglesey, ancient *Mona*. From the dark waters and peat of this lake, disturbed by wartime airfield construction, came numerous swords, daggers and spears along with a wealth of other material.

The Llyn Cerrig Bach hoard included a cluster of seven iron spearheads, 'wicked looking weapons'[1] of European La Tène design reinforced with a central ridge. One spearhead retained evidence of having been hafted to an ash wood shaft. The longest spearhead, an extreme 72cm weapon, looked fierce and unwieldy but may well have been used mainly to impress rather than to fight with, brought out for important rituals and ceremonies (Fig 4.3). However if used in battle it would have rivalled the power of a medieval pike, a long thrusting spear which lost its effectiveness only in close combat.

Fig 4.3 Equipping a warrior in north Wales c.50BC – AD 50, showing weapons to scale. The figure stands between the Moel Hiraddug shield (LEFT) discovered at a hillfort near Dyserth in Clwyd, and the Tal-y-llyn shield (RIGHT) from the slopes of Cader Idris, Gwynedd. Differences in shield size show varying interpretations of the original wooden backing, now lost. Note the regional design similarities in the plaques. The warrior holds two sizeable weapons from the Llyn Cerrig Bach votive deposit, Anglesey. The long, double-edged iron sword originally measured nearly 90cm and may reflect the demands of mounted warfare. The gruesome spearhead measured 72cm. The figure stands 1.75m (5ft 9in) tall. (T. Driver. Moel Hiraddug shield reconstructed after Hemp 1928; Tal-y-llyn shield after Savory 1964)[2]

The lake deposit also produced 11 near-complete and fragmentary iron swords. They were all double-edged and ranged from narrow-bladed examples from the third to second centuries BC, to broader examples of the first century AD date.[3] The longest measured 76cm and most of the broader swords are thought originally to have been around 90cm in length when new. The origins of the swords are still open to question. Whilst Gwynedd was a producer of bar iron in pre-Roman times (see Chapter 6), the swords are all of a style associated with southern Britain. Philip Steele[4] notes: 'Whether they were captured in battle, acquired by trade or brought to Anglesey by refugees or pilgrims is unknown'. It is quite clear that swords would have been a comparative luxury for the majority of hillfort dwellers of Iron Age Wales. Perhaps treasured examples were kept in the leader's roundhouse to be brandished during key festivals or upon the arrival of important visitors?

Fig 4.4 A modern reproduction of the formidable 90cm-long double-edged sword from the Llyn Cerrig Bach deposit, Anglesey. Hung from the waist of a person 1.8m/ 6ft tall the sword would still have very nearly touched the ground. (By permission of Oriel Môn; photography by Ian Jones)

A sword of a quite different kind was found at the Breiddin hillfort in the Welsh borderlands in the 1970s. A 40cm section of a wooden sword was discovered preserved in anaerobic conditions in a waterlogged prehistoric cistern cut into the Buckbean Pond, a boggy area within the Breiddin hillfort, during excavations in the 1970s (Fig 4.5). Whilst short wooden training swords were used by the Roman army, Iron Age wooden swords are rare. It may have been a toy, or a carefully carved votive item. Miranda Green and Ray Howell suggest it may have been specially made as: '... a functionless and, therefore, sacred object, in much the same way as other offerings to the supernatural powers could take the form of deliberately broken or miniature implements and weapons'.[5] Perhaps it was offered to the dark swampy waters of the pond following a failed raid, or the death of a prominent warrior? There is an alternative explanation: if painted and waved in anger from the top of a rampart, distant attackers may well have thought that the Breiddin's defenders were better armed than they really were.

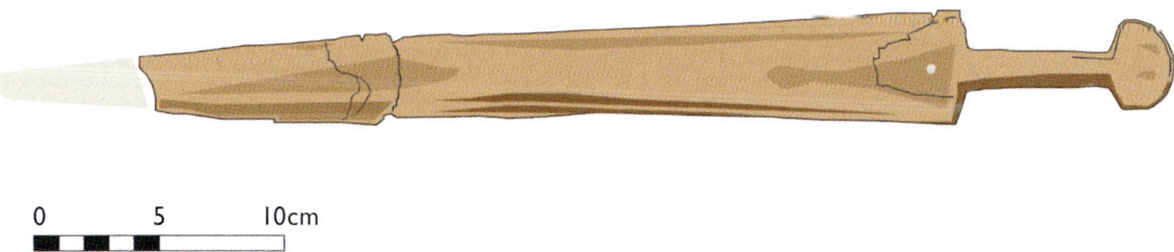

Fig 4.5 Fragile survivor: an Iron Age wooden sword from the Breiddin hillfort, Montgomeryshire, which may have been made as a symbolic, votive offering for deposition in a dark pool inside the hillfort. (T. Driver, after Britnell and Earwood 1991, Fig. 67)

SHIELDS

Finds of Iron Age shields are also rare from Wales but we have a handful of notable examples which allow us to piece together the standard war-gear of a warrior. Later Iron Age shields (50BC–AD 80) were usually around 1m in height and made of wood and leather, fronted with a central strengthening rib and decorated shield mounting which covered the central boss; the boss usually concealed the hand grip. They were generally rectangular or elongated-oval in shape. These Iron Age shields were quite different from the all-metal concentric ribbed shields of Late Bronze Age Wales (1150–800BC) which include spectacular examples from Rhos-rydd, Ceredigion (now on display in the British Museum), and two from findspots near Moel Siabod and Harlech in Eryri (Snowdonia).[6]

As with any prehistoric finds, there is enormous luck and chance involved in the discovery of these rare objects. Usually the acidic soil of Wales rapidly dissolves metal and bone once it is buried. Metal objects are often only preserved in waterlogged conditions, in completely dry voids under rock or stone or in alkali deposits such as is found in charcoal-rich cremation burials. Four shields stand out from later Welsh prehistory. At Moel Hiraddug hillfort in Denbighshire a bronze shield fitting and other objects were discovered under rubble collapsed from the innermost rampart of the hillfort during the construction of a quarry road in 1872.[7] The objects lay at or near the bottom of a rock-cut ditch, covered by rampart debris. The shield fragment has an ornamental central boss with three radiating lines and two moulded transverse arms running the length of the shield. Also found with the shield was a beautifully decorated cast plaque bearing a triskele design, other sections of metal and two pieces of a sword blade, now lost. Hemp reconstructed the Moel Hiraddug shield as a long and large shield (shown in Fig 4.3), based on the height of the metal Witham shield in the British Museum. Yet it may well have been far shorter, like the suggested 88cm tall Tal-y-llyn shield (Figs 4.3 and 4.7) which is based on a reconstruction by the archaeologist Hubert Savory (1964). The triskele symbol, described by Green and Howell[8] as 'a triple-armed, whirling motif' was widespread throughout Europe

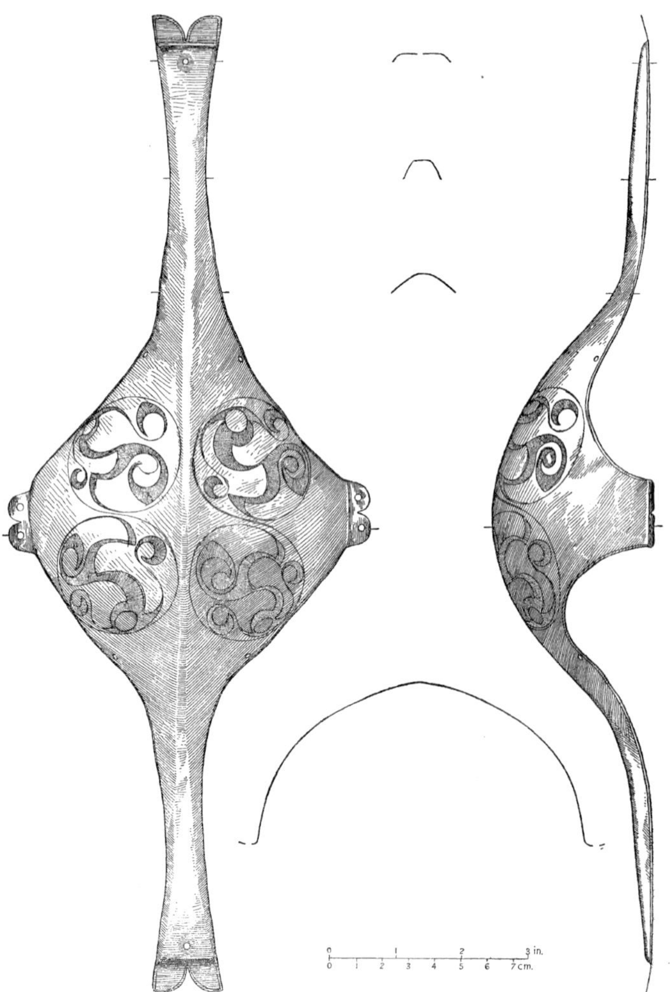

Fig 4.6 The slender and beautiful Llyn Cerrig Bach shield boss is emblazoned with a repeated set of swirling Celtic La Tène triskele designs at its centre, thought to have given the holder spiritual protection. Philip Steele argued it was 'surely the most splendid item' in the Llyn Cerrig Bach hoard. (Published by Sir Cyril Fox in 1945. By kind permission of the Cambrian Archaeological Association)[8]

and was thought to have been a potent magic symbol, particularly through its use on the surface of weapons. It is found not only on the Moel Hiraddug plaque, but is repeated on plaques and the shield boss (Fig 4.6) from Llyn Cerrig Bach and on the shield boss and associated discs from the Tal-y-llyn hoard, described below (Fig 4.7, chapter frontispiece).

Three other north Wales shields share some design similarities, although they look quite different. Parts of two La Tène-style Late Iron Age shields were found above Tal-y-llyn lake on the slopes of Cader Idris in southern Gwynedd, by picnickers in 1963. The shields had been crammed into a gap beneath a large glacial boulder along with fragments of decorative plaques of Celtic design, possibly from a casket or chariot, and a Roman lock. Originally made of wood or leather fronted with a decorative metal boss, the best-preserved shield stood 88cm tall and was made and buried in the campaigning years between AD 50 and AD 80 as the Romans ravaged the uplands of the Ordovices (Fig 4.7). Dr Adam Gwilt[10] of the National Museum Wales draws attention to the three Celtic 'triskele' designs on the shield, one either side and another on the central boss. He considers that: 'The repeated three-limbed triskele design may have given wearers spiritual protection and power'. The hoard was deposited alongside a mountain path on the way up to a remote lake, Llyn Cau, which occupies a cauldron-like setting in the side of the mountain (Fig 3.19). Perhaps the very deep, dark waters of this lake were the true focus of the mountain-side votive deposition?

Part of the other great north Wales shield was found along with the weaponry and tools of the Llyn Cerrig Bach votive lake deposit. A decorated shield boss was discovered crumpled in the original deposit but was restored by experts at the British Museum (Fig 4.6). It features a domed central boss made of hammered bronze with integral vertical extensions which curve elegantly. Like the Tal-y-llyn shields and the Moel Hiraddug cast plaque, the central boss is decorated with a cluster of four swirling triskele motifs. Philip Steele postulates that these shields represent a regional style of north Wales. He further notes[11] the power of the shared symbolism:

> The powerful triskele motif, probably seen as a protective charm, appears here in four symmetrical patterns. These writhe with energy and life ... The boss mounting is surely the most splendid item in the Llyn Cerrig Bach assemblage.

AN EVERYDAY WEAPON: THE SLINGSHOT

> *These fortifications were very cleverly engineered so that there should be no 'dead ground' down the slopes, and that the defenders upon the rampart could effectively sweep the hillsides below with their slingstones and javelins and arrows.*
>
> Willoughby Gardner, describing the hillforts of north Wales in 1926[12]

Away from the prestige and glamour of iron swords and decorated shields, the everyday weapon of the Iron Age was the slingshot. This was a smooth rounded river or beach pebble slightly smaller than a hen's egg, fired with deadly speed and accuracy from a woven or leather sling (Fig 4.8). Caches of slingshots are reasonably common finds from behind ramparts and among the roundhouses of the hillforts of Britain, and have been discovered in some numbers during historic excavations at St David's Head promontory fort, at Pen Dinas hillfort, Aberystwyth, and more recently at Castell Henllys in Pembrokeshire. Single slingshot are also a common surface find at Welsh hillforts among loose soil, rabbit holes and in amongst the spread stones of collapsed ramparts. They are all the more easy to spot if the water-rounded pebbles stand out from the local prevailing geography.

From a young age children would have honed their skills with a sling out in the fields watching over livestock, using the weapon to see off predators or steer the animals when moving. Under attack, slingshot could kill at a distance of 60–100m and they were even used as an effective weapon against Roman troops. Rawhide slings remained an essential part of the North American Apache warrior's war kit into recent centuries. The large cache of several thousand slingshot excavated behind the gateway at Castell Henllys hillfort surely formed an important source of ready ammunition in case of attack. Yet, it survived into the present day largely unused. It is not easy to fathom the reasoning for this. Professor Harold Mytum discusses the problems around this particular pile of shot:

> The sling shots represent a store of weaponry that could have been used to deter and keep at a distance those not welcome, but may also have been used in hunting and herd control ... Moreover, when the entrance was remodelled, the sling shots were buried; if defence were still a major concern ... why then lose such an important armoury?[13]

Fig 4.8 A hillfort dweller uses a leather sling to fire small water-rounded stones, or slingshot, at attackers approaching the ramparts. Ammunition could be freely collected from beaches or rivers. A slingshot could kill or seriously injure a person at 60m. (T. Driver).

THE CHARIOTEERS OF IRON AGE WALES

We continue to learn more about Iron Age Wales through unexpected discoveries and the steady accumulation and analysis of finds. But very occasionally, there comes a seismic shift in our knowledge. Never was this more true than with the discovery of the Pembrokeshire chariot burial in 2018.

Chariots are one of the great symbols of Celtic warfare which still fire the popular imagination. These extraordinary, nimble vehicles of Iron Age Britain are celebrated in Roman writings about Gaul and Britannia. The axled carts which were only 1m across, pulled by ponies with elaborately decorated bits and bridles, seem unbelievably advanced when set against the many prevailing images of prehistoric Britain as an uncivilised place of mud huts and forests. Archaeologist Fraser Hunter reminds us of the contemporary view of these wheeled vehicles:

> Just like cars today, chariots were about more than getting from A to B. Some were fast, light vehicles; others were heavier and more ornate, where being seen on the journey was as important as the destination.[19]

THE CARNYX: WAR HORN OF THE HILLFORTS

> *The impact of a battle lay not just in sight but also in sound: the tumult of the warriors, the thumping of shields, the screams of the fallen and the blare of musical instruments.*
>
> Fraser Hunter 2015[14]

Visiting the more remote hillforts of Wales today, whether high in a mountain pass or above a sea cliff, we often seek out the peace and solitude of an ancient site to help engage with the past. The truth is that hillforts, when in use, were not quiet places. They were frequently thriving, bustling, noisy settlements akin either to a large family farm or a sprawling village. There would have been shouts, songs, noises of dogs and farm animals.

Back in the Iron Age, at key times in the calendar, whether for special feasts and festivals, or to herald the arrival of visitors at the hillfort gate or to terrify enemies at the height of battle, an alarming, howling sound rang out. High above the heads of the assembled crowd there would tower a shimmering metal trumpet, crowned with the head of a bellowing animal: the carnyx.

Carnyces were a type of Iron Age trumpet widespread throughout prehistoric and Roman Europe between 300BC and AD 200.[15] They typify the idea of a 'Celtic' musical instrument and are depicted being used *en masse* on the decoration of the famous Danish Gundestrup Cauldron and on Roman triumphal sculpture and coinage. They comprised a trumpet-like mouthpiece connected to a very long tube which formed the serpent-like 'neck' of a wild animal, crowned with a monstrous head based on the head of a wild boar.

The most famous British example was discovered in a bog at Deskford in north-east Scotland around 1816 (**Fig 4.9**). Although only fragments of the head survived it is a spectacular object from early Roman Britain. Subsequent excavation of the findspot in the 1990s showed that the carnyx had been offered to the watery bog as a votive offering to the gods along with smashed pottery, joints of meat and a cache of charm-stones. The National Museums Scotland[16] describe it thus:

> ... it is a masterpiece of early Celtic art, shaped to resemble a wild boar with its upturned snout and decoration mirroring the folds of skin around a boar's face. It is a complex composite construction, wrought from sheet bronze and brass ... it represents recycled Roman metal ... [suggesting] a date between c.AD 80 and 250 for its construction. Today only the head survives: it lacks the erect crest, ears, enamelled eyes, wooden tongue and long cylindrical tube which it once had.

Fig 4.9 Modern reconstruction of the Deskford carnyx, on display in the National Museum of Scotland. It has a moveable wooden tongue and is brightly enamelled. (T. Driver)

Modern reconstructions of carnyces can be played again, bringing to life the haunting, echoing, eerie sound these war-horns brought to the Iron Age.[17] The Deskford example even had a separate tongue which rattled in the head of the beast as the horn was played. It is worth imagining the bellow and echo of these strange prehistoric instruments next time you visit the peace and solitude of an Iron Age hillfort. Other non-martial musical instruments are known but horns and trumpets remain exceptionally rare. Part of a riveted Late Iron Age horn was found among the Llyn Cerrig Bach votive hoard, one of only five known from Europe. This was a more melodic instrument than the carnyx and may have been used to play more complex music in religious or betrothal ceremonies as well as on the battlefield.[18]

Wales has produced many items of horse gear and chariot fittings from the Iron Age and Roman periods. One incredible piece stands out, the Late Iron Age decorated bronze 'terret' or rein guide dating to the Roman campaigning years of AD 50–80, discovered in 1965 at Lesser Garth, Pentyrch, south Wales (Fig 4.11). The National Museum Wales[20] describing the piece, note:

Fig 4.10 Illustration of an Iron Age chariot based on excavated evidence, manned by both a charioteer and an armed warrior as described by Caesar in his *Gallic Wars*. It is likely that very similar wicker-sided chariots were a common sight in Iron Age Wales with charioteers practising daily outside the hillfort as the demands of the farming year allowed. The warrior's extraordinary helmet is based on a well-preserved British example discovered in the River Thames below Waterloo Bridge, now on display in the British Museum. (© Jean Michel Girard/ Shutterstock).

> There was a powerful connection between warriors and their horses. Elite warriors used their chariots to display their high status. They used exquisite bronze work decorated with red glass in their horse harnesses and chariot fittings. Objects like this give us a glimpse of the people who waged war with an invading Roman army, 1,950 years ago.

Professor Ray Howell comments on its large size, 14cm x 10cm, and rates it as the most impressive object in the National Museum's collection.[21] Tacitus explicitly mentions chariot warfare in his general description of the people of Britain, but interestingly suggests that not *every* group in Britannia used chariots:[22] 'Their strength is in their infantry. Some tribes also fight from chariots. The nobleman drives, his dependents fight in his defence'.

While some archaeologists have questioned whether chariots could ever have been successfully used in the mountain country of Wales, Roman historians were in no doubt about the agility of Iron Age chariot drivers and their mastery of steep terrain. Julius Caesar, writing in his *Gallic Wars* (Book IV, 33) provides a gripping description of Gaulish (French) horsemen and chariots on the battlefield, worth quoting at length:

> Their manner of fighting from chariots is as follows. First of all they drive in all directions and hurl missiles, and so by the mere terror that the teams inspire and by the noise of the wheels they generally throw ranks into confusion. When they have worked their way in between the troops of cavalry, they [armed warriors accompanying the drivers] leap down from the chariots and fight on foot. Meanwhile the charioteers retire gradually from the combat, and dispose the chariots in such fashion that ... the warriors ... have a ready means of retirement to their own side.
>
> Thus they show in action the mobility of cavalry and the stability of infantry; and by daily use and practice they become so accomplished that they are ready to gallop their teams down the steepest of slopes without loss of control, to check and turn them in a moment, to run along the pole, stand on the yoke, and then, quick as lightning, to dart back into the chariot.[23]

This is a vivid description. We read that skills are honed through 'daily practice', leaving us to imagine these activities happening outside most larger hillforts in Wales. It is also interesting to read that chariots could be ridden easily down 'the steepest of slopes'; finds of chariot fittings are common in some of the hillier parts of Wales, from Seven Sisters in the Dulais valley in the hills north of Neath, South Wales, to the steep-sided valleys around Tal-y-llyn in the foothills of Cader Idris, Gwynedd. We also see in this description the type of bravado and horse skills that were famous among the Apache warriors of the old American west. In battle, at speed, the Gaulish warriors could evidently leap from the chariot to fight on foot; whilst driving they could also '... run along the pole, stand on the yoke' and then 'dart back'.

Fig 4.11 A simply stunning Late Iron Age bronze 'terret' or rein guide dating to the Roman campaigning years of AD 50–80, discovered in 1965 at Lesser Garth, Pentyrch, south Wales. Originally fitted on the yoke of the chariot between the ponies, this example is elaborately inlaid with opaque red glass. (© National Museum Wales. Item no. 65.82/1)

Roman historian Tacitus also records chariot warfare by the British. In Suetonius Paulinius' clash with Boudicca of the Iceni in eastern England in AD 60 or 61, where the Romans ended the Boudiccan rebellion, he writes:

> On the British side, cavalry and infantry bands seethed over a wide area in unprecedented numbers ... Boudicca drove round all the tribes in a chariot with her daughters in front of her.[24]

Before 2018, no Iron Age chariot was known from the whole of southern Britain, including Wales. The only known examples were from elaborate chariot burials of Yorkshire and examples from southern Scotland. Then in 2018 a characteristic collection of decorated metalwork, thought to represent a warrior chariot burial, was discovered by a metal detectorist in south Pembrokeshire and promptly reported. Geophysical survey of the findspot and its environs revealed a previously unknown inland promontory fort, with a circular 'ring ditch' monument just outside its gateway which was the source of the finds. Most archaeologists would have classed this circle as a Bronze Age burial mound but the spectacular finds suggested otherwise. This was in fact an Iron Age circular burial mound, a very unusual discovery for Wales where burials from the period are extremely rare.

A full excavation of the findspot was mounted in spring 2019 by archaeologists from the Dyfed Archaeological Trust and National Museum Wales. This revealed the very first Iron Age chariot burial from the whole of southern Britain, dating from the first century AD. It appears that it was buried just as the Romans launched their campaigns against Wales. Perhaps the community was so terrified about the collapse of its known world that urgent offerings were made to their gods in order to appease them. This would not be unusual; the shields from the Tal-y-llyn hoard (Fig 4.7) were made and buried beneath a boulder on the slopes of Cader Idris in the same campaigning years of AD 50–80. The discovery of the Pembrokeshire chariot burial within a circular mound on the approach to an inland promontory fort has prompted new geophysical surveys outside similar hillforts in south-west Wales, to identify further likely burial sites which have hitherto gone unrecorded (see Fig 5.33).

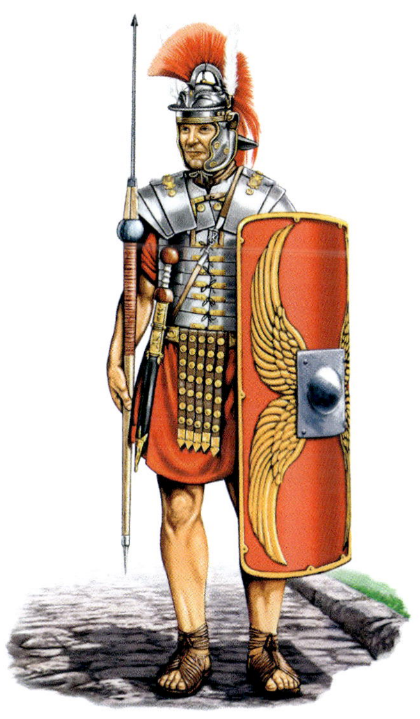

Fig 4.12 A Roman legionary armed with a javelin, short sword and shield: a disciplined and terrifying opponent in battle. While the Iron Age peoples of Wales mounted a sustained resistance to the Roman Conquest over three decades they were ultimately no match for a well-trained and well-equipped professional army. (© Jean Michel Girard/ Shutterstock)

> *Neither before nor since* [Agricola's arrival in AD 77] *has Britain ever been in a more uneasy or dangerous state. Veterans were butchered, colonies burned to the ground, armies isolated. We had to fight for life before we could think of victory ...*
>
> Tacitus on Agricola's governorship of Britannia[25]

The story of the Roman Conquest of Wales is one of determined resistance against the invaders for nearly three decades by the Welsh peoples, before their eventual assimilation into what became Roman Britain. Julius Caesar's two invasions of Kent in south-east England in 55 and 54BC did little to disturb Iron Age life in western Britain, although this unusual state of affairs may well have sent reverberations through the leaders of western peoples. The final Roman invasion of Britannia in AD 43 at Richborough, Kent, set in train a determined three-decade-long struggle for supremacy in the west, in which the Romans ultimately triumphed. They were to stay in power for a further 350 years.

Fig 4.13 The face of a conquered Silurian warrior. A fragment of a carved stone figure, excavated from the ruins of a barrack building in the Priory Field excavations inside Isca/ Caerleon Roman fortress in 2010. It shows a bare-chested man, hands tied behind his back and enslaved, wearing a defeated expression on his face. It is thought that it may have come from a victory monument somewhere in the fortress, probably celebrating the downfall of the Silures after a protracted struggle. (T. Driver)

Whilst the various peoples of Britain fought valiantly, they were no match for well-armed, disciplined, professional soldiers drawn from across the Roman empire. Yet, matters of conquest were not nearly as simple in Wales and the west as the Romans might have hoped. Despite rapid, brutal advances through north-east Wales towards Anglesey in the late AD 40s – soon after the conquest – and the successful capture of one of the great Iron Age leaders, Caratacus, somewhere on the Rivers Severn or Tanat in eastern Wales early in AD 51, Wales did not fall under full Roman control for another 26 years.

Fig 4.14 Embracing some – but not all – elements of Roman life. The low-lying Caer Lêb Late Roman defended farmstead on southern Anglesey, seen here from the north, shows all the modernity of Roman living with its sharp-angled north-western ramparts. Finds from nineteenth-century excavations included a third-century Roman brooch, Roman coin, pottery and quernstones. Yet the occupants still clearly preferred life in a roundhouse to that inside a villa building. Modern scientific excavations at sites like these could well reveal ephemeral evidence of Late Iron Age origins. (Menter Môn with funding from the Heritage Lottery Fund, Cadw and Welsh Assembly Government; illustration by Brian Byron)

In both his *Annals* and his *Agricola*, Roman historian Tacitus gives us a flavour of the conflict that was waged over three decades in the western, hilly land that was to become Wales. In the intervening 1,900 or so years it is possible that these quite vivid descriptions have paled in their impact. However, if we read them afresh and in the context of recent conflicts in Europe, with their human tales of bravery, cruelty and brutality we may begin to imagine something of the horrific events that Roman historians sought to record.

There are few more graphic accounts of the professional Roman army coming up against massed forces of Iron Age warriors than the description of the battle against Caratacus early in AD 51. Academics have favoured either Cefncarnedd hillfort at Llandinam, or Llanymynach hill, both on the River Severn, as the site of this famous battle. Archdeacon Thomas in 1906[26] favoured the Breiddin. He wrote:

Fig 4.15 A new power in the landscape. Segontium Roman fort, the precursor of medieval and modern Caernarfon. It was built in the first century AD to overlook the Menai Strait and to control a key ferry crossing-point to the thriving Romano-British settlement of Taicochion, Anglesey, on the opposite shore. Hillforts and settlements in the local landscape, including the mighty coastal fort of Dinas Dinlle some 7km to the south-west, would have quickly found their daily trading and farming life severely interrupted by the Roman Conquest. It would only restart with Imperial approval. (Crown Copyright - Royalty Free worldwide with attribution in line with Crown Copyright Licencing Agreement. Asset ID: 405815)

> The description of the scene as given by Tacitus ... is singularly appropriate to this site. The Severn with its uncertain, treacherous ford (*vado incerto*) … the frowning precipices (*imminentia juga*), the terrifying aspect of the ridge crowded with defenders (*nihil nisi atrox et propugnatoribus frequens*) ...

Tacitus' gripping narrative of the last stand of Caratacus is abbreviated below[27] but it remains an invaluable description of a direct clash between the Roman army and the assembled peoples of central and eastern Wales:

> Then Caratacus staked his fate on a battle. He selected a site where numerous factors – notably approaches and escape routes – helped him and impeded us [the Romans]. On one side there were steep hills. Wherever the gradient was gentler, stones were piled into a kind of rampart ... The defences were strongly manned.

> The British chieftains went round their men, encouraging and heartening them to be unafraid and optimistic ... After a reconnaissance to detect vulnerable points, Ostorius [Scapula] led his enthusiastic soldiers forward. They crossed the river without difficulty, and reached the rampart. But then, in an exchange of missiles [presumably sling shot and spears], they came off worse in wounds and casualties. However, under a roof of locked shields, the Romans demolished the crude and clumsy stone embankment, and in the subsequent fight at close quarters the natives were driven to the hill-tops ... The British, unprotected by breastplates or helmets, were thrown into disorder. If they stood up to the auxiliaries they were cut down by the swords and spears of the regulars, and if they faced the latter they succumbed to the auxiliaries' broadswords and pikes.

Fig 4.16 The inhabitants of Crug Hywel hillfort in the Black Mountains, at the northern edge of Silurian territory, may well have launched surprise raids on Roman troops who were learning the routes through the difficult hill country here. Equally they may have harboured the injured after clashes with the army. (T. Driver)

In Tacitus' narrative of the long-running rebellion of the Silures people against the Romans between the AD 50s–70s, he recounts the campaigns in south-east Wales of Ostorius Scapula, Governor of Britannia between AD 47–52. Most chilling of all, we read of near-genocide threatened by one of the Roman Commanders who wished to 'utterly exterminate' the Silures:[28]

> In Silurian country, Roman troops left to build forts under a divisional chief of staff were surrounded, and only saved from annihilation because neighbouring fortresses learnt of their siege and speedily sent help ... Shortly afterwards a Roman foraging party was put to flight ...
>
> Battle followed battle. They were mostly guerrilla fighters, in woods and bogs. Some were accidental – the results of chance encounters. Others were planned with calculated bravery. The motives were hatred or plunder ... The Silures were exceptionally stubborn. They were enraged by a much-repeated saying of the Roman commander that they must be utterly exterminated ... Two auxiliary battalions which their greedy commanders had taken plundering with insufficient precautions, fell into a trap laid by the Silures.

Scapula eventually died prematurely in the winter of AD 51/52 from an illness thought to have been exacerbated by exhaustion brought on by campaigns with the Silures. Following the accession of Emperor Vespasian in AD 69, renewed efforts to bring western Britannia under control were driven forward by successive Governors, Bolanus (AD 69–71), Cerealis (AD 71–74) and crucially Frontinus (AD 74–77) to whom the final conquest of Wales was entrusted. Despite this final push one problem remained in the mountains of north-west Wales: the hill country of the Ordovices. Upon the arrival of the new Governor of Britannia, Agricola, in AD 77, it was found that the Ordovices held the upper hand over an exhausted and demoralised Roman army; he whipped the soldiers into shape and took decisive action against the enemy. Tacitus recounts the conclusive battle by his father-in-law:[29]

> Shortly before [Agricola's] arrival [in AD 77] ... the tribe of the Ordovices had almost wiped out a squadron of cavalry stationed in their territory, and this initial stroke had excited the province ... In spite of all, Agricola decided to go and meet the threat. He drew together detachments of the legions and a small force of auxiliaries. As the Ordovices did not venture to meet him in the plain, he marched his men into the hills, himself in the van, to lend his own courage to the rest by sharing their peril. Thus he cut to pieces almost the whole fighting force of the nation.

The resistance of these groups was swiftly crushed. Wise leaders no doubt sought a negotiated peace with the invaders so that their life and that of their people could continue in some form. Elsewhere in the wider countryside local people

Fig 4.17 Romano-Celtic temple, Venta Silurum/ Caerwent, south Wales. In a final hammer blow, Tacitus describes such luxuries in the light of the conquest of the British: 'To induce a people hitherto scattered, uncivilised and therefore prone to fight, to grow pleasurably inured to peace and ease, Agricola gave private encouragement and official assistance to the building of temples, public squares and private mansions ... And so the Britons were gradually led on to the amenities that make vice agreeable – arcades, baths and sumptuous banquets. They spoke of such novelties as "civilisation", when really they were only a feature of enslavement.'[30] (Crown Copyright - Royalty Free worldwide with attribution in line with Crown Copyright Licencing Agreement. Asset ID: SCX-VH07-1718-0269)

adopted Roman ways of life, accepting the convenience of mass-produced cooking wares and adopting elegant pottery dishes and platters, even while they lived in roundhouses within Romano-British hillforts and defended farms. By AD 75–80 even the truculent Silures had been pacified and settled in their new market town and administrative capital in the Monmouthshire lowlands: *Venta Silurum*, modern-day Caerwent, the 'Market town of the Silures'. Venta Silurum came to have all the conveniences of a Roman town including a grand forum-basilica built by the early second century AD, the focus for the market square and seat of local government. There was also a Romano-Celtic temple, civic baths and rows of shops and houses. The town was enclosed by a great stone wall lined with towers and punctuated by gateways. These standing walls are still among the best-preserved town defences to be seen anywhere in Roman Britain. The Iron Age of western Britain had ended.

5 Shock and awe: hillfort design and construction

Fig 5.1 (PREVIOUS PAGE)

The gateway of an Iron Age hillfort in its prime. This view of Old Sarum hillfort on the Wessex chalklands of England by Peter Dunn perfectly captures the pomp and ceremony of the approach to a gateway. Carved 'totem' poles greet visitors, based upon wooden examples recovered from Iron Age shrines. The gateway is towered, allowing two stories for display and intimidation. Members of the hillfort community shout, jeer and blow carnyces (war horns) to intimidate visitors and exert power. Spikes on the upper storey carry the heads of vanquished enemies. (© Historic England Archive; IC074/013, Peter Dunn)

5

The forests are their cities; for they fence in a spacious circular enclosure with trees which they have felled, and in that enclosure make huts for themselves and also pen up their cattle ...

The Greek geographer Strabo describing the Iron Age settlements of Britain in his *Geographica* (Geography), *c.*7BC

A NEWLY-BUILT hillfort would have been quite unlike anything Iron Age people had seen before. It would have had a huge visual and engineering impact on the contemporary landscape. Timber-reinforced, stone-faced ramparts towered high above all else with gateway towers casting long shadows. Higher still were human or cattle skulls, flags, fabrics and wooden sculptures and figurines adorning the top of the gateway, as a warning to visitors and to bring luck and good magic to those entering (Fig 5.1). Professor Harold Mytum discussed the many reasons why spaces in the Iron Age were enclosed with ramparts, walls and ditches:

> The requirement was to enclose; that was the psychological, cultural and spiritual necessity. The monumental nature of this enclosure was a social need ... an enduring symbol of identity, unity, coherence and protection.[1]

Well-known hill summits would have been forever changed with the arrival of a hillfort, signalled by brash new walls of fresh-quarried stone, tips of bare earth or rubble and rock-cut ditches. During construction crowds of people would have come and gone daily, with local tracks churned up by repeated wagonloads of material being delivered to the site. Completing the top of the rampart would have been a high palisade of upright timbers newly-felled from the surrounding woodland, or alternatively walls of split planks or woven withy fences.

With the completion of the hillfort, a gate was forever closed on previously open countryside. Hitherto oft-visited hilltops with their ancestral burial mounds from earlier centuries were now firmly closed off, secured within a new inner world. Old monuments were now in new ownership. The newly-built hillfort was a bewildering assault on the senses for anyone seeing it for the first time, an architectural and engineering marvel of its time. We must always bear this in mind when we visit the collapsed, grass-grown hillforts of Wales today.

Breaking new ground: building the hillfort

Building a large hillfort was akin to the raising of a great medieval tithe barn, or even the construction of the larger churches and cathedrals of rural medieval Britain. Hillfort raising would have been an extraordinary, novel and exciting activity for most Iron Age communities, cementing the social fabric in a pre-modern world. Rather than the daily cycle of waking, farming, working and sleeping, a hillfort build would have brought people together from across the locality or wider region. In this way, the social act of building a hillfort would have worked in much the same way as a barn-raising or annual harvest worked throughout history – by kindling new friendships, alliances and even romantic attachments across different communities whilst providing the opportunity for old friendships to be renewed, all against the background of a hard day's work.

The anticipation and planning behind a new build would have been considerable. Did the community have access to all the materials they needed, from coppiced woodland, mature timber and building stone to oxen for traction and stores of rope, withies, wagons and sleds for moving heavy material? Archaeologist William Manning calculated that even a medium-sized 4ha hillfort required around 4,680 trees for all its timber components, including vertical timbers and tie beams within the rampart.[2] For a hillfort of this size, timber would need to have been harvested from 76ha of woodland and moved to the construction site, a considerable task in upland country.

On site, were there enough antler picks, buckets, baskets, ladders and ropes for everyone to work? Specialist iron fittings for the hinges and closing mechanisms of the gate could be expensive and difficult to source, whilst bronze and iron tools would be required in quantity for working wood and reducing forest timbers to planks, posts and stakes. How were the roundhouses to be roofed? The choice of reeds, straw or bundles of heather could depend on season, access to different landscapes for suitable material, and how much one had to barter, promise or pay for the material. Supplying adequate food on a daily basis for all the workers was another important consideration.

Forging the correct allegiances as the big build approached was perhaps one of the most critical roles for the leader: hosting feasts and meetings to discuss

Fig 5.2 Consulting the gods. Pairs of divination spoons from the Iron Age are incredibly rare. Only 27 individual bronze spoons are known from Britain, Ireland and France representing just 17 pairs. Two pairs are known from Wales, from Ffynogion near Ruthin discovered close to a lowland temple and the Penbryn Spoons (REPLICAS PICTURED) from inside Castell Nadolig hillfort, Ceredigion (Fig 5.33). Each pair features an upper holed spoon, believed to have been used to drip liquids or a granular substance through to the lower, cross-incised spoon. Where and how the substance fell into the quadrants below may have divined the future. It is highly likely such precious tools were only used by religious specialists or Druids. Leaders may have consulted such specialists to find auspicious days for key events, including when to commence construction of their new hillfort. (T. Driver; spoons kindly lent by Amgueddfa Ceredigion Museum)

requirements, making long-overdue visits to neighbours or estranged family members to smooth the path for the months ahead whilst gathering courage to reach out to distant experts in hillfort-building that one had heard of, but perhaps never met. Lastly there came the members of the community who were preparing to move permanently into a new home. For some this would have meant abandoning a family farm in the open countryside in favour of a new communal life behind fences and gates.

For most ordinary people, working on a big hillfort build could have been likened to the excitement of attending a large festival today, or even of catching sight of a celebrity. Here was the chance to see important people one did not

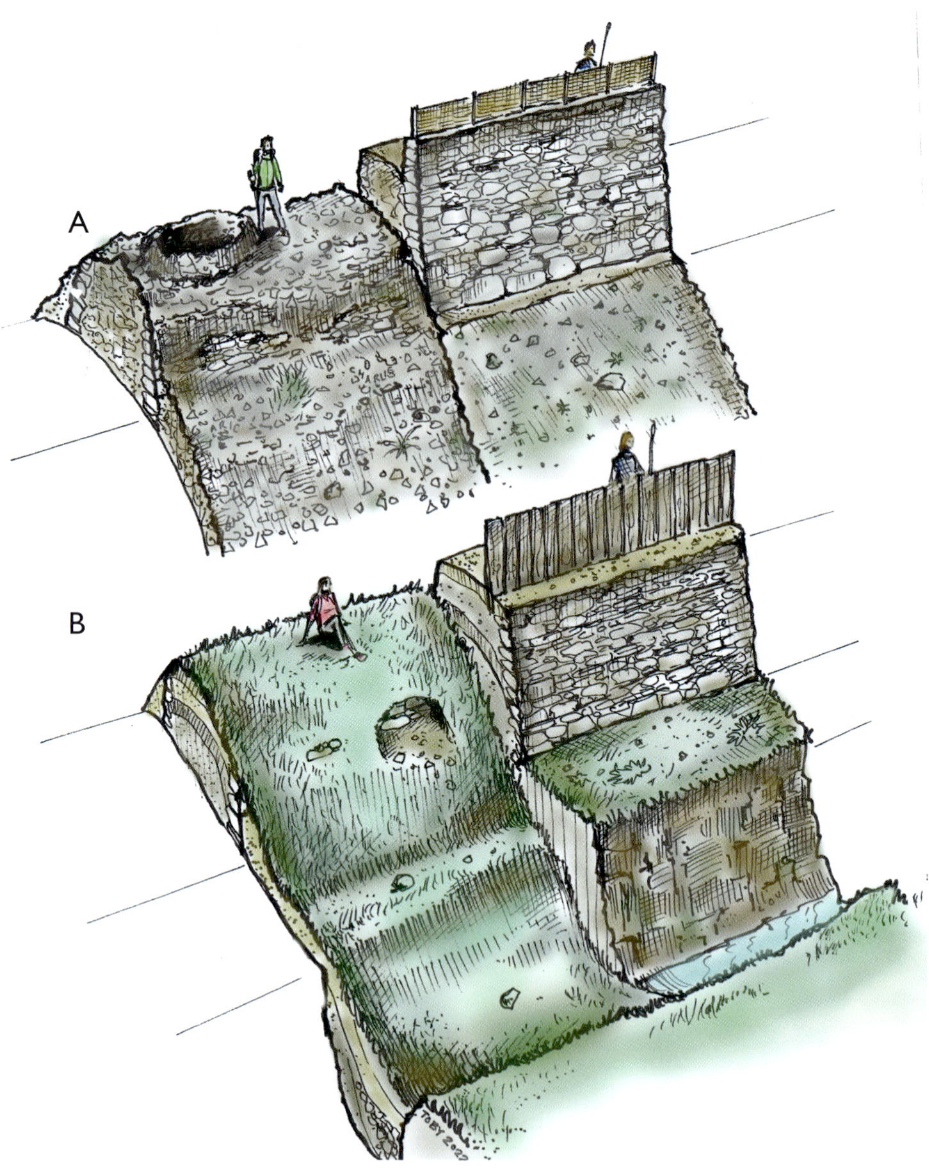

Fig 5.3 Ramparts in ruins. The hillforts we visit today are tumbled ruins of once grand monuments. This diagram illustrates, on the left, the present-day appearance of (**A**) a scree or stone-built rampart wall more typical in upland areas, and (**B**) an earth and stone rampart common throughout Wales; the original appearance of both Iron Age ramparts can be seen on the right. In both cases, sections of rampart walling may still be found along collapsed banks today. Stone ramparts (**A**) can often be further damaged by the modern construction of shelters among the tumbled scree. Outer ditches shown in (**B**) have often infilled considerably from their original appearance. (T. Driver)

normally encounter at close-quarters, whether they were the leader and his or her family, Druids or religious specialists who were called upon to make auspicious incantations and blessings, or charismatic visiting architects and engineering specialists from afar who would arrive with stories of distant lands. At a large hillfort build there was the chance to briefly step outside one's own everyday life and experiences.

What rituals were involved at the beginning of prehistoric building work? Undoubtedly beliefs ran deep. Even the Welsh and Cornish miners of recent centuries were superstitious, believing in 'knockers' or helpful spirits underground who would knock to signal a good ore vein or an imminent collapse. Cornish miners left the knockers the last part of their pasties for thanks and protection. Today the most modern construction sites still have a 'topping out' ceremony where a tree or leafy branch is tied to the highest point of the structure. At Castell Henllys, Pembrokeshire, one of the most thoroughly excavated small hillforts in Britain, excavations through the earliest, palisaded phases of the northern rampart discovered several unusual deposits. A decommissioned posthole from an earlier phase had a pig joint placed inside it and an antler pick laid on top. Close by two more antler picks were found, one carefully placed on some shale stones with yet another surrounded by a selection of quartz pebbles. These antler picks were all associated with a carefully layered gravel and clay mound which was later buried by the northern rampart.[3] Immediately prior to the construction of the main northern rampart a great, steep-sided pit was dug and filled with what is thought to have been either a body or sections of a large animal like a cow or pig. Nothing survived in the acidic soil aside from trace elements. Harold Mytum summarises the role that ritual and superstition may have had during building work:

> Whether any specialist advice was available for the laying out of circuits and the ways in which construction should take place is uncertain. This ... could be controlled by a specialist group to whom were also known the ritual and supernatural implications and obligations that would be associated with such massive interventions into the natural form of the world ... so that the desired manipulation of the landscape into an enclosed, monumental form was achieved without alienating any hidden forces.[4]

THE HILLFORT BUILDER'S TOOLKIT

The hard construction work which lay behind the building of hillforts with their multiple banks and deep ditches, often dug through the solid bedrock, is still hugely impressive given the tools that were available to the builders. 'Modern' construction tools that we would recognise, such as iron spades and picks, did not become widely available in Britain until after the Roman Conquest of AD 43. Before that tools were rather basic, but supremely effective, and had remained largely unchanged since Neolithic times.

The main tools in the hillfort builder's kit were most likely to be antler picks, shoulder-blade shovels and tough oak spades. Wealthier Iron Age communities may have been able to acquire some metal tools, but these would have remained rare before Roman times.

Red deer antlers remained one of the most adaptable tools throughout prehistory and were naturally shed each year for collection. The tines or tips furnished Mesolithic people with sharpened harpoon points and provided a tough, handy pressure-flaking tool for manufacturing flint arrowheads and scrapers from the Mesolithic through to the Bronze Age. When used whole, the red deer antler formed a durable pick; tough enough to prise its way through bedrock but with sufficient spring in the handle to absorb much of the impact. Antler picks are a common find in the Neolithic ditches of causewayed enclosures and the deep flint mines of Norfolk but have also been preserved at the bases of Welsh hillfort ditches. They have been discovered at Dinorben near Abergele, excavated between the 1950s and 1970s prior to its destruction by quarrying; at Bwrdd Arthur hillfort on south-eastern Anglesey, and from the construction layers at Castell Henllys, Pembrokeshire. Two antler sections were recovered from Iron Age layers in the waterlogged ditches of the Collfryn defended enclosure, Welshpool, but seem to have been discarded after use in the settlement for tool manufacture rather than being used as picks.[5] Bone and antler is best preserved in the limestone regions of Wales, or by chance in other alkali or waterlogged conditions; in most parts of Wales any similar bone and antler tools would rapidly dissolve in acidic subsoils.

While we do not have evidence for the use of cow shoulder blades for spades at Welsh hillforts, it is also likely these abundantly available bones continued in use from earlier times. The shoulder blade of a cow formed an excellent ready-made shovel with a short handle, while the strong upper and lower leg bones of pigs and cows provided material for a range of other tools, from tough prising tools to delicate awls and needles.

Fig 5.4 Red deer antler pick and cow shoulder-blade shovel, on display in Avebury museum as an example of Neolithic construction tools. Such tools still formed part of the hillfort builder's toolkit thousands of years later in the Iron Age. (T. Driver)

AN IRON AGE OAK SPADE FROM MID WALES

Our knowledge of hillfort builder's tools has recently been significantly advanced by the chance discovery of a Late Iron Age or early Roman oak spade from a Ceredigion metal mine. In February 2019[6] two industrial archaeologists and mine explorers, Ioan Lord and Alan Tansey, were investigating the nineteenth-century Penpompren silver-lead mine near Talybont, Ceredigion, when they discovered an old openwork above the mine that had collapsed down into the historic adit. The area was already steeped in prehistoric mining history. Just to the north lay the Erglodd Early Bronze Age mines, investigated in the early 2000s by the Early Mines Research Group. A report in the 1869 *Mining Journal* noted that in the Penpompren area 'a large amount of ground has ... been opened by the ancients; ... the great quantity of their work is evident, from ... large numbers of stone hammers mixed with the debris thrown up by more recent workmen'. Copper ore was also available in these mines along with the more common silver and lead.

The oak spade was fortunately preserved in waterlogged conditions caused by a huge amount of water draining through the old opencut from above. If the mine had been dry, the spade would have long since rotted away. The Penpompren spade measures 85cm long and has a flat wooden blade and a slightly thicker handle. Radiocarbon dating suggests the oak spade dates from between 37BC and AD 71 although it may have been in use for longer. This is the Late Iron Age/ Roman campaigning period and the find undoubtedly represents a commonly available Iron Age tool reused in Romano-British times. Research shows that five similar spades were unearthed at Darren mine (**Fig 3.24**) in Ceredigion in the 1850s, just below a prominent Iron Age hillfort where the defences intersect prehistoric mines; all but one were destroyed in the nineteenth century and the last is lost. Whilst Roman and early medieval wooden spades of different designs have been unearthed in mines in Shropshire, the Forest of Dean and Cornwall, the Penpompren spade appears to be a unique Late Iron Age survivor from Britain. Archaeologist Jeffrey Davies suggests that the spade could have been sheathed in metal sheet to prolong its use when digging through rock.

Thus we can picture the tools which equipped rampart-builders and ditch-diggers on the first day of the hillfort build. Tens or hundreds of antler picks, cow shoulder blades and oak spades stood ready to loosen earth and rock and dig down to create the defences. Large river or beach cobbles may still have been used, as in earlier periods, to smash away rock. Alongside these tools, hundreds of wicker baskets would have been made to carry away the spoil.

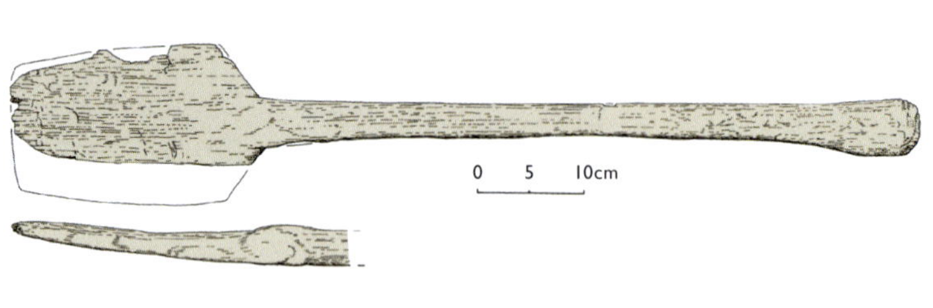

Fig 5.5 The Late Iron Age or Roman oak spade from Penpompren mine, Ceredigion, a remarkable discovery from 2019. (Drawing © Brenda Craddock)

WORKING IN GANGS

Without good organisation, chaos could reign on the construction site. Supply chains of material, from timber for structural bracing and quarried rock to give stability to the rampart to smaller supplies of facing stone for the walling, all needed to be available to the workers as building progressed. There is good evidence from several hillfort excavations that gang-work was employed to organise the otherwise formidable challenge of a big hillfort build into smaller, manageable tasks.

Fig 5.6 Caer Drewyn: a change in building style midway along the eastern rampart, with larger blocks in the foreground changing to smaller blocks a short distance beyond, may show the work of different gangs. View looking north, uphill towards the summit. (T. Driver)

Several phases of rampart at the Breiddin hillfort in Montgomeryshire showed signs of gang-working. Clear subdivisions in the rampart walling could be made out by excavators apparently indicating where different gangs had worked, often using stones of wildly different sizes. The excavator Chris Musson noticed that the core and rear facing wall of the rampart had been distinctly built in sections measuring 2.2m to 2.4m wide, suggesting a well organised line of builders each concentrating on a small section.[7] Similar evidence for gang-work can be seen at Caer Drewyn hillfort, Corwen, where the eastern rampart shows clear divisions between the use of larger blocks and smaller blocks midway along the run of the rampart (Fig 5.6).

In reviewing evidence for gang construction at Welsh hillforts, Harold Mytum ponders how the work may have been organised. He suggests either that a drag sledge pulled by humans or oxen may have dumped off loads of stone for the wall builders to work with, and that skilled wall builders may have awaited material from unskilled 'collecting gangs' scouring the hillside for available stone.[8] Evidence

Fig 5.7 An imagined scene at the build of a small mid Wales hillfort around 100BC, loosely based on Darren Camp, Ceredigion. The female leader in a prestigious purple cloak is discussing progress on the gateway tower with the visiting architect. Meanwhile rock-cut ditches are being dug with oak spades and antler picks, with smoke rising from fire-setting to break the bedrock; rubble is carried to the ramparts in wicker baskets. Timber strengthening is being incorporated in the new ramparts. A shield of north Wales design is propped inside a guard chamber of the new gateway as part of a foundation ceremony, while in the distance earlier Bronze Age burial cairns in the heart of the hillfort have been respected by the new builders. Symbolic quartz boulders flank the gateway and may have embodied gods or guardians. (T. Driver)

for this collection of smaller stones can be seen at Craig yr Aderyn/ Birds' Rock (Fig 5.8). From his own excavations at Castell Henllys, Mytum suggests various gangs worked to dig the ditches, extract gravel and clay separately for the bank, shift material and build the rampart. He writes: 'It is unclear whether the gangs carried out all stages of the [construction] work, but it seems more likely that there were ditch diggers, spoil movers and rampart builders'.[9]

BREAKING THE BEDROCK

... the antients seem to have some methods of working thro' hard rocks which is now lost.

Lewis Morris in 1744 describing presumed Roman and prehistoric early mining evidence at Cwmsymlog mine, Ceredigion.[10]

How was hard bedrock broken up and quarried before the widespread use of metal tools? Archaeologist Ken Murphy noted the marks of stone mauls on the ditches cut through resistant shale bedrock during excavations at the Ffynnonwen defended farmstead, Ceredigion.[11] Working with mauls or cobbles would have been a painful, jarring process if they were hand-held. A hafted cobble like those found at the Great Orme Bronze Age mines may have been a far more effective tool, the handle providing greater leverage and absorbing the impact.

Another way that hard rock may have been broken without leaving much archaeological trace would have been by fire-setting, a technique used in even the most basic rural Welsh mines of recent centuries. Using this technique, a vigorous fire would first be lit against the rock face and allowed to burn. Once the rock was hot, usually after a few hours of firing, water expanding within it could cause it to shatter into rubble; alternatively water would be thrown on the hot rock to quench it.

Fig 5.8 At Craig yr Aderyn or Birds' Rock a modern breach in the boulder walling of the main gateway passage (intact walling visible at lower left and right of the image) has exposed the rampart core, made up of a dense mass of smaller stones. One can imagine the hundreds of basket-loads of material this core represents, gathered from the surrounding hillside. Such a mass of stone may originally have been bolstered by internal timbers. Scale 1m. (T. Driver; original observation by Louise Barker)

The surveyor of the Cardiganshire silver-lead mines in the eighteenth century, Lewis Morris, described how this contemporary process may have been used to excavate a Bronze Age mine at Twll y Mwyn that he had visited:

> Their method seems to be this. They made a great fire of wood in the bottom of their rakes, which were always open upon that account, and when the rock was sufficiently hot they cast water upon it, which shiver'd it, and then with stone wedges, which they drove in with other stones, they work'd their way through the hardest rocks, tho' but slowly.[12]

Evidence for the use of fire-setting to break the rock in the hillfort ditches of Wales should perhaps by now have been discovered during a hillfort excavation. One would expect burned stone, charcoal and scorched bedrock in the base of a ditch. Yet the process, by its very nature, removes the face of stone which has been heated and burnt and the shattered rubble would have been carried away to build the rampart. Therefore it is questionable what archaeological trace fire-setting would leave today.

A final, perhaps equally effective, method of excavating bedrock would have been to hammer in lines of dry wooden wedges to rock crevices. The wooden wedges were then thoroughly soaked; as the wood expanded it would crack the rock. Larger wedges could be driven in deeper as the stone spilt. Such methods of 'wedging' were used into the historic period in stone quarries to split even very large blocks away from the rock face. In Iron Age Wales, this technique would have left very few visible traces.

Bluster and bravado: monumentality and hillfort design

> *The oddities of Welsh hillfort architecture go beyond the sober buildings of prehistoric people obsessed with protection and attack strategy. They speak of monumental symbolism and display, neighbourhood one-upmanship and the conjuring of fear, terror and respect in the minds of one's enemies – and friends – as they approach the hillfort.*
>
> Toby Driver, 2018[13]

Fig 5.9 An Iron Age ditch cut through the limestone bedrock at Buckspool (The Castle) coastal promontory fort, south Pembrokeshire. The fresh, rock-cut ditch edge can be seen on the RIGHT, with material piled up to form the rampart on the LEFT. The ditch would originally have been deeper and bright grey/ white in the sun, overlooked by a bright rampart wall of quarried limestone blocks. Buckspool has been newly surveyed by CHERISH Project archaeologists and lies on the Castlemartin military training area with restricted access (see Fig 5.36). (T. Driver)

In a prehistoric world of limited labour availability, with competition over resources, instability in political leadership and uncertainty over weather and crops, what pushed Iron Age communities to build their hillforts above and beyond the basic functional requirements needed for the creation of a protected home?

Archaeologists in the early to mid-twentieth century, studying the hillforts of Britain against the backdrop of two world wars, sought to explain changes in prehistoric architecture through developments in defence and attack strategy. Hillforts were widely seen as military encampments or refuges to defend a cowering population from conflict and – ultimately – doomed battles against the Roman legions. Yet there was much about hillforts which made little sense in military terms. Many hillforts in Wales had strong main gateways at their front but weak or entirely absent rear defences, leaving their 'back doors' vulnerable to attack.

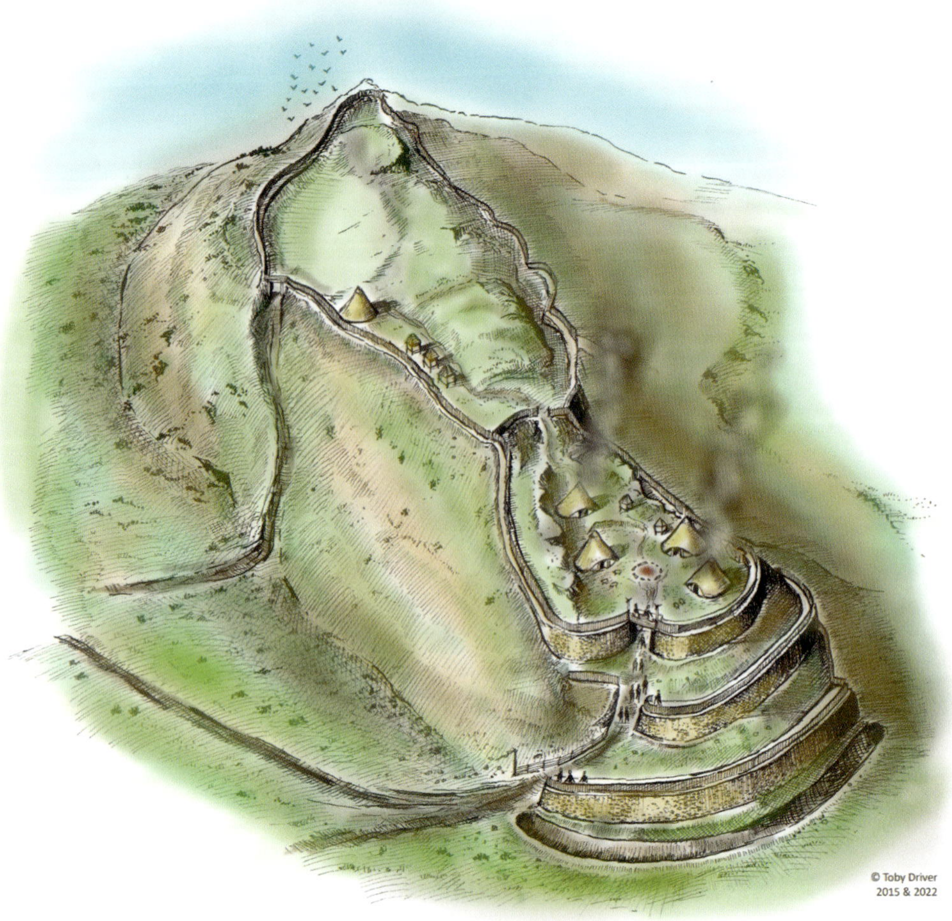

Fig 5.10 Monumentality in hillfort design is exemplified by the directional defences of Pen y Bannau hillfort, Strata Florida, Ceredigion, where three very impressive ramparts formed a multivallate defensive 'façade', but only at the northern end of an upland outcrop. The remainder of the outcrop was largely undefended. Clearly the defences were principally designed to project an impression of strength at the gateway, rather than securing the entire settlement against the threat of attack. (T. Driver)

Similarly, a number of hillforts had domed interiors with houses and people fully on view to those approaching from the surrounding landscape. To some archaeologists this rendered the hillfort strategically weak and even redundant as a military stronghold. Archaeologist Michael Avery,[14] who produced an expert overview of many of the hillfort defences of Britain, noted that a functional hillfort rampart should be high enough to obscure the view of the interior, allowing the inhabitants the advantage of '... interior lines of communication' against their assailants. Continuing this theme, in an influential 1989 academic article about hillforts, attack strategy and non-military hillforts archaeologists Bowden and McOmish[15] suggested that hillforts with highly visible interiors were untenable as military strongholds as attackers could see military preparations going on inside the fort.

Hillfort archaeologists have now come to the realisation that the majority of these prehistoric strongholds were never intended to be fully protected against sustained military attack. They were built in landscapes of fear and respect, superstition and awe, and most employed techniques of **monumentality** to make the hillfort look more terrifying and impenetrable than it actually was. Within the psychology of warfare the *appearance* of great defensive strength could have been as ruthlessly effective at preventing an attack as a real stone wall. The great hillfort archaeologist A.H.A. Hogg summed up this concept in 1975 when he wrote: '... ideally a fortress should be so strong as to make any thought of attack appear hopeless'.[16]

The gateway at Castell Henllys, Pembrokeshire, was studied in detail over many years of excavation by Professor Harold Mytum and his wider team. Superficially this strong towered structure, with a long entrance passage and cache of thousands of slingshot stored behind the rampart, looked like a strong military structure to resist and repel invaders. But there are other ways to read the evidence. Mytum discusses the problem:

> Why do the earthworks give the impression of a military arrangement to modern eyes yet would not have done so in the Iron Age? ... What should be made of the massed hoard of sling stones? The first point is that such investments do not create effective military features against most of the raiding bands that were the most likely form of threat. At dead of night such groups could easily scale the slopes; there was not even a fence to negotiate. Moreover, the side entrances were left open and exposed ... The requirement was to enclose; that was the psychological, cultural and spiritual necessity. The monumental nature of this enclosure was a social need ... an enduring symbol of identity, unity, coherence and protection.[17]

Similarly, the tactical intimidation of enemies by Iron Age warriors is recorded by Roman historian Tacitus in his description of the famous battle of Mons Graupius, late in AD 84, which took place somewhere on the approaches to Inverness. The Romans under Governor Agricola faced the Iron Age peoples, or the 'British army' of Mattingly's 1948 translation:

> The [Roman] troops were mad for action and ready to rush into it, but Agricola marshalled them with care ... The British army was stationed on higher ground in a manner calculated to impress and intimidate its enemy ... the other ranks

rose, as it were in tiers, up the gentle slope. The space between the two armies was taken up by the charioteers ...[18]

There were several ways that monumentality was employed by hillfort builders to make a hillfort appear awe inspiring, terrifying and strongly defended. Principally many gateways faced a **correct path of approach**, the direction along which most human or animal traffic was expected, or the chosen approach to the main gateway which was the most respectful path to follow. Accordingly, main gateways were usually the strongest, most elaborately built and best defended sections of any hillfort. These strong main gates, flanked by tall ramparts, often contrast with weak or absent rear defences where any serious invader could simply have stepped over a fence to gain access. This **asymmetry** in Welsh hillfort defences is a common occurrence and shows that an *impression* of strength was often more important than creating an actual impenetrable barrier. Hillforts like Twyn y Gaer in the Black Mountains, illustrated in Figure 3.20, have **directional defences** where most of the labour was focused upon building the tallest, steepest ramparts only on the side facing the most 'traffic'; or perhaps facing the territory falling within the visual command of the community. At other hillforts like Caerau, Cardiff, low contour ramparts enclosing the fort's perimeter become massive at the points where they flank the main gateways (Fig 1.26).

Fig 5.11 The huge scale of coastal enclosure is perhaps best seen at Porth y Rhaw promontory fort, Solva, in north Pembrokeshire. Ramparts here stand some 5m above the infilled ditches and are among the tallest in Pembrokeshire. Originally the ditches were deep and rock-cut while the ramparts were brightly walled with grey/ white stone blocks. (T. Driver)

Our knowledge of hillfort approaches in Wales has changed considerably since the discovery of the Pembrokeshire chariot burial in 2018. This elaborate and unusual burial was interred in a round mound flanked by trackways approaching the defences of an inland promontory fort. All those arriving at the fort would have walked past this ostentatious ancestral burial. We now know that we need to look *outside* hillfort defences to find monuments on the approaches that have been missed by generations of archaeologists. Indeed recent surveys outside hillforts like Castell Nadolig in Ceredigion (Fig 5.33), carried out since the chariot discovery, have revealed groups of previously unrecorded burial mounds on the gateway approaches which may well be of Iron Age date. Elsewhere the immediate environs of hillforts have revealed additional archaeological sites, such as a crag top enclosure recently identified outside Craig yr Aderyn/ Birds' Rock hillfort (Fig 8.24; Chapter 8).

Fig 5.12 Monumentality in action. Structured internal building techniques used during the original building of this forward-facing rampart at the modestly-sized Castell hillfort near Tregaron, Ceredigion, ensures the earthwork still stands with a steep face today. The almost unclimbable rampart face towers some 5m to 8m above the infilled ditch below, preserving a steeper angle than Maiden Castle in Dorset. The ramparts were originally fully stone-walled. The hillfort lies on private land. (T. Driver)

Whilst those living in some of the greatest hillforts of Wales presided over truly strong and impregnable defences, the majority of smaller hillforts employed a range of techniques to make their hillfort *look* stronger than it actually was. These included using **structured internal building techniques**, incorporating alternating layers of clay and stone inside the earthen bank to make forward-facing ramparts more stable and retain a steeper face than elsewhere on the circuit (Fig 5.12). We also see plentiful evidence of the use of **revetment walling as a method of display**, particularly along forward-facing ramparts or gateways. Here one sees the use of neat stone walling as opposed to the ragged and untidy walls found at the rear of the defences.

Hillforts were artificial structures in a natural landscape and this contrast was often heightened through the **conspicuous construction** of additional forward-facing ramparts, terraced outworks or scarped banks on the key approaches to ensure maximum visual impact. Hillfort builders also harnessed **topographic incorporation** to lend natural strength and spectacle to defences; the incorporation of crags, cliff lines and extraordinary natural outcrops into the meandering lines of hillfort ramparts can be seen at many sites today. At times particularly striking outcrops, as found at the hillforts of Carn Alw, Pembrokeshire (Fig 3.14) or Craig y Dinas, Gwynedd (Fig 5.15), may have been interpreted by prehistoric communities as the ancient remains of past strongholds which imbued their 'new' forts with strong ancestral powers. This is further discussed below.

Reshaping the land: types of hillfort defence

> *That the earthworks survived to the present day gives some support for assumptions that there was substantial technical knowledge and practical ability available ...*
>
> Harold Mytum discussing the ramparts of Castell Henllys hillfort.[19]

There are three fundamental ways to build a barrier to enclose a hillfort: (1) with a wooden fence, stockade or 'palisade'; (2) with a stone wall; or (3) with a tall bank built of earth, rubble or a combination of subsoil and stone. In practice, all these techniques were used singly or in combination in Wales as the local terrain or resources allowed. Thus, a common rampart type in Wales was an earth and rubble bank built using material quarried from ditches, fronted (and stabilised) by a stone revetment wall and topped with timber posts supporting a wooden fence or plank-built palisade.

We must not forget the other more simple ways to enclose or defend sections of a fort, namely by hedging. Well laid hedges, or even the placement of substantial bundles of thorns and sticks, may have been just as effective at quickly creating an animal-proof (or intruder-proof) barrier that would leave little archaeological trace today. Ian Ralston[20] notes the use of thorn hedges as particularly effective barriers in nineteenth-century India, particularly the famous 1,100-mile Great Hedge of India built in the 1840s. The late seventeenth-century masonry Fort Charles at Nevis, Barbados, also had an 'impassable' prickle pear fence between its breastworks and the sea. Tall thorn hedges are still employed to define and enclose tribal villages in the present-day Omo Valley region of Ethiopia and may have been useful barriers to visibility – as well as access – to make hillfort interiors even more private, exclusive and inaccessible. It is rare to find evidence for hedged barriers at Welsh hillforts, but excavations at Twyn y Gaer hillfort in the Black Mountains by Probert in the 1960s to 1970s suggested part of the fort existed as a fenced or hedged annexe in its early phase.

Fig 5.13 Walls of upright branches and thorn bundles enclose a traditional village in the Omo Valley of south-western Ethiopia, protecting it from cattle raiders and hostile tribes. This is an effective and widely used method of protecting a settlement in this region, particularly for guarding the cattle wealth of the community. Thorn defences may have been widely used in the Welsh Iron Age but would leave virtually no trace in the archaeological record today. (© Shutterstock/ Hecke61)

PALISADES AND TIMBER DEFENCES

Some of the earliest hillforts in Wales, constructed during the Later Bronze Age, were enclosed by timber defences. The use of timber 'stockades' during nineteenth-century military campaigns in the United States shows how effective these rapidly-constructed timber walls could be. For these nineteenth-century forts whole trees were felled, cut in half and placed upright in a narrow foundation trench with one end sharpened; sharpened posts could be placed in secondary trenches outside the stockade. Experimental construction of a section of Iron Age palisade in 1986 at Castell Henllys, Pembrokeshire, saw the building of a fence standing 1.6m tall with posts held upright in a stone-packed construction trench. A narrow timber wall-walk was added behind.[21]

At their simplest, a palisade or fence enclosing a hillfort could be built at ground level to provide a single barrier, in which case excavations may discover a line of regularly-spaced postholes or a continuous 'palisade trench' where close-set posts or planks were directly set into the ground. A timber footing trench from the first Late Bronze Age/ Early Iron Age was discovered at the start of the rampart sequence at Caerau hillfort, Cardiff, buried by later iterations of the rampart. Evidence for a similar palisade defence was found at the likely fifth- to fourth-century BC north fort at Pen Dinas, Aberystwyth.[22] A series of palisade trenches were also carefully excavated and studied from the earliest phases of enclosure at Castell Henllys, Pembrokeshire. Another defensive solution was for a fence or palisade to be erected on top of a low bank, in which case the postholes or trench will only be preserved if that bank was subsequently buried – and preserved – by later additions to the rampart.

While a timber defence of upright posts or planks may have stood alone as a basic defence, timber posts may also have been used as a framework or bracing to support a more substantial earth or stone bank. A timber element within a stone-walled rampart could have been visually impressive. Famously the Early Iron Age rampart at Maiden Castle, Dorset, which mostly comprised a massive dump of chalk, was augmented by a vertical limestone wall interspersed with massive timber uprights flanking the eastern entrance, presumably an elaborate façade designed to impress approaching visitors.[23]

One of the best known of the early Welsh hillforts to employ timber reinforced defences is the Breiddin, a great, long-lived hilltop enclosure sited on the rock summit of the Breiddin hills overlooking a bend in the River Severn to the east of Welshpool (see Chapter 8). Excavations showed that the Late Bronze Age rampart of earth and stone was reinforced and strengthened by a row of large postholes. After a period of abandonment, some 500 years later, a Middle Iron Age hillfort on the same summit was enclosed with a larger stone-faced rampart partly built over the earlier Late Bronze Age defences.

Effective as timber was in hillfort defences it would have rapidly rotted, depending on the type of wood and the dampness of its position and foundations. Some estimates suggest that a drystone wall with integral green oak timbers, such as one might find in a walled hillfort gateway incorporating upright timber posts (see Figs 5.22 and 5.24), may only have a life of around 30 years before the posts became rotten and the entire structure required rebuilding.

STONE-WALLED HILLFORTS

Among the most impressive hillforts in Wales are those encircled by stone-walled ramparts. A stone rampart wall was only possible if the prevailing geology provided suitable building materials, such as the rocky mountains and crags of north-west Wales. Serendipitous quantities of scree on some Welsh hills were frequently seized upon by the builders of hillforts, among them Caer Drewyn at Corwen and Garn Goch in Carmarthenshire, to create stone-walled forts in more rolling moorland country (see Chapter 8).

Fig 5.14 Visual command of the land and sea. The partly restored northern rampart at Tre'r Ceiri hillfort, Llŷn Peninsula, Gwynedd, with its parapet wall-walk provided panoramic views over the expanse of the Irish Sea. (T. Driver)

Today walled hillforts may be quite ruinous with tumbled masses of stone showing the general line of the walls. One of our best examples, Tre'r Ceiri on the Llŷn Peninsula, was fortunate to have been the subject of a long-term programme of excavation and restoration of its slumping walls, gateways and roundhouses, ensuring this great drystone hillfort lasts for another 2,000 years. At other hillforts, like Caer Drewyn, Corwen, good traces of drystone walling can be seen around parts of the hillfort where antiquarian archaeologists in the later nineteenth and early twentieth centuries conducted programmes of clearance to discover the buried structures of the wall (Figs 8.14 and 8.15). At times we are fortunate that the drystone Iron Age walls are robust enough to stand today without any active conservation, but they remain vulnerable to modern shelter-builders and general collapse.

The builders of walled hillforts in more rocky, upland parts of Wales, frequently used rock outcrops to great effect – the technique of topographic incorporation discussed above. Drystone walls seem to spring from the living rock where it was incorporated as a foundation (Fig 5.15). Kate Waddington cites the rocky façade of Creigiau Gwineu fort at Rhiw on the southern tip of the Llŷn Peninsula as a good example of using cliffs and crags to dramatic effect in hillfort defences.[24] At both Craig y Dinas and Birds' Rock/ Craig y Aderyn forts in Gwynedd, the forms of

Fig 5.15 Augmenting nature. This clever rampart at Craig y Dinas hillfort, Dyffryn Ardudwy, merges naturally outcropping rock with its own 'cyclopean' stone wall above. The basal outcropping rock forms naturally squared blocks, some even appearing like squared-walling stones (LOWER LEFT). Perhaps the hillfort builders recognised these squared shapes as natural rock, or perhaps they wondered if this was an ancient, long-abandoned wall of their ancestors? Whatever the case the massive Iron Age rampart wall appears inspired by the rock; huge polygonal and irregular blocks are locked together in a strong wall. The author provides a scale. (T. Driver)

naturally occurring fissures and blocks in vertical outcrops of rock are continued seamlessly in the stonework of Iron Age rampart walls. This is particularly striking in Figure 5.15 where the builders may have felt that their wall incorporated the strength and solidity of the natural bedrock. It is difficult sometimes to tell where natural rock ends and artificial walls begin – no doubt a deliberate act to make the newly built fort literally 'rise' from the earth.

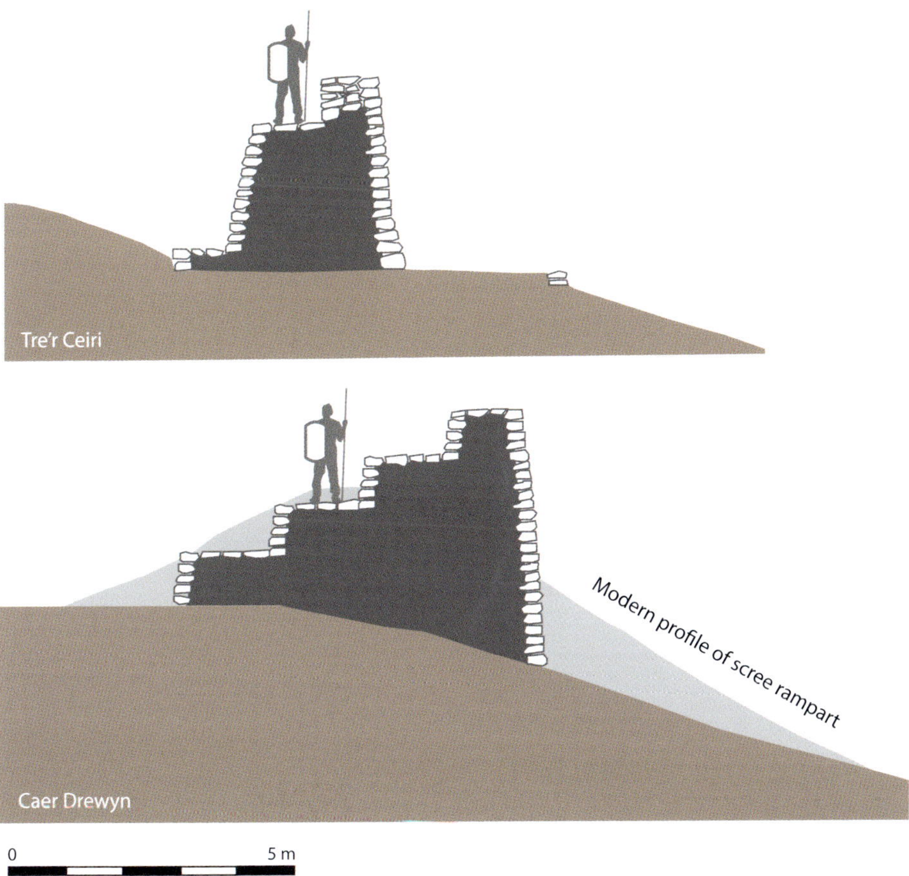

Fig 5.16 Walled hillforts of north Wales. Reconstructed sections through the stone-walled ramparts of Tre'r Ceiri hillfort (TOP) and Caer Drewyn (BOTTOM). The Tre'r Ceiri section shows the wall to the east of the roofed postern gate, high up the fort towards the summit cairn. It shows the rear foundation footing of the wall, the wall-walk and the estimated original height of the parapet wall. The external wall face originally stood some 3.35m above the ground. The wall at Caer Drewyn, Corwen, was equally impressive. Despite being largely buried by tumbled scree today, Willoughby Gardner estimated the outer face of the stepped rampart originally stood as high as 4.6m (15 feet) with a 1.5m-wide rampart walk. (T. Driver. Tre'r Ceiri after RCAHMW 1960; Caer Drewyn after Gardner 1922, Figure 5)

Fig 5.17 The circular stone ringforts or 'cashels' of Ireland represent perhaps the pinnacle of skilled early stone rampart construction. Built during the Irish Iron Age (c.500BC to AD 400) and into the Early Medieval period, the key examples like Cahergall ringfort in County Kerry, seen here, are often heavily restored as national monuments. The impressively thick walls and elaborate interior stairways coupled with single, restricted doors to the outside world mirror some of the characteristics of the Iron Age brochs of Scotland; like a broch, the interior would have been invisible from outside. (T. Driver)

EARTH AND ROCK: CREATING RAMPARTS, DITCHES AND SCARPS

By far the most common form of enclosing a hillfort was with a bank of material, created by digging down through the soil, subsoil and – sometimes – bedrock and piling it up into a great rampart. Depending on their size and steepness, such banks could represent enormous engineering feats requiring an input of labour from hundreds of people.

At their most basic these banks are often termed 'dump ramparts' formed – as the name suggests – by quarried or excavated material being carried in baskets and dumped into a huge bank. Another arrangement of earthen defences was the 'glacis' bank and ditch system, where a continuous slope was created between the crest of the rampart and the base of the ditch far below, resulting in an almost unclimbable grassy slope of material (see Fig 8.38). Usually any slumping or slippage from the rampart above, although infilling the ditch below, would leave the basic system of an unclimbable slope between the two unaffected. Some hillforts display evidence of internal rampart structures, called box ramparts, to stabilise the banks of earth and stone. These internal boxes may have been constructed

Fig 5.18 Excavations by the University of Liverpool examined a section of damaged rampart north of the eastern gateway of Penycloddiau hillfort in the Clwydian Range, one of the largest hillforts in Britain. Careful excavation of the rampart, seen here in 2018, revealed its internal structure (see also Fig 1.22). Scale bar – 2m. (© Rich Mason and Rachel Pope, University of Liverpool)

of drystone cells, or revetted with timber. Excavation of longitudinal sections of ramparts can sometimes reveal evidence of this internal strengthening. More rare is the survival of evidence for timber bracing inside ramparts and walls, but this technique was surely widely employed in Wales to ensure structural stability of tall ramparts where the prevailing building stone was of poor quality (Fig 5.7).

Evidence of monumentality at many Welsh hillforts, discussed above, suggests that considerable care and attention was invested in getting the most important ramparts structurally stable and internally robust, ending up with something far stronger than a basic 'dump' rampart. This would have been achieved by carefully layering the rampart as it went up, perhaps with 'levelling' layers of clay, laid turfs, gravel or rock, to reduce the risk of slippage or slumping.

At some sites there is evidence of the careful use of foundation layers to stabilise the rising bank. Both the eroding coastal promontory forts at Linney Head, Pembrokeshire (Fig 5.19) and Castell Bach, Ceredigion, display thick basal layers of clay in rampart sections exposed through erosion. Similar clay footing layers have also been observed in some coastal promontory forts in south-east Ireland. Work

Fig 5.19 Coastal erosion has exposed a clear cross-section through the defences of Linney Head coastal promontory fort on the limestone Castlemartin peninsula in south Pembrokeshire, allowing study of the ditch and rampart profile without excavation. This view taken during fieldwork by the CHERISH Project team in March 2018 shows the true depth of the infilled, steep-sided, flat-bottomed rock cut ditch (ARROWED, LEFT). The flat ditch base must have been designed to impress. To the right, a figure stands atop the partly collapsed rampart, which reveals – towards its base – a thick foundation layer of yellow/ brown clay. This clay layer must have been carefully sorted during rampart construction, or even imported to the site; similar use of clay footing layers are found at other west Wales forts. There is no public access to Linney Head which lies on the restricted Castlemartin Training Area. (© Crown: CHERISH PROJECT 2022. Produced with EU funds through the Ireland Wales Co-operation Programme 2014-2023. All material made freely available through the Open Government Licence. NPRN 94226)

by the EU-funded CHERISH Project has made careful new surveys of a number of these sites. A clay-bonded rampart was also investigated in some detail during the excavations of Castell Henllys, Pembrokeshire. The main rampart on the north-west side was built solely of gravel, but as it swung around to the western side excavators found a large amount of clay had been deliberately deposited in layers towards the front of the bank, '... perhaps to create stability and reduce slippage onto the scarp and into the ditch beyond'. This design innovation was combined with a downward slope at the front of the rampart, possibly to aid water run-off.[25] The clay layer observed at Linney Head and Castell Bach forts suggests that it was specially quarried off-site, or discovered during the excavation of the outer ditches and carefully sorted into piles for re-use in the rampart foundation. Both processes attest to considerable time and effort taken to internally structure these ramparts.

A final important way that hillfort builders worked with earth and stone defences was through scarping and terracing existing hillslopes. Louise Barker, in her survey of Gaer fawr hillfort at Guilsfield, noted:

> There are two main styles of [rampart] construction, those created through the sculpting of the natural slope and the more constructed form whereby a ditch was cut and bank constructed. The main factor defining these styles is the underlying topography.[26]

The addition of scarps and terraces to the built defences of even these very large borderlands hillforts was considerable. Some steep natural hillslopes at Gaer fawr, modified at their tops with the addition of scarp edges and terraces, stand nearly 6m high and may have been topped with timber defences. Other scarped ramparts, like those found at Craig yr Aderyn or Birds' Rock at Bryncrug (see Chapter 8), may have stood simply as steep, unclimbable faces.

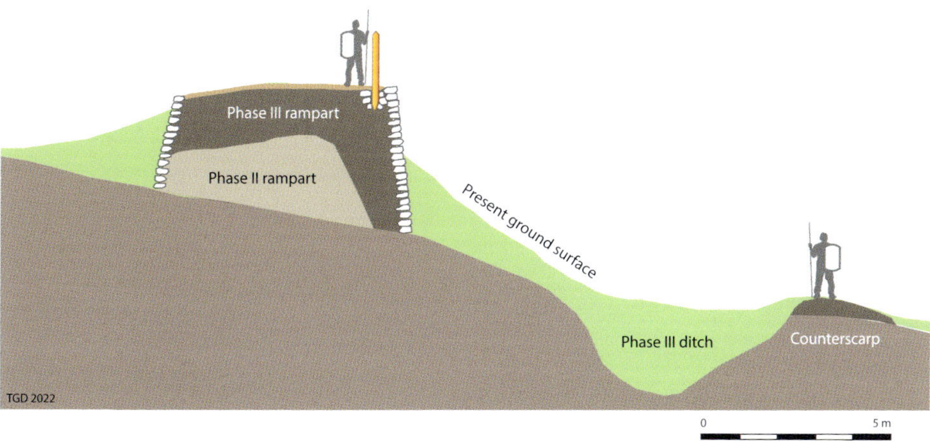

Fig 5.20 Pen Dinas, Aberystwyth. Simplified, reconstructed section through the north rampart of the south fort, alongside the north gate. The outer face of the Phase III rampart, effectively a shale rubble and clay rampart fronted with dry walling, originally stood at least 3.35m above ground level. In this picture, the warrior patrolling its ramparts would have towered some 5.5m above the head of the attacker standing on the counterscarp bank below. This rampart section was excavated in the 1930s by Professor Daryll Forde and questions remain about the exact chronology of the layers he uncovered and recorded. The line of the present ground surface also shows how far the modern profile of hillforts earthworks can vary from the original structure. (T. Driver. After Forde et al. 1963, Figure 7, Cutting A, east face)

BUILDING AND REBUILDING

While the hillforts of Wales were relatively permanent structures in the landscape, it is likely that these early fortified villages were continual construction sites and were rarely finished. We know from long-term excavations at hillforts that gateways and ramparts built of clay, earth, stone and timber were constantly prone to subsidence and collapse and may have been substantially rebuilt every 20 to 40 years. Sometimes hillfort builders only had poor-quality shales and softer

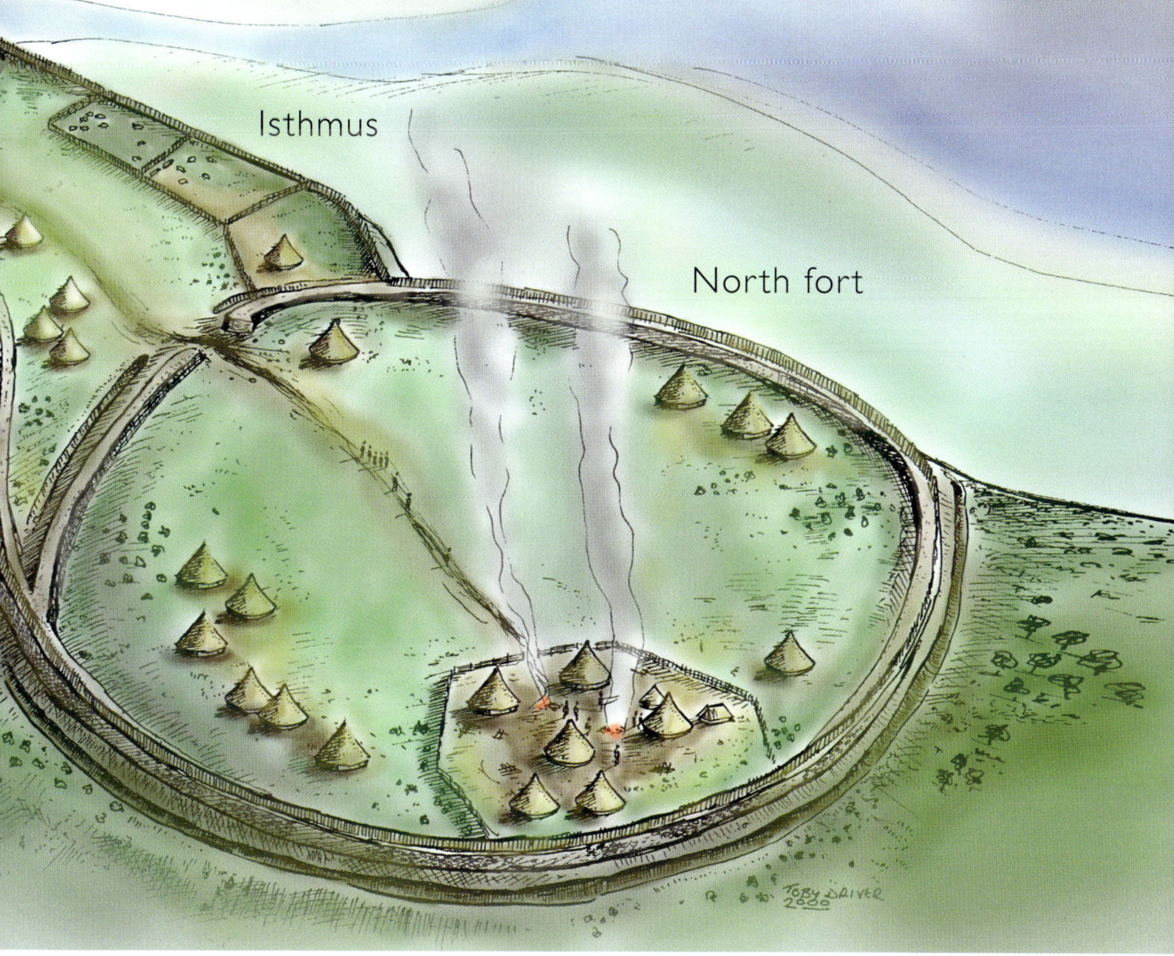

Fig 5.21 The large coastal hillfort at Pen Dinas, Aberystwyth, developed through a number of phases from the simple, large enclosure on the north (RIGHT) summit to the stepped ramparts and intermittently-rebuilt gateways of the southern hillfort (LEFT); eventually both were linked with defensive walls and a new gate across the central isthmus. The 1930s excavations provided a simple description of the likely phasing but, in practice, all parts of a large hillfort like this would have been variously under constant renovation and repair by successive leaders, interspersed with periods of temporary abandonment. A new programme of excavation by the Dyfed Archaeological Trust began in 2021. (T. Driver)

stones to build with; evidence from 1930s excavations at the isthmus gate at Pen Dinas, Aberystwyth (Fig 5.20), and more recent excavations by Professor Gary Lock at Moel y Gaer, Bodfari, show these low-quality rampart walls could bulge or collapse, often requiring shoring up or rebuilding completely. Most hillforts were probably 'works in progress' with partial wall collapses under repair, wholesale rebuilds taking place and sections of less important defences becoming disused and overgrown in the summer months.

At some sites, particularly Dinorben near Abergele (now destroyed by quarrying) and Moel Hiraddug at Dyserth (Fig 2.9), both on the north Wales coast, former gateways were blocked and bold new gateways knocked through adjacent ramparts. Such evidence may reflect the need to 'start afresh', to replace old collapsing walls and rotten timber posts with new gateways. Alternatively we may be seeing evidence of new leaders, or the sons or daughters of a retiring leader, wishing to make their mark on the hillfort. One can imagine a young leader-in-waiting seeing their mother or father stepping down as leader, finally being given the opportunity to take the hillfort and workforce in hand. Works may have involved renewal of gateways, clearance of ditches and rebuilding ramparts in a long-awaited programme of remodelling.

Fig 5.22 Reconstructed gateway at Castell Henllys. Originally the ramparts would have been far higher to each side of the gate with the passage fully enclosed and topped with a timber bridge and tower. This carefully excavated gateway was found to have developed through five main periods. The **Period 1** gateway alone, first established around 410BC, developed through five phases. **Period 2** saw a stone and timber-built gateway passage with paired guard chambers established around 370BC, the one reconstructed at the site today. After a period of neglect and collapse the gate was cleared and rebuilt in **Period 3**, around 300BC. By 250BC this gateway had rotted and collapsed and a timber gateway was built on the ruins of the old gate (**Period 4**). Shortly after, the hillfort was abandoned and only in the late Roman or post-Roman period (**Period 5**) was a new timber gateway constructed on the old opening. (T. Driver)[27]

Instilling fear and respect: gateways and annexes

> *The enduring nature of the authority under which hillforts in the Marches were constructed, at least in the early period, and its wide scope, are above all proclaimed by their entrance features ...*
>
> Hubert Savory, 1976.[28]

The hillfort gateway was the most important part of the defensive circuit. It was the focal point for anyone arriving and the culmination of everybody's journey towards the hillfort, whether from many miles distant or returning from local lands. It was usually where the very best design and defensive ingenuity were focussed and was the most frequently rebuilt and redesigned section of the hillfort's defences. It was the critical point for conveying the power, strength and

Fig 5.23 Following the 'correct path' into a hillfort gateway. On rare occasions, as here at Castell Perthi-mawr hillfort, Cilcennin, Ceredigion, the faint earthwork of an original prehistoric trackway (or holloway) survives leading up to the hillfort gate. The trackway was worn by decades or centuries of foot and animal traffic in prehistory and only survives because the hillslope has been more lightly ploughed in recent times. The hillfort lies on private land. (© Crown copyright: RCAHMW. NPRN 300148. AP_2015_3930)

social standing of the owner of the fort and their community. It was the point at which – it was hoped – enemies would cower and retreat while friendly visitors would gape in awe and respect.

From one kilometre out one's presence as an unexpected visitor would have led to alarm, shouts and a flurry of activity on the distant rampart. Getting closer, passing well-tended fields, grazing livestock and other signs of land ownership, the dominating presence of the hillfort walls high above you would increase considerably. The final approach to many hillforts followed a 'correct path', a particular route along which people were expected to arrive. The full defensive might of the hillfort would be focussed to overlook this route, employing all elements of monumentality to their best advantage.

Occasionally archaeological evidence of the original approach survives in the form of a well-worn holloway up and into the main gateway. Good examples can be followed to this day into Pen y Crug hillfort, Brecon (Fig 8.27) and at Caerau hillfort, Cardiff. The hillfort of Castell Perthi-mawr, Cilcennin in Ceredigion (Fig 5.23), on private farmland, also retains a worn holloway up and into the main gate. At some upland hillforts entrance approaches were formalised in stone as constrictive walled corridors and passages (Fig 5.25), described further below.

FROM PUBLIC TO PRIVATE SPACE: ENTERING THE GATE

Approaching to within 60m of the gateway one would come within dangerous range of slingshots fired from the rampart walk (Fig 4.8). There would be shouts and commotion from the rampart walks and gateway tower, itself adorned with cattle – or human – skulls, along with wooden carvings and other embellishments.

If one was friendly and had permission to enter, you would have been relieved to hear echoes from inside the wooden gates as they were unbolted and opened. Once the gates swung open you entered into a long dark passage beneath the wooden gateway tower, a constricted 'squeeze' through the narrow, liminal darkness of the passage under close scrutiny.

In a typical Welsh hillfort the gateway passage would have been dark and stone-walled (Fig 5.25), lined with massive timber posts supporting the roof. Footsteps and voices from the rampart walk above would clatter over your head. The experience of passing through this dark gateway passage could be likened to one's experience of airport security today, with the consequent relief on the other side. At some hillforts there were guard chambers to either side, or shallower 'gateway recesses', sometimes corbelled over with low roofs. At Moel y Gaer Bodfari, a 'hooked inturn'

Fig 5.24 Reconstruction of the Phase III south gate of the south fort, Pen Dinas hillfort, Aberystwyth, as it might have appeared around 100BC. The asymmetric gateway stood on sloping ground, standing 3m high and towering over the approaches. Inside, new excavations by the Dyfed Archaeological Trust in 2021 established that the entrance track was flanked left and right by roundhouses shelved into the steep, rocky hillslope. (T. Driver)

inside the main northern gateway was not a guard chamber as such but provided a distinct recess perhaps with a similar function; a small circular hut can also be seen within the inturn of the main gate at Craig yr Aderyn/ Birds' Rock hillfort (Chapter 8). Earlier interpretations of hillforts as military strongholds suggested that guards stood in these chambers, but new thinking about hillfort gateways proposes instead that these may have been ceremonial niches in this unusual liminal space between 'public' and 'private'. Perhaps one would yield any weapons or be asked to make offerings to the community and the gods.

Certainly the most exotic finds are often excavated within or close to gateways. During the 1899 excavations of Foel Trigarn hillfort in the Preseli hills of Pembrokeshire, four workmen spent five and a half days digging roundhouse 21, set just inside the main west gate. Exotic finds included five spindle whorls of stone and slate, fragments of a slate armlet and one of wood, a stone ring, half a finger ring, two blue glass beads and another of yellow glass and seven halves of light green glass beads; also a well-made sandstone lamp, a possible corroded bridle-bit of iron and much wood charcoal.[29] The implication is that at least some of these finds, unparalleled in range and quantity from other house sites excavated at the hillfort, may have been left as offerings by those arriving.

Once the dark gateway passage was safely passed one would break back into daylight, joining the bustle and noise of a busy hillfort interior and safe within the private world of the community. For friend, guest or returning member of the community this would have been a significant experience.

Some structural details of stone-walled gateway passages survive today where they have not become buried in later collapse. At St David's Head coastal promontory fort one passes through a gateway passage of massive upright boulders, lined with a combination of fine and coarse boulder walling, to gain access to the fort's interior. At Tre'r Ceiri hillfort on Llŷn the main north-west gateway (Fig 5.25) has been cleared and drystone walls stabilised and reconstructed during recent conservation works allowing one to walk up the long entrance passageway and in through the

Fig 5.25 Squeezing along the stone-lined passageway on the final approach to the grand north-west entrance at Tre'r Ceiri hillfort on the Llŷn Peninsula. By this point visitors had already negotiated a steep, winding approach path through a lower gateway and here would have encountered a crossing bridge ahead at the final point of entry. A stone bastion on the right-hand side of the inner gate narrowed the entrance further. This gateway has benefitted from conservation and partial reconstruction in recent years. (T. Driver)

constricted main gate. Perhaps more impressive at Tre'r Ceiri is the cleared, restored and re-roofed northern postern gate (Fig 8.11, one of three) sited towards the summit of the hill. Here one can walk beneath an original (reinstated) Iron Age roof and out through this 'back door' which gave access downhill to nearby springs.

Stone gateways of megalithic proportions can be seen at the mighty Y Gaer fawr, Garn Goch in Carmarthenshire (Fig 5.26 and see Chapter 8). The 1.7kms of ramparts and the gateway structures of this hillfort were wholly built from scree and slabs and survive in places reasonably well, albeit in a ruinous state. With eight gateways, two main gates and six postern gates, Garn Goch is unusual in a British context: only four other hillforts have more entrances.[30] The north-east main gateway was originally a monumental structure, comprising: '... twin passages, 14m. apart. Each was 2m. wide and 10m. or 11m. long, lined with very large upright slabs, and perhaps roofed ...'.[31] The main south-west entrance is more ruinous but sat at the foot of the enormous 4–5m-high scree mound which marks the western rampart of the fort.

In the south-east rampart is a narrow slab-lined postern gate which the archaeologist A.H.A. Hogg, who surveyed the hillfort in the 1970s, thought had probably been cleared since prehistory (Fig 5.26). He noted that it was walled with large upright slabs or columns '... like most of the others, but is unusual in that it is not straight.'[32] It is the peculiarities of this entrance that make it so interesting to study. This postern gateway is approached up a steep hillslope on the southern side of the fort. The towering outer slab stands at head-height, 1.5m high. One proceeds

Fig 5.26 Approaching the tall portal slab standing 1.5m high which marks the start of the narrow, slab-lined south-eastern postern gateway into Y Gaer fawr, Garn Goch. This is one of the best-preserved Iron Age gateways to be seen in Wales. It is likely the gate passage was kept clear of stone and used into the Middle Ages to provide access to a nearby medieval farmstead inside the fort. The ranging rod measures 1m (see also Fig 5.31). (T. Driver)

into the passage and up a step, and past a narrow stone pillar (Fig 5.31) 1m high, standing proud of the passage wall on the left. This could have been a practical door jamb in the passage, but also resembles 'tomb guardians' stone pillars inside Neolithic tombs. It may have served a similar purpose to greet visitors through this entrance. As one passes along the passage towards the interior, the direct exit is blocked by a prominent 1.25m-rectangular pillar which forces you to move to the left. It seems access into the hillfort, at least through this monumentalised postern gate, was strictly controlled and choreographed.

Fig 5.27 The Ultimate Iron Age gate at South Cadbury hillfort, Somerset. A recent study[32] has reinterpretated groups of rusted iron fittings found during the excavation of hillfort gateways in England, revolutionising our understanding of the original appearance of the actual gates which closed these points of entry. The example shown is the reconstructed south-western gate of South Cadbury hillfort where, in 1970, several pieces of iron representing pivot mechanisms, angled brackets, bolts and other fittings were excavated. Through a lengthy process of deduction these disparate pieces of iron have been carefully reconstructed into a narrow pivoting-gate and with an inset piece-gate, closed by horizontal timber bars. This Late Iron Age gate is far smaller than would have been seen at the great hillfort gateways on Early to Middle Iron Age Wales but gives a good idea of the sophistication of contemporary carpentry techniques. (Copyright: John Swogger and Rachel Pope)

FUNNELLING THE TERROR: CORRIDORS AND PASSAGES

Gateway passages or corridors were built at many Iron Age hillforts in Wales, extending and complicating the journey to the gate itself. Many cropmarks of plough-levelled defended farmsteads, particularly those built as arrangements of concentric circles with an inner defended settlement and outer field, have passages linking the inner gate to the countryside beyond. These are commonly referred to as 'antennas'. A distinctive type of Iron Age farmstead in south-western Wales was classified as the 'concentric antenna enclosure' by the archaeologist Terry James, who discovered many of them during aerial reconnaissance across Pembrokeshire and Carmarthenshire in the drought summer of 1984 (Figs 5.37 and 6.18). Throughout England similar enclosures are called 'banjo enclosures' for obvious reasons. Cropmarks show the ditches of monuments which have long been ploughed away and, therefore, these cropmarked 'antennas' were most likely to have been ditched trackways or the remains of trenches for palisades or fences.

Fig 5.28 An extraordinary entrance: A group of small hillforts was excavated at Llawhaden in Pembrokeshire by the Dyfed Archaeological Trust between 1980 and 1984. Within the group, two small 'ring forts', Woodside and Dan-y-Coed, sat side by side on a high plateau and were threatened by plough cultivation. Excavations at Woodside revealed a first phase entrance of long 'antenna' banks and ditches, once supporting timber fences, which funnelled visitors along a surfaced trackway. It was further defended by two separate towers over the outer and inner gates. Double posts at the outer gate tower suggested that a further storey may have risen above the tower. Yet this grand entrance led into a very small fort with only two or three roundhouses. It was clearly designed to impress and overawe anyone making the long approach into the interior. This entrance arrangement was later blocked in the second phase by two outer concentric banks and ditches, although the inner gate remained.[33] (T. Driver)

At upstanding hillforts, such 'antenna' or passageway entrances may still stand as imposing earthen or walled structures. Entering these passageways today one can get close to the experience and ceremony of approaching the hillfort gateway along a narrowing, controlled corridor. Several hillforts in north-west Wales have long passages into their gateways, penetrating surrounding masses of scree and rock. Particularly good examples can be seen at Craig y Dinas hillfort, Ardudwy (Fig 5.29) and at the eastern gateway of the smaller fort, Y Gaer Fach, at Garn Goch, Carmarthenshire. Sometimes passageways allowed access through dangerous perimeters, as with the passage entering through the chevaux-de-frise of point rocks and boulders at Carn Alw, Pembrokeshire (Fig 5.35). It is worth noting that many of these passages are only 1m or 2m wide in places, preventing the access of carts, wagons or chariots. The excavated walled gateway passage at Porth y Rhaw coastal promontory fort, Pembrokeshire, was narrowed in its second phase to 1.7–1.8m wide, with a 1.4m-wide gateway defined by rock-cut postholes – barely wider than a modern pair of French doors (Fig 7.6).[35] The main aim of these passages seems to have been to make access difficult, controlled and intimidating.

The scale of some gateways went beyond the mere appearance of strength, instead offering true tactical superiority in their form and approaches. At Gaer fawr, Guilsfield, a large and powerfully built hillfort of the Welsh Marches, three heavily defended gateways protected the innermost areas from unwanted visitors.

Fig 5.29 Looking in towards the main gateway at Craig y Dinas hillfort, Ardudwy, along the narrow entrance passage which guided visitors 70m from the open moorland below. The passage was created through the mass of scree and boulders from which the main ramparts were built. In places it narrows to barely 1m wide, and it would have been impassable to carts or wide loads. (T. Driver)

Gateways carefully funnelled approaching people along contrived ramps and corridors, each one a 'killing zone' where enemies could be easily attacked. The complexity of each gateway was finally revealed during a new survey of the fort in 2007 (see Chapter 8),[36] showing the huge value in detailed new surveys and interpretations of comparable Welsh forts.

At the lowest level of Gaer fawr's defences the west gate was approached by a narrow corridor overlooked by a 35m-long platform on which stands a mound, very likely a slinging platform or tower base to overlook the approaches. Higher up at the summit of the fort, strong south-west and north-east gates gave access to the hillfort's interior. The out-turned south-west gate first channelled attackers along a 100m-ramped approach, looping around within the maze-like ramparts. As attackers curved around to the north-east, they were faced with a final 24m-long 'killing zone' up to the main south-west gate (Fig 5.30), defined by ramparts set 5m apart. There are strong similarities between Gaer fawr and the impressive, curving 34m-long entrance passage which enters the main south-east gateway at Pentwyn hillfort, Crucorney (Fig 3.21), accessible on the Offa's Dyke Path. Here, the passage curved around to the left, exposing one's right-hand sword arm to hostile attack from above. Perhaps only with a protective 'testudo' or tortoise formation, when Roman troops packed closely together with their shields locked across their front and top, would an attack up and into such a defended passage have been possible.

Fig 5.30 The killing zone at Gaer fawr, Guilsfield: a view looking out from the site of the south-west gate, downslope along the narrow 5m-wide approach 'corridor' along which any attackers would have been funnelled, making them vulnerable to attack from either side. Peaceful visitors and important guests would still have felt intimidated and 'off-guard' entering along this heavily-defended, constricted corridor. (T. Driver)

GUARDIANS AT THE GATEWAY

There is further evidence that the point of entry to a hillfort may have been a highly ceremonial place imbued with symbolism. White quartz blocks were often deliberately built into hillfort gateways, apparently to heighten their appearance and to make the entrance stand out from afar. These distinct blocks may even have been seen as 'guardian' stones to which respect had to be paid. The Irish word for quartz is *grianchloch* which translates as 'sun stone' and it is often found adorning Neolithic burial monuments.

During a phase of the Castell Henllys gateway a revetment wall of large quartz blocks which had been '... carefully selected to be both impressive and effective' was built on the southern side of the inner palisaded gate.[37] This showy wall was retained in several subsequent phases of the development of the gate. Quartz was also conspicuously employed in the building of the *chevaux-de-frise* outside the gate.

Fig 5.31 A low-standing stone, 1m-high, set inside the south-eastern postern gate of Garn Coch hillfort could be considered as a carefully positioned 'guardian' stone. It appears to lack a structural role and similar stones have been found inside the passages of Neolithic tombs. (T. Driver)

Quartz blocks similar to those found at Castell Henllys can still be seen in the gateway of the unexcavated Ceredigion hillfort of Cnwc y Bugail near Trawsgoed (Fig 5.32)[38] while quartz revetments can be seen eroding from the ramparts of many other mid Wales hillforts including the accessible paired hillforts at Castell Allt Goch and Castell Goetre at Long Wood, Lampeter. A number of quartz blocks can also be seen tumbled among other walling stones at the main gateway of Craig yr Aderyn hillfort in Gwynedd (see Chapter 8). Excavations by the Dyfed Archaeological Trust in 2005 at the cropmark defended enclosure at Troedyrhiw, near Cardigan, revealed blocks of an original quartz-reveted gateway which had tumbled into the ditch during the hillfort's collapse. The excavators, Ken Murphy and Harold Mytum, described this as follows:

> The brightly coloured white and orange quartz would have made the approach visible, even at dusk ... Large blocks of other rock also lie across the landscape, so the selection of quartz would seem to be deliberate ... Associating the quartz with the entrance of the enclosure may have held some symbolic significance at this liminal area, such as some form of protective function, or as a sign of a certain status.[39]

Perhaps one of the most striking uses of quartz in a hillfort gateway was the ungainly incorporation of a large quartz boulder in the otherwise neatly-walled gateway of Darren Camp hillfort, Ceredigion. Only one side of the gateway was excavated by the Early Mines Research Group in 2005, but the discovery suggests both sides of the Iron Age gateway may have been flanked with large boulders.[40]

Despite the widespread use of quartz at many sites, there are plenty of hillforts built in landscapes rich in quartz that show no evidence for its incorporation in gateways or walling. Are we seeing instead the cultural traditions of the peoples of west Wales who strove to bring strong magic, protection and conspicuous display to their gateways? Alternative 'guardian' stones may be observed in the form of very large boulders or upright standing stones positioned at some hillfort gateways including an unusual setting of three large boulders unearthed in the 1930s excavations of the isthmus gateway at Pen Dinas, Aberystwyth.[41]

Fig 5.32 Showy and symbolic. Large quartz boulders protrude through the turf of the unexcavated gateway at Cnwc y Bugail hillfort, part of a group of three small hillforts near Trawsgoed, Ceredigion. (T. Driver)

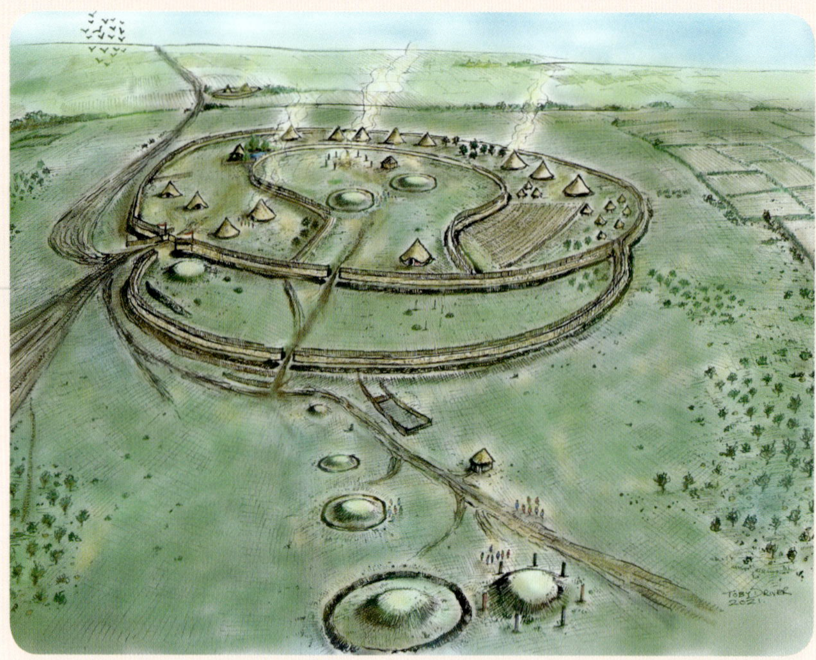

Fig 5.33 Reconstruction drawing of Castell Nadolig, Ceredigion, in the Late Iron Age, with the locations of burial mounds based on the results of geophysical surveys. Various prominent burial mounds dominated the approaches to the hillfort, and the interior. View looking south-west. The hillfort lies on private land. (T. Driver)

In the Iron Age, boundaries between the everyday worlds of domestic life and farming and the otherworlds of death, ritual and ceremony were frequently blurred. Watery places including springs, lakes and bogs together with isolated, liminal and dangerous places from mountain peaks to deep caves were seen as places where the gods resided and where the worlds of the living merged with the otherworlds (**Figs 3.15**, **3.18** and **3.19**). Sometimes these caves and dark places were enclosed within hillforts (see **Figs 7.17**, **7.23** and **8.27**). Whilst Wales has its share of votive deposits of prestige metalwork and other finds, actual burials from the Iron Age had hitherto proved elusive.

With the chance discovery and excavation in 2018 of a chariot burial in south Pembrokeshire, enclosed within a circular burial mound on the approaches to an inland promontory fort, archaeologists realised that scores of Iron Age burials may have been missed by generations of archaeologists. The chariot burial was not discovered inside a settlement but on the approaches to it. Were it not for the chariot discovery, the circular mound which contained the extraordinary burial would have been easily dismissed as being of Early Bronze Age date and unrelated to the nearby hillfort. Following this momentous discovery, attention turned to the immediate environs of other west Wales hillforts to seek out further evidence of Iron Age burial. Geophysical surveys by the Dyfed Archaeological Trust indeed confirmed other – as yet undated – burial mounds outside a number of hillforts.

Following on from these Pembrokeshire discoveries, new fieldwork by the Royal Commission at Castell Nadolig hillfort, Ceredigion, was designed to investigate the original findspot and wider context of the Penbryn Spoons (illustrated in **Fig 5.2**). These rare artefacts, now on display in the Ashmolean Museum in Oxford, are thought to be linked to divination and the work of a religious specialist or Druid residing at the hillfort.[42] Castell Nadolig is the second largest hillfort in Ceredigion but has never been excavated. New high-resolution geophysical surveys of both the hillfort and its immediate environs revealed several previously unrecorded burial mounds. A pair of burial mounds discovered inside the hillfort may indeed have been the original findspot of the Penbryn Spoons, thought to have been unearthed when a boulder-burial was cleared by the tenant farmer in 1829. The biggest surprise was a group of burial mounds sited on the approaches to the fort, reimagined in **Fig 5.33**. These are now plough-levelled and were rediscovered by the geophysical survey. Only future excavation could establish whether some or all of these mounds held Iron Age burials, but the implication is that Castell Nadolig, for a time at least, was a centre for prehistoric ceremony and burial on the Cardigan Bay coast. Castell Nadolig lies on private farmland with no public access.

A CURTAIN OF STAKES AND STONES: THE *CHEVAUX-DE-FRISE*

The French term 'chevaux-de-frise' literally means 'Frisian horses' or 'horses from Friesland' and refers to the Frisian people of north-western Europe who were masters in the art of deploying cavalry in battle. Anti-cavalry defensive devices to guard against attack on horseback, including barriers of wooden spikes or spears, have since continued the name and were widely used in the American Civil War. The identification of curtains of sharp, upright stones around a number of Iron Age hillforts in western Britain, western Ireland and even Galicia, north-western Spain, appeared to enshrine the same defensive purpose of repelling mounted attack.

Fig 5.34 A chevaux-de-frise of small upright stones flanks the south rampart of the San Millán hillfort (Castro de San Millao) near Cualedro (Ourense), Galicia (north-west Spain), inhabited during the fifth or fourth centuries BC through to the late Roman period. It is so well preserved that it is difficult today to walk through the curtain of stones unless one follows the cleared path to the main gate. Such close parallels with similar defensive structures in Pembrokeshire, including Carn Alw fort, and elsewhere in Wales suggest the maritime movement at least of ideas or specialist hillfort architects between the two regions, if not the emigration of entire groups of people. (By kind permission of Manuel Gago)

There are a handful of very clear examples at Welsh hillforts. These have been added to in recent years through the discovery of a previously buried chevaux-de-frise outside Castell Henllys and the identification of new examples following archaeological survey. Two of the best to see are at Pen y Gaer, above Caerhun on the Conwy valley in Eryri (Snowdonia), and at Carn Alw fort on the north side of the Preseli hills, Pembrokeshire. Beyond the outer rampart of Pen y Gaer hillfort

(Fig 1.10) are two areas of chevaux-de-frise on the south and western side. These are set with pointed stones varying between 30cm and 90cm in height but most are not very high at all. It is very likely that these stony barriers were augmented with perishable defences, conceivably sharpened upright stakes – renewed during times of strife – or even wide areas of blackthorn to protect the approaches.

The broad curtain of upright stones, boulders and slabs at Carn Alw is impressive to see today (Fig 5.35). This wide chevaux-de-frise survives on the open moorland of the Preseli hills and principally protects the west and south sides of a prominent, steep outcrop around part of which has been constructed a scree rampart for a small fort. The chevaux-de-frise is penetrated by an earlier, slab-lined main entrance passage on the north-west, which was later blocked in favour of a side passage into the fort. The surrounding moorland seems to have been 'picked clean' of useable stone to provide rocks for the chevaux-de-frise. The original surveyors

Fig 5.35 Carn Alw hillfort, Pembrokeshire, view from the west. The southern arc of the chevaux-de-frise on the right shows the very clear demarcation between the dense outer perimeter of stones and the virtually stone-free tract of moorland beyond from where slabs and boulders have been collected in the Iron Age. The earlier slab-lined main passage through the defence and into the fort shows as a broad green corridor (RIGHT OF CENTRE). This was later blocked in favour of a minor side passage. (© Crown copyright: RCAHMW. NPRN 94240. AP_2012_2917)

Harold Mytum and Chris Webster found the stone spread to be at its most dense around the outer five metres of its perimeter, meaning that the 'front face' of the perimeter looked more impressive on the approaches.[43]

Perhaps the best studied chevaux-de-frise in Britain is that excavated at Castell Henllys, Pembrokeshire, described in detail by Harold Mytum in his 2013 published report.[44] It only survived into the modern day as it was buried by a later extension of the rampart. This stony barrier comprised hundreds of low upright stones, none much higher than half a metre, aligned edge-on to the north towards the direction of approaching attackers. There was a high proportion of quartz in the stones at the western end of the feature, closest to the main gate, suggesting that display was important. Given the detailed excavation and analysis of this chevaux-de-frise, Professor Mytum is well placed to discuss whether it was primarily a defensive feature, or a purely symbolic one. He writes:

Fig 5.36 Old works of the ancestors? Distinct rows of naturally outcropping, sharp limestone bedrock flank and defend the approach to Buckspool (The Castle) coastal promontory fort, south Pembrokeshire. Was this pre-existing, 'natural chevaux-de-frise' seized upon by Iron Age builders looking to build a new promontory fort? It may have been interpretated as signs of an 'old work', a defunct defence built by earlier generations. It could have functioned as a perfectly effective defence if augmented with sharp wooden stakes or thorn hedges. Buckspool lies on the Castlemartin military training area with restricted access. (T. Driver)

[the stones] ... would not have been highly visible except in shortly cropped grass, and so this area may have been used for the grazing of sheep ... The width of the *chevaux-de-frise* would have been sufficient to slow a charging Iron Age horse (the size of a modern pony), which might have had difficulty in clearing such a spread of stones, but they were hardly a major deterrent. Running warriors or ponies would probably have been merely inconvenienced ... At best it may have slowed down the attackers as they picked their way between the stones ... [but] Not a single slingshot was found between the stones ... The military role for the *chevaux-de-frise* therefore seems at best partial. It is possible that the *chevaux-de-frise* primarily served a symbolic role, marking the boundary of the settlement and the approach to the fort.

Fig 5.37 Striking cropmark of a 'concentric antenna enclosure', or Iron Age farm, photographed in July 1990 in Pembrokeshire, 2km west of Llandissilio. The long, narrow 'antenna' entrance passage measures nearly 50m long. Compare with Fig. 5.28. (© Crown Copyright: RCAHMW. 905528/18. NPRN 401987)

6 Ways of living: houses, farms and hut groups

Fig 6.1 (PREVIOUS PAGE)

Safe and secure: the Iron Age and Romano-British roundhouse. This reconstruction painting shows one of the domestic buildings at Din Lligwy, Anglesey, and some of the activities which may have taken place inside. Iron fire-dogs (Fig 6.21) support a cauldron over a stone hearth, the focus of the house. In the background, weaving is taking place. The daub-plastered walls and small window may not have been luxuries found in every roundhouse in prehistoric Wales, but similar stone walled roundhouses were common along western coasts. (Menter Môn with funding from the Heritage Lottery Fund, Cadw and Welsh Assembly Government; illustration by Brian Byron)

6

ALONG the rocky coasts of Wales, and across the mountains of central and north-west Wales, durable standing remains of prehistoric houses can still be seen inside hillforts and promontory forts. Standing roundhouse footings inside Garn Boduan and Tre'r Ceiri hillforts on the Llŷn, or at the guardianship hut groups at Din Lligwy and Holyhead Mountain on Anglesey, are remarkable survivals. Today one enters the houses through the same doors which Iron Age inhabitants used; inside one sees the same stones lining the interior, the same boulders used as seats. At some coastal promontory forts like Clawdd y Milwyr/ St David's Head, upright stones ('orthostats') define the circular walls of prehistoric houses which were formerly infilled with timber, clay and small stones (Fig 7.8).

Modern visitors to hillforts on a wet and windy day usually marvel at the tenacity of Iron Age people who endured such a hard life in such exposed places. Sabine Baring-Gould, excavating the houses within St David's Head coastal promontory fort in 1898, noted the lack of shelter they offered:

> ... the hut circles must have been terribly exposed in foul weather, and in winter gales from the east and south, almost untenable. A summer gale with rain in August brought this very forcibly home to the explorers.[1]

By visiting authentic reconstructed roundhouses at museums like Castell Henllys in Pembrokeshire or St Fagan's Museum, Cardiff, we can gain new respect for the builders of Iron Age Wales (Figs 3.16 and 6.13). It is hard not to be impressed by the permanence and grandeur of a great Iron Age roundhouse. Even on a cold winter's day, these cosy and well-insulated homes would have kept out the worst of the weather. Warmth was provided by a roaring fire, members of one's extended family and even perhaps a few animals on the coldest winter days. Reconstructed roundhouses have taught us an enormous amount about how Iron Age families lived and worked 2,000 years ago. Yet there are still questions about the nature of living inside some of the hillforts of Wales. Whilst the earliest buildings inside Tre'r Ceiri hillfort were large roundhouses, these became ever more subdivided in Romano-British times with rough huts and shelters piled around them. In its later phases the interior of Tre'r Ceiri may have resembled a crowded jumble of informal dwellings, a world away from the pristine individual houses presented through reconstructions at outdoor museums today.

Hillforts dominated the landscape of later prehistoric Wales but were home to only some of the population. Away from these walled villages, first millennium BC Wales was in places heavily farmed, cleared and managed yet in other parts still wild, wooded and undiscovered. Within this wider land stood family farms, specialised cattle enclosures and scattered roundhouses. In parts of north-west Wales, settlements formed entirely of round and rectangular houses – known generally as 'hut groups' – were the most common form and survive within millennia-old hillside field systems.

Fig 6.2 A treasured possession fresh from the earth. A neat spindle whorl, used for drawing out yarn from wool, excavated during the Pen Dinas hillfort community excavations by the Dyfed Archaeological Trust in 2021. It was recovered from a crevice in the bedrock floor of one of the roundhouses where it had been lost or discarded some 2,000 years ago. (T. Driver)

HOUSES THROUGH THE MILLENNIA

The forms of houses in Wales changed through the millennia. Structural traces of the temporary shelters and camps of nomadic Mesolithic hunter-gatherers rarely survive, but we have good evidence that certain locales were revisited over successive years. At Mesolithic sites like the Nab Head coastal promontory in Pembrokeshire, where hundreds of perforated shale beads were manufactured and presumably exchanged far and wide over many years, it is likely that more permanent shelters were erected.

During the Neolithic, the widespread adoption of farming in Wales brought with it the first permanent settlements and early villages. Timber houses and halls were normally rectangular and post-built, influenced by the traditional buildings of Neolithic Europe. The shapes of the houses of the living were often echoed in the rectangular or trapezoidal plans of long barrows and cairns for the communal burial of the dead. Long barrows with dark inner passages and stone chambers are often referred to as 'houses for the dead', from which the bones of deceased ancestors were periodically removed to take part in ceremonies among the living. Neolithic houses are still very rare in Wales but excavations by CR Archaeology at Llanfaethlu on Anglesey between 2014 and 2017 revealed the first multi-house early Neolithic settlement in north Wales. Postholes of four buildings were revealed with a strong resemblance to Irish sites, an unprecedented discovery in a region

Fig 6.3 Roundhouse 20 at The Wick farming settlement on the south side of Skomer Island, Pembrokeshire, sits at the heart of well-preserved prehistoric fields picked out here in April evening sunlight. A recent programme of excavation and scientific dating on the island by the Royal Commission, working with the universities of Sheffield, Cardiff and Aberystwyth, has shown that Skomer's earliest fields were laid out in the Bronze Age, and were later developed during Iron Age and Romano-British times. (© Crown copyright: RCAHMW. NPRN 415556. DS2016_077_013.)

which had previously only revealed the remains of a handful of single buildings. The largest house at Llanfaethlu, House 1, measured 21.6m by 7m, representing a sizeable 6,000-year-old timber hall, far larger than many modern houses. Finds from the settlement included human remains, worked flint and hundreds of sherds of Neolithic pottery.[2]

During the Bronze and Iron Ages domestic buildings changed drastically from a generally rectangular plan to the widespread adoption of circularity. Without excavation and dating it is still very difficult to identify original Bronze Age roundhouses in the landscape as opposed to later Iron Age and Romano-British examples, as their appearance from surface evidence alone can be very similar. It is likely that many upland 'hut groups' in landscapes like Eryri (Snowdonia) have 4,000-year-old Bronze Age houses at their heart. On Skomer Island, Pembrokeshire, a likely Bronze Age settlement at The Wick on the south of the island is represented by a series of earthen terraces tucked below a rocky outcrop thought to have held transient remains of timber or turf buildings. Here the shape and form of the earthworks suggests its date, but excavation could prove otherwise.

With the coming of the Romans rectangular homes were once again in vogue signalling a new, modern way of living brought by the conquerors. The merging of 'native' and Roman styles can be particularly seen where circular and rectangular buildings co-existed at some Romano-British hut groups and farms, like Din Lligwy on Anglesey (Fig 6.4) and the excavated settlement of Graenog, Gwynedd. Studies by the Welsh Roundhouse Project[3] noted that, 'The evidence as it stands indicates that rectangular structures appear in the latter half of the Roman period', particularly during the third and fourth centuries AD. The Project authors noted however that most dating had been based on finds of Roman pottery at these sites, which always survives better than prehistoric pottery. A lack of radiocarbon dates coupled with the overwhelming survival of more durable Roman pottery means that some rectangular buildings may date from earlier times; we need more modern excavations to answer this question.

Many Romano-British farmsteads continued to mix elements of Roman and Iron Age ways of life in their architecture (Fig 6.5). The intermixing of cultures can be particularly seen at some of the rectangular Romano-British farmsteads of southern Ceredigion and Montgomeryshire, discovered over several decades of aerial photography and then investigated on the ground through geophysics and excavation. Whilst many of the defended farmsteads have a circular plan some were built within rectangular ditches and banks apparently reflecting Roman influence.

Fig 6.4 Blending old and new; the Din Lligwy hut group on Anglesey is a substantial Late Roman farming settlement with thick walls built of upright limestone blocks and rubble infill. Excavations in the early twentieth century revealed Roman coins and pottery dating mainly to the fourth century AD but traces of an earlier settlement close by suggested Iron Age origins. The rectangular buildings seem to have been used as barns or workshops – some contained smelting hearths and iron slag – alongside domestic Iron Age style roundhouses. (Menter Môn with funding from the Heritage Lottery Fund, Cadw and Welsh Assembly Government; illustration by Brian Byron)

Excavations at the rectangular Troedyrhiw defended farmstead near Cardigan by the Dyfed Archaeological Trust yielded Iron Age pottery from the gateway postholes but some 200 sherds of Romano-British pottery from the upper ditch fills. This included the ubiquitous Roman cooking ware, Black-burnished pottery, widely traded from its place of manufacture in Dorset. This pottery demonstrated the adoption of Roman culture by the owners of the farmstead, even though day-to-day ways of living essentially continued from the Iron Age. When the nearby Blaensaith rectangular defended farmstead was examined using geophysical survey it revealed clear Iron Age-type roundhouses within a Romano-British style rectangular farmstead. Villas showed the ultimate adoption of a Roman way of life among the wealthy rural farmers of mid, south and eastern Wales. Villas were usually built by Romanised locals displaying their '*Romanitas*', or their adoption of Roman ways of life, and sat at the heart of great farming estates.

Fig 6.5 Late Iron Age or Romano-British defended farmstead discovered through aerial photography at Trehill near Marloes in south Pembrokeshire in the drought summer of 2018. The rectangular ditches, defining an enclosure 56m across, are clearly marked in the ripening crop showing a simple gateway facing east (LEFT). Inside, cropmarks show traces of a single large roundhouse. The size of this prehistoric farmstead compares well with the adjacent modern farm. The cropmark lies on private farmland. (© Crown: CHERISH PROJECT 2022. Produced with EU funds through the Ireland Wales Co-operation Programme 2014-2023. All material made freely available through the Open Government Licence. NPRN 423108. AP_2018_4926)

The Iron Age roundhouse: changing perceptions

> *Occasionally the huts are double, one chamber leading into another ... The walls of the huts, which are very rudely built, are usually 4ft wide, and vary in height from 3ft to 6ft ... we found on sheltering in this during a northerly gale, that the wind penetrated the combined walls of some 15ft in an unpleasant manner, and compelled us to seek a less draughty retreat ...*
>
> Sabine Baring-Gould and Robert Burnard describing the excavation of several roundhouses on St David's Head, Pembrokeshire, in 1904.[4]

Iron Age and Romano-British roundhouses were remarkable structures. We have learnt much, over several decades of modern experimentation and reconstruction, about how they were built and the resources a typical roundhouse consumed during its construction. Roundhouses provided secure, storm-proof, warm accommodation in even the most inhospitable mountain environments of Wales. They conveyed the status of their occupant in their size or position within the hillfort and range in size in Wales anywhere between 2m to 15m in diameter. At times their very siting and construction could be imbued with meaning and ritual, such as the common eastward orientation of many roundhouse doors to face the rising sun. Each large roundhouse was a major building project for an Iron Age community, requiring tons of timber and thousands of bundles of roofing materials – whether reeds, straw, bracken or heather.

Perceptions of prehistoric houses have changed throughout the twentieth century as archaeological thought and science have developed. For example, early in the twentieth century the many large, deep storage pits discovered inside hillforts during excavations across the chalklands of southern England were mistaken for 'pit dwellings'. It was believed these deep, steep-sided pits were where Iron Age folk resided, presumably in darkness and squalor. From the 1930s such pits were recognised more correctly as grain silos, a highly organised solution to the storage of a large agricultural surplus alongside roundhouses within the great Wessex hillforts of Danebury and Maiden Castle.

Our ideas of what prehistoric roundhouses looked like were also influenced by early twentieth-century colonial travellers to Africa and Asia. The roundhouses of prehistoric Britain were usually reconstructed in drawings as roughly built 'huts' based on those in hotter climates and were usually shown with shaggy thatched roofs with rough sticks protruding at their apex in the manner of a woodland shelter. These early views were certainly influential in shaping contemporary views of the abilities of our prehistoric ancestors.

Fig 6.6 Subtle 'surface archaeology'. A pair of Iron Age house platforms or 'hut scoops' within Flimston Bay coastal promontory fort, picked out in low sunlight. The platforms are cut into the bedrock of the hillslope on the uphill (RIGHT) side producing a levelled area for building. (T. Driver)

Fig 6.7 The great Romano-British stone-walled roundhouse at Dinas Dinlle coastal hillfort, Gwynedd, excavated from a deep layer of accumulated sand by the Gwynedd Archaeological Trust over three seasons. The roundhouse was constructed in the second and third centuries AD during the Roman period. It measured 13m across, one of the largest recorded in Wales, and had unusually thick walls measuring up to 2.4m wide. This 3D photogrammetric post-excavation model shows the structural details well, including the unusual threshold of quarried slate slabs. The remains of the roundhouse have now been consolidated for public view. (Copyright: Gwynedd Archaeological Trust)

We now understand these buildings far better after decades of experimental reconstruction. We know for example, that roundhouse roofs did not have a hole at their apex to allow smoke out like a chimney; this would simply cause an updraft and could set the thatch alight. Instead, roofs were fully enclosed with smoke from the hearth gradually seeping out through the thatch. This provided ideal conditions for smoking food hung from the rafters and also for keeping parasites in the thatch at bay: look for the sooty tar coating the undersides of the thatch inside many modern reconstructions.

Yet the smoky, damp atmosphere inside a roundhouse may also have been an unhealthy environment to live and sleep in, particularly throughout the winter months. These houses are reminiscent of the damp, smoky interiors of mining barracks in Wales of recent centuries. In the cold, damp buildings of our recent industrial past, the poor living conditions frequently gave rise to chest complaints and diseases like bronchitis and pneumonia. It was often impossible to dry wet shoes and clothing for the next working day. We can imagine varying conditions inside the Iron Age roundhouses of Wales; relative levels of wealth, building materials, prevailing weather patterns and ways of life would have varied so much from region to region and dictated the conditions of living inside the home.

Unless a hillfort interior has been ploughed, the remains of house sites can usually be made out. One should look out for 'house platforms' or 'house scoops' where an oval or circular levelled area within the fort indicates where the building once stood. Sometimes these are best sought out in the raking light and low vegetation of a winter or spring day (Fig 1.8). If excavated, these levelled platforms often reveal rock-cut terraces into which have been cut narrow grooves for timber walls, deep postholes to support a roof and – sometimes – stone-lined drains in the floor to keep the house dry (Fig 6.9).

Fig 6.8 'Iron Age sheep', a Soay/ Hebridean cross, have been introduced to Old Oswestry hillfort on the Welsh border by English Heritage as a way of managing vegetation at this large site. This is a timeless scene which evokes the livestock seen on most family farms of Iron Age Wales. (T. Driver)

DEFINING HOUSEHOLD SPACE

The coming together of groups of people from the Later Bronze Age onwards to live closely with one another inside defended settlements marked a major change in the ways people thought about domestic life. From the sporadic upland family farms and small hut groups of the Bronze Age, people in the Iron Age were now living in sometimes crowded interiors of what can be considered to be early villages or towns.

In south Wales, on the edge of modern Cardiff, archaeologists Dr Oliver Davis and Professor Niall Sharples of Cardiff University directed the community excavation of one of the largest hillforts in south Wales – Caerau, Ely from 2012.

Fig 6.9 All modern conveniences. Excavations by the Dyfed Archaeological Trust inside Pen Dinas hillfort, Aberystwyth, in 2021 revealed curving rock-cut platforms which once contained post-built roundhouses. The very rough shale bedrock must have made for an uncomfortable floor, suggesting perhaps a plank floor originally covered the rock. This view shows small slabs of a covered drain emerging from the earth on the roundhouse floor (CENTRE), a novel feature which would not have been out of place in a medieval building. (T. Driver 2021)

Two of the earliest houses discovered dated from the seventh to sixth centuries BC, the Early Iron Age; all that remained of these houses were a pair of conjoined gullies.[5] These gullied roundhouses were later replaced by a substantial post-built roundhouse rebuilt on the same spot at least four times. Normally such gullies were thought to be 'eaves drip' channels or drains around the house, to channel water pouring off the thatched roofs.

The excavators suggested instead that the encircling gullies could be evidence that early householders, attempting to acclimatise to the novelty of living within a hillfort, wanted to delimit the private space around their household:

> It is interesting that these houses were contained within gullies ... given that later roundhouses at Caerau did not possess them suggests that they may have had a social rather than a functional purpose ... placing a house within one could be interpreted as an attempt to delimit space, and by implication a socially, independent unit within the hillfort.[6]

From surface evidence, the interiors of some hillforts were particularly crowded with roundhouses; yet without excavation it is difficult to be sure just how many dwellings were occupied together at any given moment in prehistory. The great stone hillfort of Garn Boduan on Llŷn (Fig 6.10) contained at least 170 roundhouses, almost a proto-town. The pockmarked interior of Foel Trigarn hillfort in Pembrokeshire (Fig 3.6) contains at least 227 levelled platforms for buildings; in places the platforms were built up one against another. Whether these were all house platforms, or whether some 'four poster' raised granaries for the conspicuous display of grain wealth is impossible to tell without excavation.

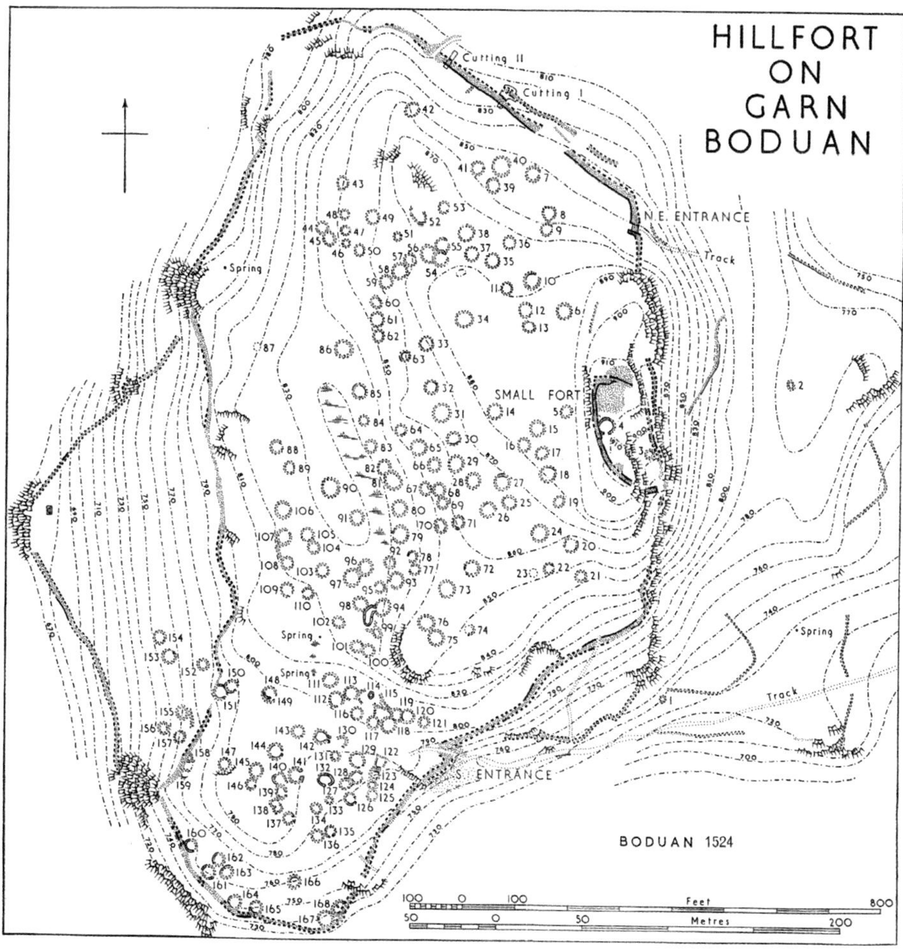

Fig 6.10 Garn Boduan, Llŷn Peninsula; a prehistoric and early historic hilltop town. The defences comprised at least two periods and there were around 170 huts inside, served by two main gateways, numerous smaller entrances and several springs. During Late Roman or even post-Roman times, a small fortified 'citadel' was founded on the eastern summit. (© Crown copyright: RCAHMW. NPRN 95271)[7]

Even if only a proportion of buildings inside Garn Boduan and Foel Trigarn were contemporary, parts of these densely-occupied hillforts would have resembled the crowded lanes of a medieval town, with roof eaves touching one another above muddy paths. Initial excavation of Pen Dinas hillfort at Aberystwyth by the Dyfed Archaeological Trust in 2021 uncovered part of a crowded group of house platforms set just inside the south gate of the south fort (Figs 6.9 and 5.24). Each one was stepped up the steep, rocky slope leading from the gateway so that the door of the house above would have opened to the roofline of the house below. Such building practices inside steeply sloping fort interiors bring to mind the rural dwellings of Alpine or Tibetan hill villages. One can only imagine what drainage was like in these crowded interiors following heavy rain, a problem hinted at by the well-built floor drain discovered inside one of the Pen Dinas houses (Fig 6.9).

Tre'r Ceiri hillfort on the Llŷn Peninsula is another interior displaying signs of crowded living. This grand hillfort, more fully discussed in Chapter 8, has been the subject of several investigations. It was newly-surveyed by the Royal Commission for their ground-breaking *Caernarvonshire Inventory* of 1960 (Volume II: Central), building on the work of earlier surveyors and excavators including Harold Hughes (see Fig 8.9). There are around 150 huts in the main hillfort and many more on the surrounding slopes, nearly half of which have been cleared or excavated by antiquarians who documented the main finds from each structure. The busy interior of the hillfort is the result of multiple phases of occupation and the building sequence can be 'decoded' based on close observation of the physical relationship of earlier and later buildings within the clusters (Fig 6.11).

The earliest buildings appear to have been simple roundhouses which ranged from 2.5m to 7.9m in diameter. There are only a handful of these, suggesting the hillfort as first built had only a moderate number of residents; only 10% of excavated roundhouses produced Roman-British pottery, suggesting the majority were occupied in Iron Age times. These roundhouses were then subdivided, most with central partitions; however, one in the western interior (the combined buildings 53, 89 and 90; Fig 6.11) was cut into thirds with the insertion of a Y-shaped interior wall. Thus spacious roundhouses were converted into far smaller buildings. The third phase of development was the construction of D-shaped or irregular smaller huts, mostly accreted (joined onto) earlier buildings. The archaeologist A.H.A. Hogg found that nearly two-thirds of excavated D-shaped huts produced Romano-British pottery. These structures were then added to again with rectangular structures, possibly during post-Roman times. Later uses may not have

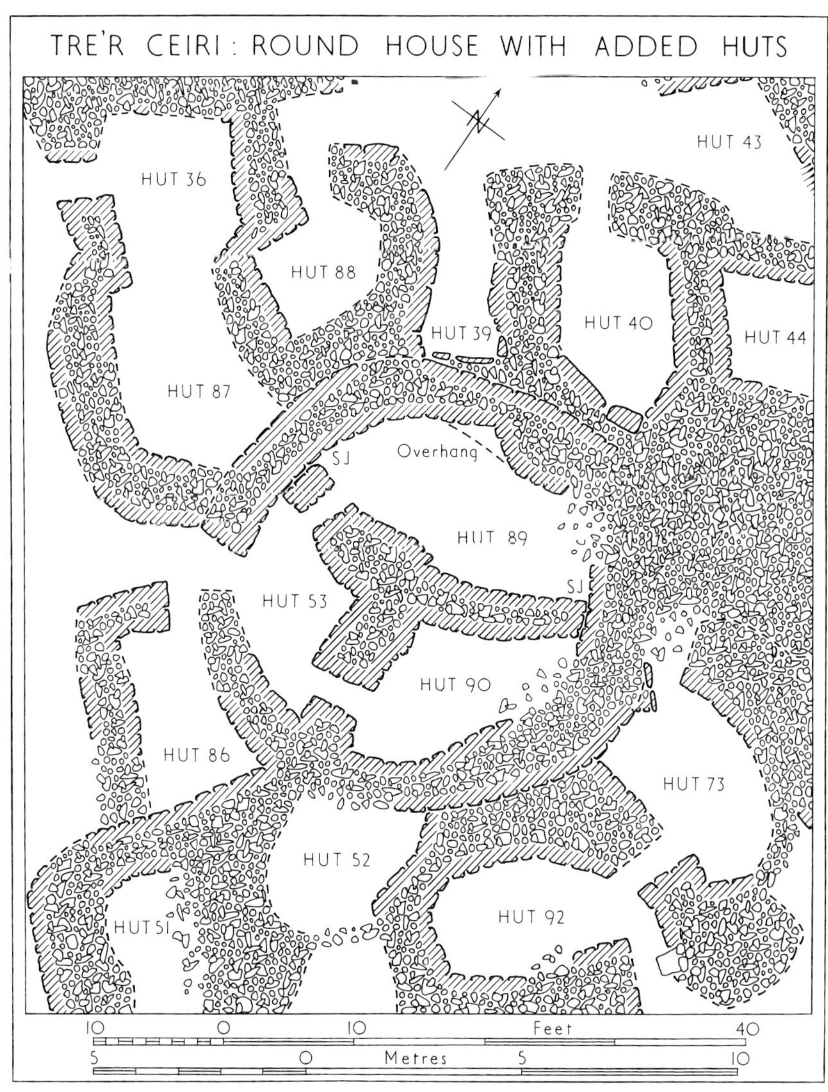

Fig 6.11 Reducing household space at Tre'r Ceiri hillfort: plan of the hut cluster focussed on buildings 53, 89 and 90, prepared for the 1960 *Caernarvonshire Inventory*.[9] The changing sizes of dwellings at this north Wales hillfort, from spacious Iron Age roundhouses to subdivided shelters of Romano-British or post-Roman times reflects considerable changes in the aspirations of the population. An expanding hillfort with regional command may have attracted a growing Iron Age population. In later times perhaps the hillfort saw more transient phases of occupation? Rather than permanent family homes we may be seeing the growth of temporary 'cells' akin to a monastery where people visited, slept and then departed after their reason for visiting had passed. Do these tiny later rooms at Tre'r Ceiri show this great hillfort became a centre for meetings, ceremonies and gatherings at key times of year when the fort became temporarily crowded?[10] (© Crown copyright: RCAHMW. NPRN 95292. DI2008_0128)

been straightforward. The Late Iron Age or Roman beaded collar from hut 41, illustrated in Fig 2.13, is unlikely to have been a casual loss and probably indicates a burial. Hughes[8] noted the investigation of two further burials around 150m away from the south-west gateway.

The interiors of other Welsh hillforts display evidence for order, even planning. The National Trust's Dinas Dinlle hillfort in Gwynedd has been under long-term study by the EU-funded CHERISH Project and the Gwynedd Archaeological Trust. As it is not possible to excavate the entire interior of this large hillfort, a Ground Penetrating Radar (GPR) survey was commissioned in 2020. Excavations in the previous year had shown that large stone structures and Romano-British roundhouses (Fig 6.7) survived buried beneath deposits of windblown sand, making ideal conditions for 'hard' structures to be identified by radar within the 'soft' background of the sandy subsoil. The resulting survey showed an organised interior with a stony, surfaced trackway leading in from the main gate and splitting into at least three lanes as it headed towards the roundhouses. This ordered interior, with a cobbled lane leading to great thatched roundhouses, would have been a world away from the more crowded upland hillforts which had to contend with damp peaty ground, rocky slopes and a wetter year-round climate.

Fig 6.12 Crowded living. One of a number of subdivided roundhouses inside Tre'r Ceiri hillfort, where sizeable Iron Age roundhouses were dramatically changed with the insertion of dividing walls. A 1m scale rod shows the relatively limited size of the new divided interior. (T. Driver)

RECONSTRUCTING IRON AGE ROUNDHOUSES IN WALES

Only through experimentation can we truly learn the skills and raw materials required to build these roundhouses. Before the 1990s, reconstructed roundhouses in Britain were comparatively rare but by 2015 there were around 126 reconstructed examples across Britain and Ireland,[11] all providing valuable insights into our past. At the St Fagans National History Museum near Cardiff, an original 'Celtic village' of three reconstructed roundhouses had stood for around 20 years before it was finally closed in 2013 and a replacement considered.[12]

The three original roundhouses were built as careful reconstructions based on archaeological evidence by Peter Reynolds, who had developed similar pioneering buildings at Butser Ancient Farm in Hampshire. The St Fagans roundhouses were based on excavated examples from Moel y Gaer hillfort, Rhosesmor, in north-east Wales, Moel y Gerddi upland farm in north-west Wales and Conderton in the English Borders. Much was learnt from these early experimental builds. All had to be re-roofed after only eight years and one had to be demolished after only nine years. The sheltered, damp woodland location of the village had exacerbated the demise of the buildings. The terrace cut into the slope withheld ground water and the shaded thatched roofs of the houses never fully dried out causing them to rot. Yet it was estimated that the original Celtic village hosted around 250,000 visitors a year, with 6–7,000 on peak summer days.

To replace the Celtic village, the National History Museum turned to a reconstruction of a conjoined roundhouse originally excavated at Bryn Eryr on Anglesey.[13] While many roundhouses in Britain had been reconstructed with timber and wattle walls or stone walls, comparatively few had been attempted with thick walls of earth or clay – a building method well adopted in the Welsh Iron Age. A drier, more open location was also chosen. Wall height was difficult to estimate accurately. Just using pure clay for the Bryn Eryr walls would have limited them to around 0.5m high, but by producing a strong mix of coarse aggregates, straw and stone dust a strong building material traditionally known as 'clom' in Wales was made. As this mix was often used to make very strong cottage walls up to 2.4m high in medieval and later Wales, it seemed the best solution for the walls of the new roundhouse.

Today the reconstructed roundhouses at Castell Henllys and St Fagans provide great evocations of Iron Age domestic life. They are robust and elegant buildings. Yet it is worth remembering that their present form has been shaped – at least in part – by the demands of the visitor experience. They are cleaner and less cluttered than a long-standing and long-occupied prehistoric house. It is likely that Iron Age Wales had both well-built, opulent, grand examples of roundhouses like these but also its fair share of rather tumbledown and poorly-built homes of the rural poor.

Fig 6.13 The recently-built Bryn Eryr conjoined roundhouses at the St Fagans National History Museum near Cardiff, January 2020. The roundhouses were designed to be a faithful reconstruction of the original structure excavated on Anglesey, as well as providing a robust and spacious new educational facility for schoolchildren and visitors to the outdoor museum. (T. Driver)

DRAWING FROM THE LAND: BUILDING AND ROOFING THE ROUNDHOUSES

Iron Age roundhouses consumed vast resources from the surrounding land; the build would have galvanised the entire community. Whereas nowadays a house builder will visit a well-stocked builder's yard and arrange for deliveries of tons of materials to site, the Iron Age community needed to cultivate resources months or years in advance. It needed to own the land where the raw materials grew, or at least develop careful alliances and exchange networks with those who had what they needed.

The great reconstructed roundhouses at Castell Henllys, which stand in the exact spot of their Iron Age predecessors, have taught us much about the raw materials needed to complete a build. The largest roundhouse at Castell Henllys required 30 coppiced oak trees, 90 coppiced hazel bushes, 2,000 bundles of water reed and two miles of hemp rope and twine to complete the main structure of wattle walls, posts, ring-beams, rafters and the thick thatched roof on top.[14] Even for a wealthy farming community these resources were considerable.

In order to get the long, straight, pliable lengths of wood for weaving wattle panels and other tasks one needed to coppice a tree. Coppicing involves cutting trees back to a stump to allow new, young straight lengths of wood to grow. Hazel

Fig 6.14 Detail of the doorway into one of the recently rebuilt roundhouses at Castell Henllys, Pembrokeshire, showing the elaborate construction methods, different materials and high quality of workmanship required to build a long-lasting Iron Age home. (T. Driver)

is one of the most common trees to be coppiced and needs to be cut every seven years to produce the right timber for building a roundhouse.[15] If sufficient woodland was owned to provide the timber, there still came the task of cutting down trees, harvesting the coppiced wood and transporting it all to site.

Roofing the roundhouse again required an enormous effort, planned well in advance. Whether the thatch was of reeds from wetlands, the stalks of cultivated wheat, bundles of gorse and heather or even seaweed in the coastal zone, huge quantities of material required cutting in advance and storing ready for the build. For the St Fagan's Bryn Eryr roundhouse (Fig 6.13) it was calculated that 3.5ha of spelt straw had to be grown to cover the conjoined roofs. Harvesting and threshing using traditional methods turned out to be a major task, dominating the late summer and early autumn, as Steve Burrow[16] comments:

> However the harvest was managed, the inhabitants of Bryn Eryr will have found their late summer and early autumn dominated by the gathering and processing of the crop ... a task which must have involved many people – probably drawing on a population from beyond the farmstead itself – and which would have consumed the attention of the community. There were few short cuts in a process which involved moving and processing tonnes of material. Indeed it was a task which probably took much more effort than the cutting and preparing of timbers for the roof.

HUT GROUPS AND FAMILY FARMS OF THE IRON AGE COUNTRYSIDE

Roundhouse styles varied by region, by available building materials and by geology. Roundhouses occur inside hillforts, but also in open country as 'hut groups' which were effectively early farmsteads or proto-hamlets. These are most commonly found in the upland and unimproved marginal lands of Wales, from the south Wales valleys, parts of western and upland Pembrokeshire and into north-west Wales. It is highly likely that hut groups existed across the more fertile lowland parts of Wales in between enclosed hillforts but have been destroyed or obscured by later cultivation. Hut groups are a distinctive reminder that not all the population of Iron Age and Romano-British Wales lived in hillforts. Indeed, in parts of north-west and south-west Wales hut settlements dominated the landscape, to the extent to which people have questioned whether nearby hillforts ever fulfilled a role as permanent settlements. The name of this type of settlement is something of a dated term, coined when upland roundhouses were seen as mere 'huts' and assumed to have been poorly built; in fact many of these groups of buildings were prestigious homesteads of their time.

Hut groups are found widely across Wales, usually surviving in more marginal or upland regions. They are known from the moorlands and coastal regions of Pembrokeshire, particularly on Skomer Island (Fig 6.3), the slopes of Mynydd Carn-ingli and the Preseli Hills. There are scattered roundhouses on the moorland tracts of Gower but more examples occur across upland south Wales, particularly on the uplands of the heads of the Valleys where scree-built roundhouse settlements associated with straggling moorland field systems are more numerous than hillforts. Prehistoric roundhouses and fields are also known from the Denbighshire uplands around the Berwyn mountains, though they are less numerous than examples in the west.

Hut groups were usually defined by a group of round and rectangular buildings enclosed together within a walled farmyard. Wider hut settlements, conversely, can straggle on for hundreds of metres across hillslopes and moorland between the small fields and paddocks of long-lived farming settlements. Hut groups frequently stood at the heart of heavily-farmed landscapes, often marked by great grids of fields stretching from the coastal lowlands to the very edge of the upland moors (Fig 6.17).

Following the last glaciation, vast tracts of rural Wales were littered with rocks and boulders. Evidence for small-scale, family clearance of stones can be seen particularly well in the fields and hut groups of north-west Wales and across the

Fig 6.15 Reconstruction of the long-lived hut group at Ty Mawr, Holyhead Mountain, Anglesey. About 20 structures are visible today, of a wider original settlement of some 50 houses. Excavations in the nineteenth century and in the 1980s showed that it originated in the Neolithic and Early Bronze Ages, with occupation continuing into the Romano-British period. Roundhouses were enclosed within stone courtyards along with 6-post storage buildings for grain, echoing similar hut groups in south-west Cornwall. Perhaps pioneering maritime families from here had even made the crossing to Cornwall? The hill in the distance is Caer y Tŵr hillfort, which may have been a gathering place for people and livestock for miles around. (Menter Môn with funding from the Heritage Lottery Fund, Cadw and Welsh Assembly Government; illustration by Brian Byron)

uncultivated uplands of the south Wales valleys and Denbighshire, where clusters of 'clearance cairns' frequently dot the paddocks and field enclosures. Each low cairn of stones, often only 1m or 2m across, stands a few metres apart from the other. We can imagine families, even children, picking up heavy stones and moving them just as far as was needed to allow small-scale ploughing for crops between the stony mounds. These are particularly clear from the ground during the winter months at the Cors y Gedol Iron Age and Romano-British settlement, above Dyffryn Ardudwy in Gwynedd.

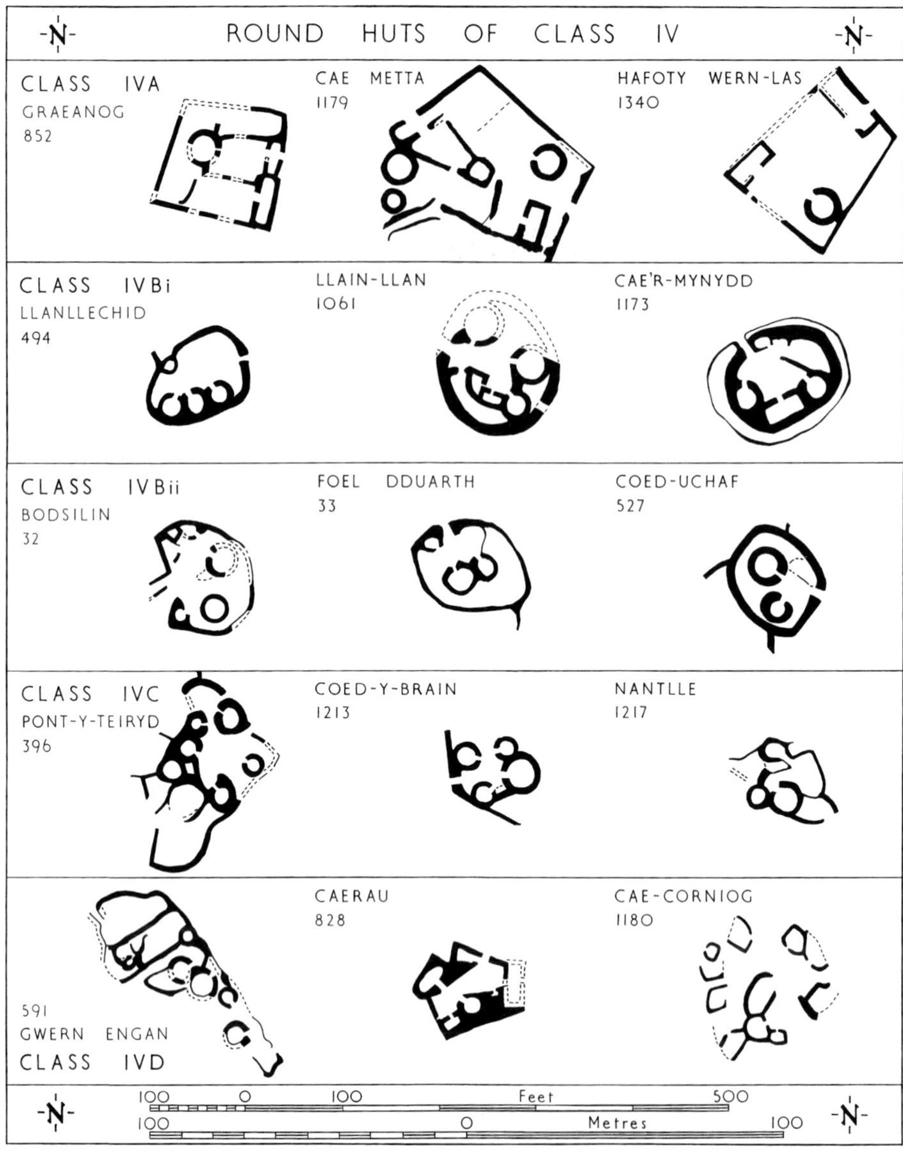

Fig 6.16 The categorisation of Iron Age and Romano-British hut groups for the 1964 Royal Commission *Inventory of Caernarvonshire West*. The diagram shows class IV thin-walled homesteads, which mostly had freestanding huts but include more tightly-grouped examples in class IVC and IVD. The great variety of building traditions, some spanning several centuries, can be appreciated in this diagram.[17]
(© Crown copyright: RCAHMW. NPRN 301046. DI2012_0272)

Among the earliest large-scale field systems in Wales were co-axial fields, long parallel boundaries which subdivided the open prehistoric landscape in many places for the first time. These are a characteristic form of land division from the Later Bronze Age, 3,000 years ago, and were first properly recognised in a major study of the Dartmoor landscape by Professor Andrew Fleming. Co-axial fields have been recognised in Wales surviving along western coastal fringes, particularly on St David's Head (Fig 7.18) and across the southern parts of Skomer Island (Fig 6.3), both in Pembrokeshire. These early field boundaries look their age as they frequently survive today as very low earth and stone banks, sometimes barely perceptible unless seen in the low raking light of a winter's day. Elsewhere, only the upright standing stones of the 'core' of these early walls or hedge lines may survive.

Fig 6.17 A well-preserved early farming landscape of hut groups and terraced fields to the north of Moel Faban, Bethesda, in Gwynedd. The terraced fields, developed over centuries of plough cultivation, have curvilinear earthworks of smaller hut groups at their edges. These Bronze, Iron Age and Romano-British fields are more intact on the left-hand side of this air photograph. To the right, the smooth green pasture has been cleared of boulders and 'improved'. Today this entire landscape is protected as a Scheduled Monument and lies on private land. (© Crown copyright: RCAHMW. NPRN 24301. AP_2005_2914)

Fig 6.18 A large cattle ranch, or specialised livestock corral, discovered as a cropmark at Brechfa, just west of Llandissilio in Pembrokeshire. The enclosure, one of three on a north-south ridge linking the northern high ground to headwaters of the Eastern Cleddau, is built on a vast scale. The outer circular ditch, once holding a timber palisade or hedge, measures 225m across; the inner enclosure once contained roundhouses. A muddy holloway enters the enclosure from the lower left side, preserved as a cropmark beneath modern fields. This Iron Age corral dwarfs the modern farm in the background, suggesting estate-level livestock management in pre-Roman Wales. (© Crown copyright: RCAHMW. NPRN 401988. DI2006_1566)

From the Middle to Later Bronze Ages and into the Iron Age the formerly wild landscape of Wales was successively cleared, enclosed and subdivided into new farming territories for pioneering families. Although the Later Bronze Age climatic downturn made upland farming difficult for several centuries, environmental evidence suggests that clearance of the lowlands accelerated from around 400BC onwards as competition for better-grade agricultural land increased.

North-west Wales is an area particularly rich in hut groups and their associated fields. In some places these roundhouse settlements were traditionally known as Cytiau'r Gwyddelod or 'Irishmen's huts', a mistaken memory perhaps arising from post-Roman re-use by settlers moving east from Ireland. Much of the coastal hill-fringe zone of Eryri (Snowdonia) and the Llŷn Peninsula, from the Conwy valley in the east all the way west to Bangor and south to Harlech including the Mawddach estuary and the slopes of Cader Idris, are scattered with the remains of complex prehistoric and later field systems interspersed with hut groups. Within these Iron Age, Romano-British and medieval farming landscapes are dotted ritual monuments – Neolithic dolmens, long cairns and Bronze Age stone circles and cairns – attesting to far earlier farming use of these western-facing hillslopes.

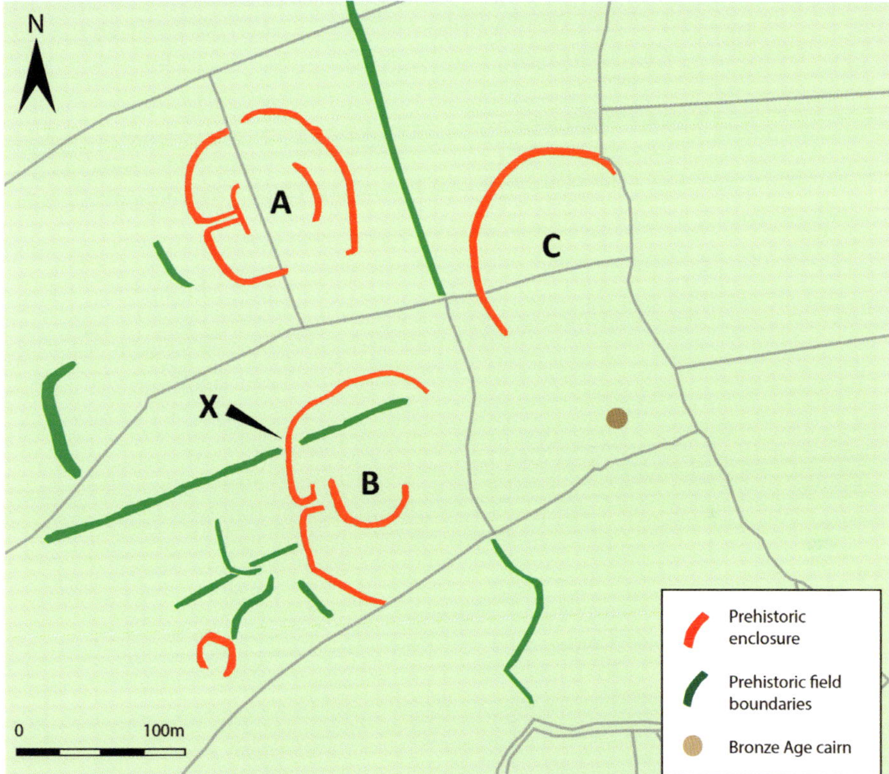

Fig 6.19 Organised stock management in Iron Age Gwynedd. These three great enclosures of Iron Age type occupy the upland coastal plain of Hendre Coed Uchaf, above Llanaber in Ardudwy at 210m above sea level. Two enclosures, A and B, have 'antenna' entrances facing downslope towards the sea. The third, C, is a more simple enclosure. None have been excavated but their arrangement suggests organised management of cattle or sheep on the hill pastures here. The enclosures are surrounded by prehistoric terraced fields and boundaries (green) formed by centuries of plough cultivation. At point 'X', the wall of enclosure B cuts through a pre-existing field boundary suggesting much earlier Bronze Age origins for the field boundary – and wider field systems – here. (T. Driver. Sources: Bing Maps, Lle Portal LiDAR and Royal Commission aerial photography)

Specialised settlements: ironworking and innovation in pre-Roman Eryri (Snowdonia)

Britain yields gold, silver and other metals, to make it worth conquering.
Tacitus, in *Agricola*, 12, describing the mineral wealth of Britannia.[18]

Walking across one of the bleakest tracts of moorland in Eryri (Snowdonia), at Crawcwellt near Bronaber in the shadow of the Rhinogydd mountains, one comes across reconstructed circles of stone in the lee of outcropping rocks which mark the site of one of the earliest ironworking settlements in Wales. The Crawcwellt West roundhouse settlement was excavated by Peter Crew for Eryri National Park between 1986 and 2000, revealing a detailed story of metalworking artisans smelting and working iron ore won from the surrounding bogs. These 'open' roundhouses on moorland, linked by only a few low, wandering stone walls, show the same specialist metalworking expertise found nearby at the small hillfort of Bryn y Castell, Llan Ffestiniog, 13km to the north-east (Fig 8.16). Together the careful excavation of these two settlements has shed much new light on the development of local metal technologies before and after the Roman Conquest of Wales.

Fig 6.20 Crawcwellt West roundhouse settlement, Bronaber, Eryri (Snowdonia), March 2022. View looking south-east across two of the roundhouses, J2 (FOREGROUND) and J1 (BEYOND), excavated and partly reconstructed by Eryri National Park. The exposed moorland setting of these houses can be appreciated in this view. (T. Driver)

BEFORE THE IRON: BRONZE AGE METAL MINING IN WALES

The moderns have made no tryals in the upper grounds, where the antients have found vast treasures as appears by the great trench or open cast, continued even over the hill to the east.

Lewis Morris in 1744 describing the open cast workings at Darren Camp hillfort, Ceredigion, dating back to the Bronze Age.[19]

We do not know who the first innovators were to discover that certain base ores buried in the earth could be transformed into metal. The technology arose in the Near East and spread via established routes of contact and exchange across central Europe to arrive in south-west Ireland during the Bronze Age around 2400BC, associated with Beaker pottery at the Ross Island mine. The knowledge then spread to Britain from around 2200BC with new mining sites appearing at Parys Mountain, Anglesey, Copa Hill, Cwmystwyth, mid Wales and several other locations. All British Bronze Age copper mines had closed by the Late Bronze Age.[20]

The knowledge of how to convert particular rocks into metal transformed society. In the preceding Neolithic, people had made tools from hard volcanic rocks, fine-grained flint, wood and bone, which were all fairly readily worked by those with the right skills. Specialist manufacturing sites did exist: where fine-grained rocks were particularly suited to making high quality axe heads, for example from the volcanic outcrops of Graiglwyd above Llanfairfechan, north Wales, there was a focus of axe making with the products traded across Britain.

The gradual introduction of new metal technology to Britain of first copper, then bronze (an alloy of copper and Cornish tin, from around 2150BC) and eventually iron, created new specialists, new trades in raw material and artefacts and new wealth divides across prehistoric Britain. Transforming base rock into a highly polished axe was nothing short of magical alchemy.

Prehistoric Wales was rich in copper and iron ores, and a main producer of copper ore from the Early Bronze Age from three main locations: the upland valleys of north Ceredigion; the spectacular, deep opencast mines and galleries of the Great Orme; and Parys Mountain in north Anglesey. The knowledge gained about the winning of copper ores from these Early–Middle Bronze Age miners must have survived into later centuries as the Romans in their campaigning and invasion years of the first century AD quickly established control of key mining sites.

One of the earliest Bronze Age mining sites to be explored in modern times was the Comet Lode on Copa Hill ('copa' in Welsh refers to 'summit', not the metal), Cwmystwyth, Ceredigion, excavated by Simon Timberlake and the Early Mines Research Group between 1989 and 2002. It was found that between 2000BC and 1600BC, seasonal miners leaving their lowland farms opened a trench mine or opencast on the hillside using firesetting to crack the rock and red deer antler picks and cobble stone tools to break the rock. Once the ore-bearing rock was crushed, weathered copper minerals like malachite could be picked out from the associated iron oxides and lead and copper sulphides. Some 8m below the modern ground surface archaeologists found fragments of woven baskets, rope, a wooden launder or drain and charcoal, all of which have provided a range of radiocarbon dates and a robust chronology for the mines. The larger Great Orme Bronze Age mines were discovered in 1987 and are now open to the public. They were one of Europe's largest prehistoric mines worked for around eight centuries into the Late Bronze Age with copper exported to central and northern Europe.[21]

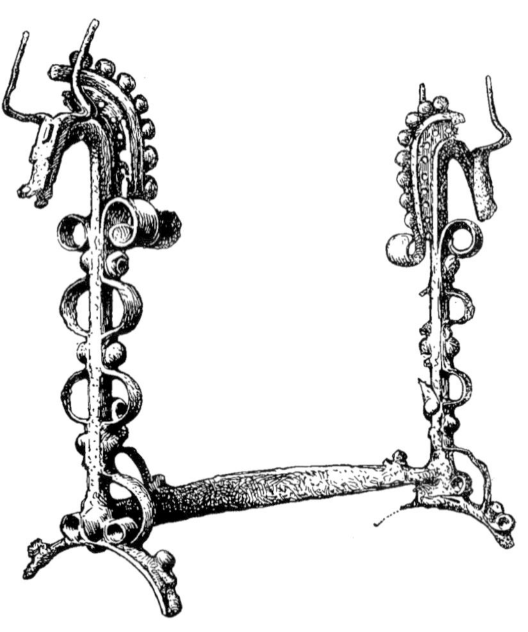

Fig 6.21 The famous Iron Age wrought-iron fire-dog from Capel Garmon was discovered whilst digging a ditch through a bog on Carreg Coedog farm, just alongside the A5 in Denbighshire.[22] The fire-dog was found as a ritual deposit, lying flat on its side with a stone at each end; the anaerobic bog conditions had thankfully preserved the iron. The bulls head terminals are unique among the known fire-dogs of Britain as they have elaborate manes giving them an ambiguous, horse-like appearance.[23] Following extensive experimental ironworking, Peter Crew concluded it was perhaps the product of local craftsmen, requiring an astonishing total of 3½ person-years' work for the production of the iron and the fabrication of the fire-dog.[24] (By kind permission of the Cambrian Archaeological Association)

Fig 6.22 The specialised 'snail-shaped' roundhouse in the north-west corner of Bryn y Castell hillfort, just inside the later gateway. This building started life as a circular roundhouse before the southern wall was demolished and moved inwards. This created an overlapping entrance wall designed to provide shelter for metal smiths inside, whilst funnelling wind into the furnaces. When excavated, the building was full of smithing debris. (T. Driver)

CENTRES OF INDUSTRY: CRAWCWELLT WEST AND BRYN Y CASTELL

The two excavated ironworking settlements of Eryri (Snowdonia) – the roundhouse group of Crawcwellt West and the small hillfort at Bryn y Castell (described more fully in Chapter 8) – still stand out in Welsh prehistory as hugely significant locales. Standing inside either one, you can sense the spirit of innovation, determination and problem-solving that the metalworkers here took on to provide later prehistoric Wales with iron for chariot fittings, fire-dogs, tools and weapons.

Ironworking was a completely different technology from working copper ore or making bronze. The first stage was for the iron ore and charcoal to be smelted together in a small clay furnace achieving temperatures up to 1,250 degrees. This resulted in an impure bloom which had to be successively hammered and reheated to refine it into a compact 'billet'. This billet was refined further down to the

Fig 6.23 Roundhouse H at Crawcwellt West, looking west towards roundhouses J1 and J2 in the middle distance. Set some distance away from the main settlement, this building was used for ironworking between 300BC and AD 200. Iron ores and charcoal were smelted in a clay furnace. Resulting blooms had to be repeatedly hammered on the anvil stone inside the house (visible as a small boulder in this view) and reheated to refine them. About 1 ton of slag was dumped outside. The view looks west to the mountain gap of Bwlch Drws-Ardudwy between Rhinog Fach (LEFT) and Rhinog Fawr (RIGHT). (T. Driver)

finished bar iron, which could be worked into objects or traded. Experimental metalworking by Peter Crew showed that the finished bar iron may be less than 10% of the original ore weight. He writes: '... to make 1kg of fully refined bar iron, under prehistoric conditions, needs 100kg of charcoal and a total of 25 man-day's work'.[25] This explains the enormous quantities of waste slag found at both sites.

Crawcwellt West roundhouse settlement is seemingly remote on its moorland expanse but lies due east of two important mountain gaps through the Rhinogydd mountains – Bwlch Drws Ardudwy and the 'Roman Steps' – both used by generations of traders and drovers to cross to and from the west coast. The settlement comprises two groups of roundhouses, with a series of stake-walled roundhouses in the west (site A) and a series of stone roundhouses with some stake-walled buildings in the east (sites J and H), linked by field walls and small paddocks. Long-term excavation revealed ironworking over the period 300BC to around AD 200, perhaps by two different groups in the west and east sides.

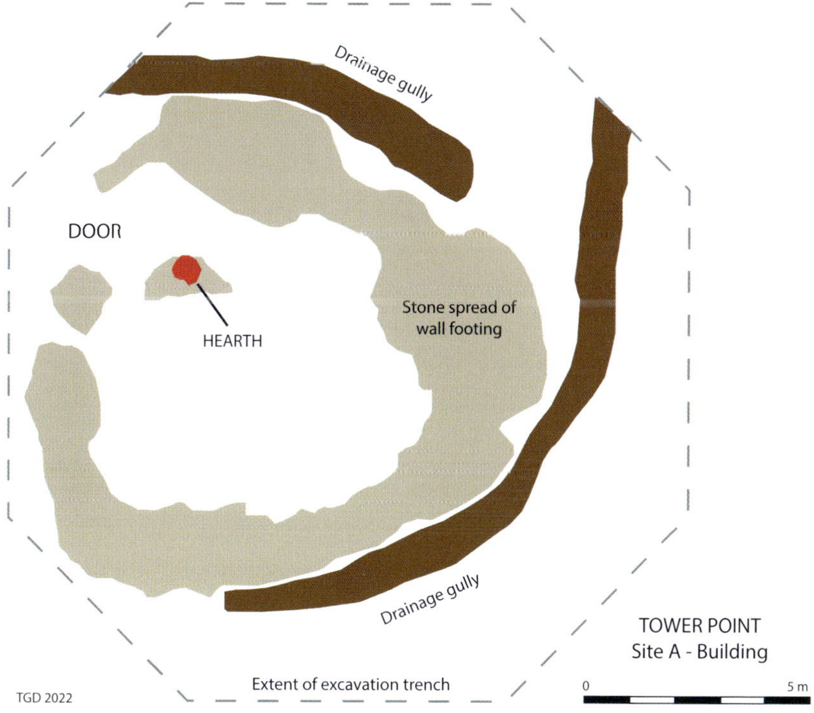

Fig 6.24 Remains of an unusual roundhouse at Tower Point coastal promontory fort, Pembrokeshire. This oval building, measuring 11m by 9.5m was excavated by Professor Geoffrey Wainwright in 1970. It sat on a terrace inside the fort with two stormwater gullies encircling it on the east and north sides. The house wall was merely a low bank of scattered stones and the only internal feature was a single hearth surrounded by 'baked clay' just inside the north-west doorway. The house walls may have been built of turf on a stone base. With new knowledge of the 'snail-shaped' roundhouse at Bryn y Castell hillfort, we can perhaps reinterpret the Tower Point building as a prehistoric smithing workshop with the hearth sited to maximise draught. However the total lack of metal slag means it may have had another specialised function or was abandoned early on in its life. (T. Driver, after Wainwright 1972)[26]

Several of the roundhouses were specifically used for iron production evidenced by successive clay furnaces set into the floor, and mounds of waste slag outside. Overall around 6.5 tons of waste slag was recovered from excavations at Crawcwellt West, which Peter Crew estimates to have resulted from around 1,200 cycles of smelting and smithing over several centuries, requiring 8 tons of ore and around 50 tons of charcoal; overall around half a ton of fully refined bar iron would have been produced.[27] These astonishing figures show the scale of the operation here, and the huge number of trees which would have needed felling and processing to provide the charcoal, depleting the surrounding hills of woodland. Bryn y Castell hillfort in the hills to the east, near Llan Ffestiniog, was used between 300BC and the Roman Conquest for the similar smelting and production of iron. It is highly likely there was communication between the two settlements whilst they were occupied.

Daily life in these settlements was not wholly dominated with the smoky, antisocial task of iron production. Excavated finds from Crawcwellt West included exotic and expensive blue glass beads, a fragment of glass bangle and spindle whorls for drawing out yarn, suggesting a wealthy and productive farming settlement which specialised in a few ironworking cycles a year, perhaps on a seasonal basis. The nearby find of the special Trawsfynydd tankard from the Late Iron Age or Early Roman period also shows that a lifestyle of ostentatious feasting, drinking and celebrating would not have been unfamiliar to the inhabitants of this scattered moorland settlement. Similarly, excavations at Bryn y Castell hillfort yielded fragments of a glass bangle, gaming pieces and slate gaming boards reflecting everyday life in a small Late Iron Age hillfort. The specialised practice of ironworking was undoubtedly more widespread across later prehistoric Wales. Two snail-shaped roundhouses inside Garn Boduan hillfort (Fig 6.10) on the Llŷn Peninsula were surveyed with magnetometry in the early 1980s, yielding very similar high readings to those produced over the snail-shaped building at Bryn y Castell, suggesting ironworking.[28] An unusual building within Tower Point coastal promontory fort (Fig 6.24), Pembrokeshire, may also have been designed for a similar function.

Crawcwellt West settlement remains valuable for the survival of very ephemeral buildings, which would have been quickly destroyed by any later episodes of ploughing. The sequence of nine Iron Age stake-walled buildings at Crawcwellt were only uncovered through meticulous, long-term excavations over many years at a site which has never been disturbed by later activity. Archaeologist Kate Waddington suggests that any actual walls between the thin wattle panels may have been made of clay or turf rather than stone and would have long since disintegrated.[29] In nearby Bryn y Castell hillfort, careful excavation also revealed two unsuspected stake-walled houses in the central area of the fort (Fig 8.16). The excavator Peter Crew noted: 'The evidence for these buildings is so slight that a single ploughing would have completely destroyed it'.[30] It is unlikely that similar slight remains of these more humbly-built dwellings would be identified as cropmarks during aerial survey or even as anomalies during geophysical surveys. Thus we can be fairly sure that many similar traces of prehistoric houses have been lost forever from our knowledge of Bronze and Iron Age Wales.

7 Worlds apart: coastal promontory forts

Fig 7.4 (PREVIOUS PAGE)

The exceptional symmetry of the triple curving defences at Watery Bay Rath, south Pembrokeshire, probably results from more than one phase. Despite appearances, erosion has been minimal at this promontory fort. The unusual low bank skirting the cliff edge appears to be an original prehistoric feature to protect the interior. The addition of a short bank to the east (TOP) of the fort, the other side of the small stream, suggests this water source was enclosed within the defences. Small scale excavations in 2011 yielded limited information about the interior (see text). (© Crown: CHERISH PROJECT 2022. Produced with EU funds through the Ireland Wales Co-operation Programme 2014–2023. All material made freely available through the Open Government Licence. NPRN 305362. 155_CHE_5_Feb_2018)

7

As a place of refuge in the face of an enemy, it must have been well-nigh impregnable. It was secure from the sea ... A direct assault on the strong rampart would have been a forlorn hope ...

Reverend Sabine Baring-Gould, describing the defences of St David's Head coastal promontory fort in 1899.[1]

Of all the many hundreds of hillforts, defended farmsteads and hut groups which dominated the landscape of later prehistoric Wales, there was nothing quite like a coastal promontory fort. Few classes of prehistoric site are as spectacular to visit today as the coastal promontory forts of Wales. Perhaps it is their sense of isolation, of being cut off from the modern world high above the salt spray, that is their chief attraction today. Despite the effects of coastal erosion and two millennia of change in the Welsh landscape, these rugged outposts still look out across timeless seascapes. In visiting them we can imagine something of the lives and outlooks of their ancient inhabitants.

In their most basic forms coastal promontory forts were simply hillforts, or defended family farms, built against steep coastal cliffs. Construction effort was saved as ramparts were only required on the 'landward' approaches. Building at the coast edge also made sense in terms of the farming economy. Sea levels around the Welsh coast stabilised around 4–5,000 years ago, meaning that the coastline in Iron Age and Roman times was similar to its position today. The people of the promontory fort had ready access to fields, pasture, livestock and other resources from the land, as did their inland neighbours, but they also benefitted from a largely frost-free coastal belt. Looking to the sea coast they also had access to the eggs and meat of nesting seabirds, intertidal resources of shellfish and seaweed and fish from the sea. The occupants of more influential coastal forts could also enjoy trading links with the wider world by establishing their fort as a port of trade, receiving in exotic goods from afar and also setting sail to make important connections with other communities on the Isle of Man, south-west England, Ireland or further afield.

Fig 7.1 Schematic map of coastal promontory forts lining the western coastlines of Wales and Cornwall, and the coast of south-eastern Ireland. (T. Driver; after Lock and Ralston 2022, Figure 3.8, with additions)

Some of the benefits of living in defended homes at the coast edge were described, perhaps with some frustration, by Caesar in his *Gallic Wars*, speaking of the coast-dwelling Iron Age Veneti peoples of Armorica (northern Brittany; Book III, 12):

> The positions of the strongholds were generally of one kind. They were set at the end of tongues and promontories, so as to allow no approach on foot, when the tide had rushed in from the sea – which regularly happens every twelve hours – nor in [Roman] ships, because when the tide ebbed again the ships would be damaged in shoal water. Both circumstances, therefore, hindered the assault of the strongholds; ... whenever the natives were in fact overcome … they would bring close inshore a large number of ships ... and take off all their stuff and retire to the nearest strongholds ...[3]

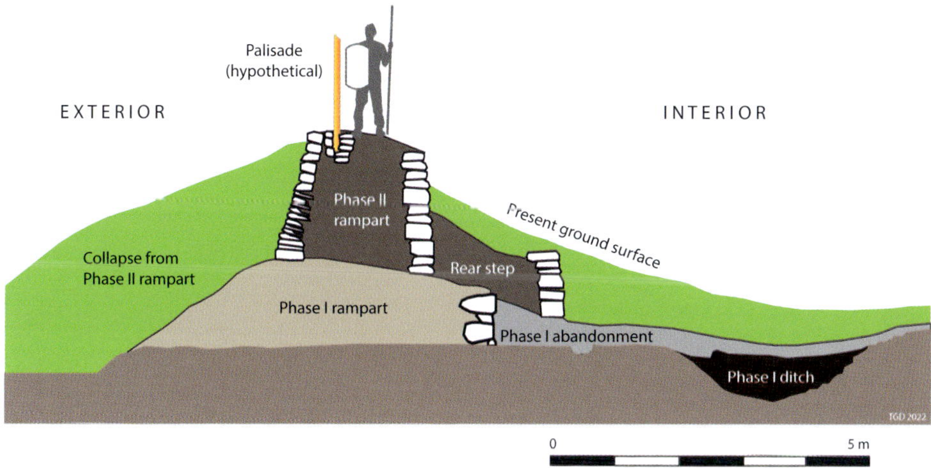

Fig 7.2 Tower Point coastal promontory fort, Pembrokeshire. Excavations by Geoffrey Wainwright in March 1970 cut a section through the northern inner rampart of this promontory fort. The cutting revealed an ambitious rampart structure with two clear phases. The Phase I rampart was a low bank of clay and broken shale. The defences were then abandoned for some time before being refortified with a tall Phase II rampart wall. This was supported by and accessed from a rear walled step providing a 'murus duplex' arrangement. A huge amount of stony material collapsed down from the front of the rampart forming the modern earthwork we see today. (T. Driver, after G. Wainwright 1972)[2]

Yet the reasons for living in some coastal locales may also have transcended straightforward domestic or defensive considerations. It is along the coast that we see some of the strangest Iron Age settlements in Britain. Some were built in dangerous locations. Elsewhere the builders of coastal promontory forts apparently laboured hard to build ramparts around massive coastal outcrops or deep chasms which left little practical space for settlement. Were these more unusual or dangerous coastal locales ceremonial rather than domestic spaces? They may have been reserved for particular rituals or may have been such sacred locations that they were only used at specific times of year. These themes will also be explored in this chapter.

EXCAVATIONS AT THE EDGE OF WALES

Although the majority of coastal promontory forts remain entirely unexcavated, there have been several 'modern' excavations in the post-war era. These include Dale fort promontory fort (excavated in the 1960s and 1970s) and Tower Point, Marloes (excavated 1970), both in Pembrokeshire. The Dale fort work was instrumental in producing a Late Bronze Age date for a pre-rampart occupation layer, while the Tower Point excavations led by Professor Geoffrey Wainwright revealed

Fig 7.3 Gribin promontory fort, Solva, viewed from its maritime approaches just inside the sheltered natural harbour that it dominates. Two other Iron Age defended sites, a ridge fort and a large concentric fort lie further up the slope behind it. The characteristics of Gribin fort, defined by a single wall running around the top of the slope – just visible on the skyline – suggest it may have been refortified in the Early Medieval period. (T. Driver)

an instructive cross-section through an earthen bank, telling us much about rampart complexity at these western forts (Fig 7.2).

Threat-led excavations during the 1980s and 1990s included new work on the Pembrokeshire promontory forts of Great Castle Head, Dale in 1993 and Porth y Rhaw, Solva in 1997–8 by the Dyfed Archaeological Trust. Both coastal promontory forts had lost considerable parts of their interiors to coastal erosion. Great Castle Head produced the expected assemblage of Iron Age and Roman pottery, but also medieval pottery suggesting this had been the first Dale castle. The find of a First World War cap badge also confirmed its use as a look-out post for coastal defence. More recently, the selective trenching of both Gateholm Island settlement and Watery Bay Rath (Fig 7.4, chapter frontispiece) coastal promontory fort in south Pembrokeshire by Wessex Archaeology for the Time Team in 2011, produced mixed results. Only prehistoric flint was found inside Watery Bay fort, but sherds of prehistoric and Roman pottery were recovered from nearby Gateholm Island along with metalworking evidence and an amber bead.[4]

The most recent coastal promontory fort excavations in Wales, at Dinas Dinlle near Caernarfon (2019 and 2021–22) by the CHERISH Project and Gwynedd Archaeological Trust (Figs 1.27 and 6.7), at Caerfai, St Davids (2021–present; Fig 1.21), by the CHERISH Project and DigVentures, and a return to Porth y Rhaw, Solva (a new programme of work 2019–22; Fig 7.5)[5] by the Dyfed Archaeological Trust have all been in response to increased threats posed by a changing climate and a race to save buried structures and deposits before they are lost to the sea.[6]

Fig 7.5 Rescuing archaeology before it is lost: the Pembrokeshire coastal promontory fort of Porth y Rhaw, Solva, with excavations in progress on the eastern (RIGHT) 'horn' by the Dyfed Archaeological Trust, summer 2022. The trench revealed the complete plan of a large roundhouse. The extent of erosion across the interior of the fort can be appreciated in this view, along with the multiple lines of huge ramparts on the landward side. (© Crown: CHERISH PROJECT 2022. Produced with EU funds through the Ireland Wales Co-operation Programme 2014–2023. All material made freely available through the Open Government Licence. NPRN 94210. CHE_AP_2022_1725)

The combined effects of coastal erosion and increased severe rainfall have been particularly damaging at Dinas Dinlle coastal fort in Gwynedd, which saw recent cliff collapses after storm events.[7] In the most severe storms, such as those which battered Welsh coasts in the winter of 2013/14, waves were photographed overtopping 40m-high cliffs along the Castlemartin peninsula, picking up and scattering boulders across the interiors of several promontory forts.

One of the best understood promontory forts is Porth y Rhaw. Both programmes of excavation here were targeted at the eroding eastern 'horn', on which survives a series of overlapping roundhouses built and rebuilt over the centuries. Excavations in the 1990s revealed at least eight roundhouses, some rebuilt several times. More recent excavations revealed the stone-walled entrance passage of the main gateway and completely excavated one of the larger roundhouses. It was found to have a

Fig 7.6 Staff and volunteers of the Dyfed Archaeological Trust make a detailed record of the well-preserved stone-lined entrance passage of Porth y Rhaw coastal promontory fort, Solva, during the 2019 excavations. The initial stone-lined gateway passage was 2.5m wide, but was narrowed in a second phase to 1.7–1.8m wide with the main gateway only 1.4m wide. The trackway was metalled with pebbles.[9] This was a surprisingly narrow passage and gate, tightly funnelling visitors into the fort. (Copyright: Dyfed Archaeological Trust)

purple slate threshold stone, and stone-covered drains around the building to carry away rainwater. Radiocarbon dating suggested a foundation at Porth y Rhaw in the Early to Middle Iron Age, as at Great Castle Head, with ceramic evidence indicating occupation continuing into the Romano-British period to the fourth century AD. The occupants were industrious: metal and glass were both worked on site with evidence for the manufacture of glass beads. Roman tableware pottery was also present showing a good level of Romanisation of these coast-edge people of the first centuries AD.[8]

Culture shock: prehistoric life at the coast edge

Building at the coast edge was fundamentally different to what every other inland hillfort community in Wales was doing in the Later Bronze and Iron Ages. Out on the coast the environment, farming conditions, the weather and even the light are greatly different to the inland hills and valleys of central Wales. We experience this even today when people who normally live many miles from the sea arrive for a day out or a holiday at the Welsh coast. The experience is transformative. Bright coastal light, blustery winds, low windblown trees and the incessant crash of waves signal a world far removed from Powys, the Welsh Marches or the English Midlands. Cliff edges ring with unusual sounds, from seagulls and the call of choughs to the ghostly howls of seals in the autumn. The contrasts in prehistory would have been far greater. Although a proportion of the Iron Age population would have been mobile, travelling to local or regional places and events, long journeys to distant lands would have been rare. There would have been a sense of culture shock when those who had been born and raised inland and out of sight of the sea arrived at a coastal promontory fort.

Fig 7.7 A vivid depiction of Late Iron Age life at the coast edge. The illustration shows a typical Galician coastal fort or 'castro' of north-west Spain, with strong parallels to many of the coastal promontory forts along the western seaways of the British Isles including Wales. All the advantages of coast edge living are depicted, from crop cultivation and rearing of livestock to fishing coastal waters and awaiting sea trade from distant lands. Gold panning is taking place at the river mouth. (Illustration © Franjo Padín)

Ways of life and attitudes to risk of the people of the promontory forts were different from those living inland. In 1811 Richard Fenton[10] mused that the houses on St David's Head were home to 'ferocious sea kings', a marvellous quote of its day. Islanders of recent centuries who grew up on the Blasket Islands of Kerry, or the Western Isles of Scotland, learnt as young children to scale cliff faces to gather eggs, to swim and climb offshore stacks to show their prowess, or to brave stormy seas in hidebound boats for fishing or essential journeys to the mainland – sometimes with fatal consequences. Professor Andrew Fleming[11] described some of the challenges inherent in growing up in the risk-laden island archipelago of St Kilda off the remote north-western coasts of Scotland:

> Children were trained to climb on house walls using ropes, from an early age; climbing ropes were always tested before use ... Climbing fatalities would have been traumatic, particularly in such a small community, but they were not particularly frequent.

While islanders would often experience scarcity and uncertainty in their supplies of food and water throughout the seasons, the combination of land and sea did offer a particularly diverse larder. Professor Fleming quotes Neil MacKenzie listing the winter stores of a typical family on St Kilda which combined fare from the land and the coast edge:

> At the beginning of winter, a cow was killed, and thereafter 12 sheep, mostly wethers [a castrated male sheep]. There would be two or three barrels of young fulmars ('which are tender and fat as bacon') and a barrel or a barrel and a half of young gannets; there would also be six stones (*c.*65kg) of cheese and some fish and eggs, the milk of two cows, and a considerable quantity of barley, with some oats and potatoes.[12]

Further back in historic times islanders and coastal communities would have had to endure the constant threat of unwelcome visitors, in the forms of raiding and piracy. How were these differences in ways of life – and death – reflected in the Iron Age settlements of the Welsh coast?

Fig 7.8 The author standing within the remains of an Iron Age roundhouse at St David's Head coastal promontory fort, Pembrokeshire. These houses were described by Richard Fenton in 1811: 'Within these ramparts ... amidst the rude shelter of ... Old Octopitarum towards the sea ... are seven or eight circles formed by a line of rude stones with an entrance to each, probably the tents of the ferocious sea kings ...' (see also Fig 1.1).[13] (T. Driver; photograph by Louise Barker)

PRESENCE AND ABSENCE: COASTAL PROMONTORY FORTS AROUND THE WELSH COAST

Coastal promontory forts shared a particular distribution along the Atlantic seaboard of Europe from the indented north-western tip of Spain (Galicia) and north-western Brittany to the south-west facing peninsulas of Cornwall and Pembrokeshire, the southern and western coast of Ireland and north to the Isle of Man, Galloway and into Scotland (Fig 7.1). The *Atlas of the Hillforts of Britain and Ireland*[14] lists 73 coastal promontory forts in Wales against 54 in England and the Isle of Man and 236 for Scotland. These 73 sites in Wales are those with more monumental hillfort-like defences as befitted the study but the true number is far higher. A 2011 study of the coastal promontory forts of Pembrokeshire by the author and Louise Barker listed at least 106 for Wales[15] and there are more than 60 in Pembrokeshire alone. New discoveries continue to be made around the Welsh coast, particularly through aerial reconnaissance.

Coastal Wales saw distinctly regional ways of life in later prehistory, with communities in the north-west, north-east, south-west and south-east living very differently from one another. Nowhere was this more evident than in the distribution of coastal promontory forts (Fig 7.1). Not all of the Welsh coast was suitable for promontory fort construction. The low-lying estuarine saltmarshes of the Severn Estuary east of Cardiff Bay, and the Dee estuary between Chester and Point of Ayr in north-east Wales were tidal wetland environments in prehistory. Hillforts and Roman forts were sometimes built on prominent hill spurs set back from these low-lying foreshores but suitable elevated coastal promontories were all but absent. Coastal promontory forts like Sudbrook near Chepstow were the exception and may have commanded coastal trade for miles in every direction. Nor did the low-lying coastlines and sand dunes of the north Wales coast between Prestatyn and Colwyn Bay, the Meirionnydd coast from Morfa Harlech south to Barmouth, or the south Wales coast between Porthcawl and Swansea offer any useful bluffs or promontories for defended settlement.

Thus we find coastal promontory forts principally constructed on the harder rocky coastlines which were highly indented with steep promontories, bluffs, rocky peninsulas and useful sheltered beaches and bays for tying up boats. There are a handful of coastal forts along the Glamorgan coast between Penarth and Porthcawl, including the severely eroded Nash Point promontory fort and Castle Ditches at Llantwit Major sited on the softer Carboniferous Limestone cliffs. When we come to Gower, coastal promontory forts are far more numerous, particularly on the southern stretch of limestone cliffs between the Mumbles and Rhossili Bay including varied and unusual promontory forts sited on contorted headlands like The Knave, Thurba Head and Yellow Top. Gower is a distinctive landscape largely cut off by water on three sides and may well have been home to a particular group of people distinct from the Silures or Demetae.

West of Gower there are very few coastal forts overlooking Carmarthen Bay; most of the coastline is estuarine saltmarshes and dunes at the mouths of the Loughor and Tywi rivers, but there are exceptions. The Iron Age and Early Medieval fortification of Coygan Camp (now destroyed by quarrying) commanded a rocky knoll protruding into East Marsh and Laugharne Burrows east of Pendine. It is not until we reach the cliffs of Pembrokeshire on the west side that we enter a zone of promontory fort building *par excellence*. From Tenby in the south around to the mouth of the Teifi estuary at Cardigan in the north there are some 60 coastal promontory forts;[16] more probably await identification.

Fig 7.9 Imaginative reconstruction of the innermost settlement of St David's Head coastal promontory fort in Late Iron Age times. Strong stone-walled ramparts (RIGHT) flank a narrow main gateway passage giving access over the rocky isthmus. Once inside, visitors weaved through great outcrops and rock slabs to a grassy saddle of ground on which were constructed a group of circular houses and other rock shelters. A ship of Romano-Celtic type, loosely based on a wreck from St Peter Port in Guernsey, is shown just leaving the safe beach landing of Porth Melgan. (T. Driver)

IRON AGE PORTS OF TRADE

The coast and sea offered new possibilities to Iron Age communities seeking to trade their goods or exchange them for exotic or prestige commodities from afar. Whilst overland travel could be difficult and time-consuming, sea travel in good conditions with favourable winds and currents could be more rapid, opening up interregional or international markets. Caesar described the international sailing prowess of the Veneti peoples of Armorica in his *Gallic Wars* (Book III, 8):

> These *Veneti* exercise by far the most extensive authority over all the sea-coast in those districts, for they have numerous ships, in which it is their custom to sail to Britain, and they excel the rest in the theory and practice of navigation ...[17]

When it came to trading, certainty was everything; certainty of time for those travelling a long distance for a particular event and certainty of place for those trying to find a particular location after a long sea journey. Simply gathering livestock and tradable goods on a clifftop and waiting for a ship to sail close enough to be signalled would not have worked. Likewise if a leader in Cornwall, on Lundy Island or in coastal Wexford wished to set sail to the coast of Pembrokeshire to buy particular goods required for a wedding or a festival, they would have needed to know when to set sail and that the required goods would be there, ready, on arrival.

For these reasons communities needed to establish a known point on the coast where goods could be gathered and defended, which was recognisable from the ocean and well-known to passing ships, which had safe anchorage and which ideally had someone in charge – a 'controlling authority'. This was a port of trade. Coastal promontories were ideal locations, as well as offshore islands which were seen as safe places on the boundaries of land and sea where parties could meet and exchanges could take place.

Professor Barry Cunliffe describes the role of an Iron Age port of trade in his discussion on the location of the great trading hub of *Ictis* in prehistoric Cornwall, renowned among classical traders and described by the ancient Greeks:[18]

> Islands and promontories were safe places that all parties to the exchange could agree were extraterritorial. Here all who came were safe and could go about their business without political restrictions or harassment ... People would come from considerable distances to these places at prearranged times, fixed by tradition and widely known, certain of finding someone with whom to strike a profitable deal.

Cunliffe discusses the likely location of *Ictis* (thought to be either St Michael's Mount or Mount Batten in Plymouth Sound). He notes that one of the great advantages of St Michael's Mount, '... is that its commanding mass can easily be recognised from far out to sea – a quality that would have commended it to sailors unused to British waters'.[19]

There are strong candidates for Iron Age ports of trade around the Welsh coast. Suitable islands and promontories which incorporated later prehistoric defences, some cut off at high tide, could include Worm's Head (Fig 2.14) which has a rampart on Inner Head and Burry Holms island on western Gower which is cut in half by a strong rampart. Further west, Deer Park promontory fort at Marloes in

Fig 7.10 Trading with the wider world: reconstruction of Caerfai coastal promontory fort, St Davids, Pembrokeshire, around 50BC, based on the results of recent excavations by the CHERISH Project and DigVentures. (© Crown: CHERISH PROJECT 2023. Produced with EU funds through the Ireland Wales Co-operation Programme 2014-2023. All material made freely available through the Open Government Licence. NPRN 305396. Artwork: Wessex Archaeology)

Pembrokeshire commands the sea channels from the mainland opposite Skomer Island and has a wide maritime aspect. In north Wales, Trwyn Porth Dinllaen promontory fort on Llŷn commands a contorted, defended finger of land which curves around to enclose a sheltered bay (Fig 2.1).

When looking for distinctive locales which formed recognisable 'seamarks' for mariners to identify from a distance, we find coastal forts like Pendinaslochdyn in Ceredigion, which occupied a flat-topped cone-like hill, the tallest eminence on the Ceredigion coast;[20] or that on St David's Head, Pembrokeshire, where the high crags of Carn Llidi outcrop coupled with the twin hills of Ramsey Island would have made very recognisable landforms when approaching from out at sea. In north-west Wales, Caer y Tŵr hillfort on Holy Island, Anglesey, crowns a prominent hill with highly visible white rocky cliffs facing out to sea (Figs 2.3 and 7.11). All these places would have been characteristic, recognisable and powerful locations for overseeing trade on the Atlantic coast of Wales. It is perhaps significant that Caer y Tŵr is an apparently empty hillfort with few identifiable house sites. The only real structure appears to be a late Roman watchtower on its summit. It may be that this great walled enclosure was specifically designed for people to meet and trade under the temporary shelter of tents, or similar light structures, rather than enclosing a permanent defended village.

Fig 7.11 Coastal seamarks. The white, rocky cliffs which form the south-western side of Caer y Tŵr hillfort on Holyhead Mountain look out across the Irish Sea. From maritime approaches the high, white-domed rocky summit stands out from the heather-clad lower hills and moors. It no doubt formed a characteristic 'seamark' guiding mariners to the fort to trade with local communities. Similarly recognisable coastal 'seamarks' further south along the Welsh coast include Pendinaslochdyn hillfort, Llangrannog, on its flat-top peak and Carn-ingli hillfort, Pembrokeshire with its characteristic stepped profile. (T. Driver)

Perhaps particularly dramatic and unusual natural locales, or anomalous rampart design, picked out likely ports of trade from more mundane defended farming settlements on the coast? The author, researching with archaeologist Louise Barker for a 2011 paper on the coastal promontory forts of the Castlemartin peninsula, south Pembrokeshire, identified the more unusual coastal fort of Bosherston Camp near Stackpole as a likely port of trade:

> It commanded ... one of Pembrokeshire's few coastal estuaries providing a level river promontory both sheltered and once navigable from the sea ... As if to reinforce the unusual nature of this position, Bosherton Camp is unlike any other south Pembrokeshire later prehistoric fort. Triple parallel defences cut an uncommonly straight line across the level promontory providing a dramatic and somewhat brutal architectural solution to defence ... as a long-lived trading base of some importance the position would seem ideal.[21]

We know from written records of the sea journeys of Pytheas and Roman navigators, and the crucial find of a Mediterranean anchor stock close to Bardsey

Fig 7.12 Bosherston Camp near Stackpole in south Pembrokeshire commands an estuarine promontory once navigable from the sea. Its unusual straight triple ramparts are unlike any other south Pembrokeshire promontory fort. It is a strong candidate for an Iron Age port of trade. (© Crown: CHERISH PROJECT 2022. Produced with EU funds through the Ireland Wales Co-operation Programme 2014-2023. All material made freely available through the Open Government Licence. NPRN 305433. CHERISH 2018 March 28 [511])

Island (Fig 2.15), that the Irish Sea and Cardigan Bay were busy with sea traffic during the Late Iron Age. We also know that these ships were likely to have been prospecting for tradable commodities along the Welsh coast before the first century AD Roman Conquest. Exotic finds may provide evidence for trade and exchange on these windswept promontories, but what form would they take?

A particularly interesting and rare find was collected from Worms Head in an area of eroding cliff in the years before 1920, by Captain E. Cunnington and reported by his mother in the pages of the journal *Archaeologia Cambrensis* in 1920.[22] Two halves of a small Old Red Sandstone mould for casting Early Iron Age jewellery were collected from an eroding midden, which also produced sea shells, animal bones, potsherds and fragments of bronze and iron (Fig 7.13). The findspot was at the western end of the middle islet, between the Inner and Outer Heads.

Although the mould was published in 1920, it was not thoroughly examined until Hubert Savory published a longer note on it in 1974.[23] The main central brooch design from which an original could be cast was circular and decorated with a continuous scroll surrounding the ring. Savory noted similarities with Iron Age La Tène designs from other parts of Britain and Europe and also that such metalwork is normally imported. While the mould is certainly made of local sandstone, Savory speculated that the metalworker may have come to Worms Head from another country. He also noted that the Carmarthen Bay area had produced quite a range of later prehistoric imported objects including ceramics and bronze bracelets more at home in central Europe, suggesting a pattern of trading to the settlements and harbours of the Bristol Channel:

> This remote part of the coast must always have been difficult to access by land, but easily reached by sea both from other parts of Britain and from the Continent ... We may, after all, be dealing with the luggage of a newly arrived party of immigrants rather than a workshop, and it is desirable that what remains of the site should be explored in the hope of clearing up this uncertainty.[24]

Green and Howell[25] further discuss the implications of Continental-style finds from the nearby coast-edge hillfort of Coygan Camp, near Laugharne in Carmarthenshire:

> At Coygan Camp, a pair of La Tène bracelets on a copper core were found in the excavations conducted between 1963 and 1965. The bracelets are similar to examples from the Continent and, perhaps even more interestingly, also to two smaller ones which were excavated in the inner defensive ditch at Llanmelin ... It is tempting to see both sets of bracelets as trade goods ...

Maritime havens and landing places may also have been important features of the Iron Age and Roman coast where contemporary defended settlements were set back from the shore. Exotic prehistoric stray finds collected from particular beaches could indicate a history of trading on the foreshore. A key location in south Wales is Swansea Bay where decades of finds from the intertidal muds have included prehistoric and Roman traded goods, weapons and ritual objects. A late first- or early second-century AD bronze roundel from Aberporth beach, for example, is thought to be a Roman casket ornament, originally mounted on a wooden or leather backing. Its retrieval '... from the seashore near Aberporth' in the late 1960s may indicate a loss from a Roman-period 'beach market' but it could also be flotsam washed up from a submerged wreck.[27]

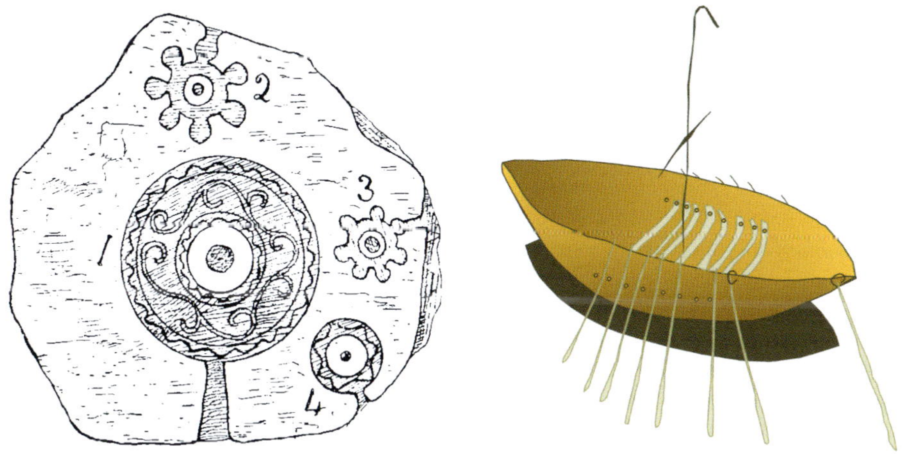

Fig 7.13 (LEFT) An exotic find from Worms Head. This small sandstone metalworker's mould measuring 12cm across was carefully carved to allow jewellery of continental design to be cast. It was found by chance before 1920 in an eroding cliff between Inner and Outer Head. Its discovery on a maritime headland, where there is also an Iron Age promontory enclosure, suggests overseas trade links during the Iron Age.[26]

Fig 7.14 (RIGHT) Golden offerings to appease a sea deity. On a February evening in 1896 a hoard of Late Iron Age gold objects was stumbled upon at the edge of Lough Foyle, Broighter in County Londonderry by two farmers. Among gold necklaces, a bowl and a magnificent torc was a unique gold model of a first century BC boat. Just 18cm long, this was a model of a sea-going craft of the type which no doubt traded on the Atlantic seaways. It had nine rowing thwarts or benches, a stepped mast amidships and a steering oar to the stern. Archaeologists have speculated that the nautical nature of the find and its location beside a sea lough may mean it was a votive offering to an underwater deity, possibly Manannán mac Lir.[28] (T. Driver)

THE LURE OF ANGLESEY

Was Anglesey, known as *Mona* to Greek and Roman navigators, a special locale in the Iron Age? Invasion of the island was attempted twice by the Roman army, once early on in their campaigns by Scapula in AD 48 and then again in AD 60. Tacitus described the second successful attack by Suetonius Paulinus on *Mona*, noting: 'although thickly populated [it] had also given sanctuary to many refugees'.[29] In his other text on Agricola, Tacitus noted the invasion was carried out because: '... the island of Anglesey ... was feeding the native resistance.'[30] On this second invasion the Romans were met by a terrifying display:

> The enemy lined the shore in a dense armed mass. Among them were black-robed women with dishevelled hair like Furies, brandishing torches. Close by stood Druids, raising their hand to heaven and screaming dreadful curses. This weird spectacle awed the Romans into a sort of paralysis ... But then they urged each other (and were urged by the general) not to fear a horde of fanatical women. Onward pressed their standards and they bore down their opponents, enveloping them in the flames of their own torches, Suetonius garrisoned the conquered island.[31]

Anglesey had copper, which was extensively worked in later prehistoric and Roman times, with ingots being found with a western distribution on mainland Wales. While the Great Orme was one of the earlier sources for Bronze Age copper in north-west Europe it has long been assumed that Parys Mountain on northern Anglesey became the focus of Iron Age and Roman mining.[32] Another major reason for Anglesey's reputation in prehistory, perhaps as important as its copper, was the sacred, cult focus at Llyn Cerrig Bach lake.[33] Archaeologists including Cyril Fox linked the hoard with the Druids of the island and suggested that the votive lake may even have seen its final acts of deposition as the horror of the AD 60 conquest unfolded.[34] Although not often explicitly stated, Llyn Cerrig Bach is actually a coastal votive site, set just inland of the shore on the western trade approaches to *Mona* near present-day Valley Airfield. Its great significance may have been known to sailors approaching the coast.

The presence of this rare votive site on the western seaways may also have precluded the development of defended coastal settlements along this stretch of Anglesey's coast in the later Iron Age. There are only two significant promontory forts between the Menai Strait and Ynys Gybi/ Holy Island, despite a deeply indented coastline and numerous later prehistoric hut group settlements. Caer y Tŵr hillfort on Holy Island is the dominant hillfort on western Anglesey and may have been a key locale for social gatherings and trade in pre-Roman times.

Understanding coastal promontory forts: demarcating the coast edge

Promontory forts were liminal places at the threshold between land and sea. Just as inland hillforts enclosed a space and prevented direct access to a hilltop, so coastal promontory forts physically cut off key parts of the Welsh coast making them private and inaccessible to outsiders. Formerly unenclosed sections of coast, with whatever landscape features or resources they contained, became locked off

Fig 7.15 The prehistoric and Roman wealth of Mona or Anglesey was based on its copper ore, mined since prehistoric times at the spectacular Parys Mountain in the north of the island near Amlwch. (Crown Copyright – Royalty Free worldwide with attribution in line with Crown Copyright Licencing Agreement. Asset ID: NVW-E14-2122-0471)

in the ownership of the occupying family or community. The builders of a coastal promontory fort were not only taking ownership of an advantageous coastal location but were also permanently altering it through the addition of artificial banks, ditches and walls dug from the living rock. At times coastal ramparts were enormous; the 4m-high multiple banks defining Porth y Rhaw coastal promontory fort, Solva (Fig 5.11), are among the most massive hillfort ramparts anywhere in Pembrokeshire. Professor Barry Cunliffe described the unique circumstances of building a defended enclosure at the coast edge:

> Perhaps it was the sense of being at the interface between land and ocean where the powers of both could be harnessed: it is not too fanciful to regard cliff castles as liminal places giving access equally to the land and the sea.[35]

With enclosure came ownership. Cornwall has a similar coastal landscape to Pembrokeshire in prehistory. Peter Herring[36] proposed that the region of West Penwith in far south-west Cornwall may originally have been divided into four main territories, each having a main coastal promontory fort spaced approximately

10km apart. Ownership extended beyond the land to the surrounding maritime territory, along with any nearby coastal landing points for trade and oversight of shipping from the new vantage point. We are reminded of Caesar describing the Veneti peoples exercising 'the most extensive authority over all the sea-coast in those districts' of Armorica.

Sometimes ownership and control of several kilometres of the coast edge appears to be visible today as an 'exclusion zone' around major coastal forts where nearby promontories suitable for the construction of forts were left empty. Did the controllers of particularly powerful coastal forts prohibit construction by near neighbours on their stretches of coast? Good examples of coastal 'exclusion zones' can be seen along the apparently empty coastlines bordering Pen Dinas, Aberystwyth, Ceredigion, Greenala Point fort in south Pembrokeshire (Fig 7.16)[37] and Sudbrook coastal promontory fort in Monmouthshire (Chapter 8).

Fig 7.16 The Iron Age communitiy of Greenala Point coastal promontory fort near Freshwater East in south Pembrokeshire may well have exerted control over the neighbouring coastline to the exclusion of any other fort. No other coastal promontory forts were built for several kilometres to either side despite the presence of suitable headlands. During a new Royal Commssion survey it was discovered that the gateway was built of stone blocks, not only of locally-available Old Red Sandstone but also of imported limestone from nearby. (© Crown copyright: RCAHMW. NPRN 94956. AP_2009_0283)

Enclosure of a coastal promontory introduced zones of access and privacy between the open farmland of the countryside and the interior (Figure 7.18). Access to 'public' and 'private' spaces on the promontory or headland was subject to control via annexes, outworks and gateways as with many inland hillforts. Thus at some coastal promontory forts strong outer ramparts or advantageous outcrops combined with narrowly eroded necks of land could have been used to define and control public spaces for markets, trading, festivals and all manner of meetings. Visitors allowed to these 'outer' public events may not have been allowed to pass through the secure inner gates.

Innermost ramparts and gateways controlled access to the private interior of the fort. These barriers protected not only the family houses and stored grain wealth of the community but also special, exotic or sacred features 'locked off' within the fort. These may have included a significant outcrop or blowhole (Fig 7.23) or an earlier burial cairn or a chambered tomb with long-held ancestral or symbolic importance to the community. Such liminal points, the most isolated, special and distant parts of the promontory, became incredibly difficult to reach without observing the correct protocol, or being granted the correct permissions, to enter through the outer and inner spaces.

Understanding coastal promontory forts: sacred capes and ritual outcrops

> *Deposition [of artefacts] in earth and water – including no doubt the sea – suggests that reverence for the natural world played an important part in the belief systems of the people. It is not unlikely that other natural phenomena – a striking rocky crag or an ancient tree – were also treated with reverence ...*
>
> Professor Barry Cunliffe, 2010.[44]

In Iron Age Wales we find that dangerous, remote or distinctive coastal features were often enclosed with defences. We find coastal promontory forts which contain very little usable settlement space, but whose interiors were instead dominated by sheer rock outcrops. At other sites, domestic interiors crowded with roundhouses have deep and dangerous blowholes at their hearts. Some settlements traditionally described as defensive 'forts' are entirely hidden in coastal hollows, overlooked on all approaches and strategically weak. How should we interpret these sites?

CONTROLLING COASTAL ACCESS: ST DAVID'S HEAD COASTAL PROMONTORY FORT

How do we understand the use of space and access to different zones within prehistoric coastal promontory forts? A good case study is St David's Head (Penmaen Dewi) coastal promontory fort, the *Octopitarum Promontorium* of Roman maps commanding the 'eight dangers' offshore. Here we are fortunate that the outer landscape of fields and walls beyond the ramparts of the fort has been preserved and has not been swept away by later agriculture or development.

This spectacular headland clearly held an earlier sacred significance to prehistoric communities; the Neolithic chambered tomb of Coetan Arthur forms a striking landscape feature on the headland and the nearby crags of Carn Llidi hold further Neolithic chambers. It has also been proposed[38] that the massive, rock-built parts of the promontory fort defences may date to Neolithic times. Farming on the headland began early in prehistory. The 'co-axial' or parallel field systems on St David's Head, running between Carn Llidi and the outer defences of the fort, have their origins in the Later Bronze Age; similar fields can be found on nearby Skomer Island.[39]

During the Iron Age access to the rocky headland seems to have been divided up into a series of controlled zones. The farmland on the east side, representing the 'public' outer territory of the promontory fort, was deliberately separated off from the inner headland to the west by a great defensive wall, 'Clawdd y Milwyr' or the Warrior's Dyke, an unusual feature at this promontory fort. One main gate and at least one minor postern gate permitted access through this wall which looked down on a deep dry valley at the edge of the fields. The wall and steep coastal slopes also separated the advantageous landing spot of Porth Melgan beach, with its 'public' role for trade and communication, from the inner headland.

Once through the Warrior's Dyke one entered a controlled inner space, a rocky boulder-strewn headland largely empty except for Coetan Arthur chambered tomb. This tomb almost certainly had a continuing importance in the Iron Age, forming a focus for ceremonies. There are also springs here.

Fig 7.17 St David's Head coastal promontory fort encloses an intriguing cavern, Goats Cave. Richard Fenton described it in 1811: '... a remarkable natural cavern called Ogov Geivyr, the cave of the goats, where sheep in winter seek shelter ... as well as goats.'[40] It is not a recorded historic copper mine but may have been explored in prehistory for ore. If it is a purely natural cave rather than a mine it is possible it was used for secretive prehistoric rituals within the promontory fort. (T. Driver)

The space could conceivably have been used for holding livestock – the wealth of the community – as well as for public fairs, markets or ceremonies safe outside the inner promontory fort.

If one was permitted to enter through the ramparts and main inner gate of the promontory fort one entered a heavily defended private world (**Fig 7.9**). The excavated footings of around 6 or 7 roundhouses along with rock shelters, excavated in 1899 by Baring-Gould,[41] clearly demonstrate domestic daily life (**Fig 1.1**). However there is every possibility that the headland itself, and particularly the 'liminal point' of the great outcrop and seawashed rocks beyond the roundhouses, was of ceremonial or sacred significance to the inhabitants. An important internal feature is Ogof Geifr or Goats Cave on the south side of the rocky headland (**Fig 7.17**). Caves in prehistory were often seen as sacred spaces and portals to otherworlds. The cave may also result from coastal metal mining of copper ore, as it appears a quartz seam has been dug into in the recesses of the chamber. If the Iron Age inhabitants had a copper mine within their fort it could have held considerable significance for the wealth and power exerted by their community.

Similar zoned landscapes of 'public' farmland, a controlled inner space and private promontory fort interior can be seen both at The Neck coastal promontory fort on Skomer Island[42] and at the Deer Park coastal promontory fort, both in south Pembrokeshire.

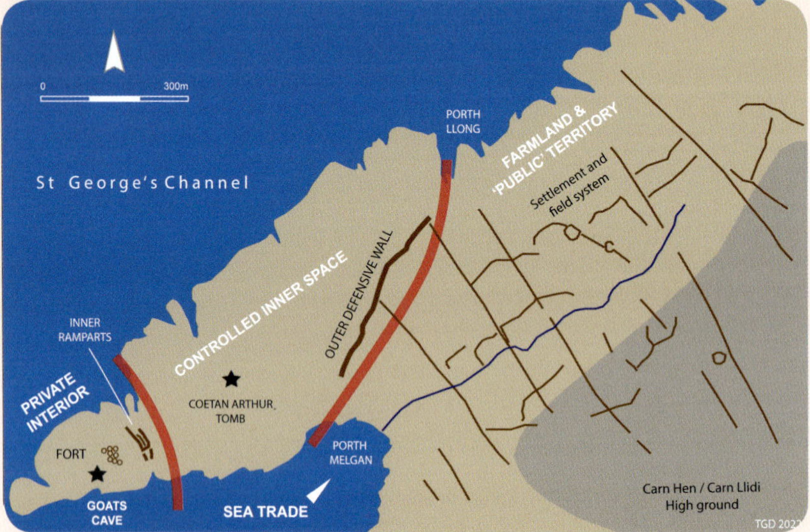

Fig 7.18 Potential zones of Iron Age land division and control suggested by the author at St David's Head coastal promontory fort, Pembrokeshire. This model is a useful way to interpret zones of 'public' and 'private' enclosure at comparable coastal promontory forts along the Atlantic coasts of Britain and Ireland.[43]

On the southernmost coastline of Cornwall, in the parish of West Penwith near the hamlet of Treen, is an extraordinary coastal promontory fort which offers clues by which we might unlock the coastal forts of Wales. Treryn Dinas is said by archaeologist Peter Herring to be 'West Penwith's largest, most complex and possibly most important Iron Age defended site'.[45] As one approaches it seems straightforward: the outer ramparts are large and impressive and enclose a great section of the headland. They are monumental defences and could have repelled an attack. They also define a 'controlled inner space' between the outermost ramparts and the interior for meetings or markets, as is found at St David's Head and elsewhere.

Fig 7.19 Treryn Dinas, Cornwall. The modest innermost rampart cutting across the narrow neck of this Cornish cliff castle in the middle distance demarcates the towering rock outcrop beyond. The spectacular outcrop, complete with a rocking stone and prehistoric offerings, was the focus of this complex Iron Age site. Note the figure for scale (see also Fig 7.22). (T. Driver)

Treryn Dinas gets really interesting as one passes through these outer defences and approaches the spectacular coastal outcrop, the focus of the entire fort. This great outcrop is separated from the mainland and outer ramparts by a narrow neck or isthmus crossed by an inner rampart wall pierced by a gateway. In front rises a great mass of shattered granite. This coastal outcrop was and is a special place. It is full of towering granite forms, slender pillars and deep echoing passages which weave between cliffs. It is home to the famous Logan Rock, an 80-ton granite boulder which used to rock when even the slightest pressure was applied.

Archaeologist Adam Sharpe[46] quotes a visitor from 1865 who noted that 'the Logan Stone has ever been connected with the supernatural' and it was for a time a well-visited tourist attraction. When visiting the site in 1992, Adam Sharpe fortuitously discovered a sherd of Iron Age pottery and also part of a Bronze Age funerary urn tucked in a gully leading up to the Logan Rock. The burial urn had been deposited in a cleft in the rock in what looked to be 'a natural cist', along with fragments of cremated bone. It is clear that Bronze Age communities revered this place, burying their dead in rock gullies below the rocking stone, with the practice continued in Iron Age times.

The outcrop was thus enclosed and revered by later prehistoric communities. The rock forms of Treryn Dinas are also intriguing. Some appear as groups of anthropomorphic or 'human-like' forms. There are parallels with sacred outcrops from other cultures around the world.[47] Perhaps the rock formations at Treryn Dinas were seen as the personification of ancestors or gods by prehistoric communities?

Fig 7.20 Treryn Dinas cliff castle, Cornwall. Strongly anthropomorphic ('human-like') forms in the rock outcrop enclosed beyond the Iron Age defences. Archaeologist Peter Herring described the Treryn Dinas outcrop as '... not only bare rock, but a rockscape of such startling form – with vertical piles of clean, rounded granite, culminating in ... the Logan Rock ... that those who built this rampart were deliberately enclosing ... a very special place.[47] (T. Driver)

There is ample evidence that coastal promontory forts were special, sacred places in prehistory. Professor Barry Cunliffe, describing Cornish 'cliff castles', notes their many roles:

These are promontories jutting out into the sea, separated from landward approach by one or more lines of banks and ditches. It used to be thought that such sites were defended refuges, but more recently the possibility has been raised that they might have been sacred sites – liminal places at the interface between land and sea, perhaps serving also as guiding landmarks for mariners. The ancient Mediterranean was after all well supplied with 'sacred capes.[49]

In ancient Polynesian societies, coastal headlands and cliffs were seen as springing-off points for ancestral spirits. Closer to home Professor Andrew Fleming,[50] in his study of life on St Kilda and the islands off western Scotland in recent centuries, recounts similar beliefs. A reef of largely submerged rocks off the south coast of Soay island has the curious name: *Sgier Mac Righ Lochlainn* or the Skerry of the Son of the King of Norway. This name is thought to have derived from the

Fig 7.21 Lunar symbolism from a dark coastal cave. This 8cm-high Late Iron Age or Romano-British bronze figurine, dating from between the first century BC to the second century AD, was found in Culver Hole Cave, southern Gower, in 2016 and reported to the Portable Antiquities Scheme. Professor Miranda Aldhouse Green notes its similarities to other statuettes including a coastal example from Aust on the Severn Estuary. She writes that the figure: '... should be interpreted, perhaps, not as necessarily that of a god or goddess but rather as some kind of religious official or priest, who could be male or female. If the headdress does represent the crescent-moon, its context deep in a dark cavern lends further nuances to its significance, as an illumination in the perpetual night of a cave'. (Portable Antiquities Scheme, Unique ID: NMGW-0322B4. This work is licensed under the Creative Commons Attribution 4.0 International License)

older word *Lochlann*, a name for the Otherworld beneath the waves. In Hebridean myths, and those of Ireland and the northern isles, the 'children' of the King of 'Norway' or *Lochlann* were in fact seals who often came ashore and adopted human forms as seal men and women. In other myths it is drowned souls who appeared as seals; there are obvious links to Selkie and mermaid stories of old. Fleming notes that the Soay reef is a liminal place, sometimes dry rocks, sometimes submerged. He writes: 'If the Otherworld lies beneath the sea, seals are its perfect emissaries'.[51] One can imagine similar stories being woven around the seals and sea creatures of the Welsh coast in prehistory. Stories of mythical drowned lands are also common in Wales, in particular the legend of Cantre'r Gwaelod. The imagination of storytellers was no doubt fired by the peat-blackened stumps of prehistoric submerged forests seen emerging on the beaches of Pembrokeshire and Cardigan Bay at low tide or after storms.

Returning to Wales, how applicable are such beliefs derived from historic Scotland, and indigenous communities halfway around the globe, to the Iron Age west? Professor Barry Cunliffe recounts classical writers who noted that a number of the major coastal promontories along the south and west coasts of Iberia were sacred to the gods.[52] Similar landscape characteristics have been noted in the deposition of precious metalwork and hoards in later prehistory, by Miranda Green and Ray Howell:

> The repeated deposition of prestigious goods in watery contexts undoubtedly reflects ... the episodic renewal of allegiance to the spirit powers perceived as residing in remote, liminal, dangerous and inaccessible places ...[53]

Thus we may look at key liminal promontories like St David's Head and consider alternative interpretations for these extraordinary places. Herring notes, of Treryn Dinas:

> Certainly the spirits of earth, water and air are all close at hand on a stormy day among these great rocks. What little is known of Iron Age belief suggests that the gods and goddesses of nature were of great importance then ... A case can then be made out for the apparently non-secular function of the inner enclosure at Treryn Dinas being closely associated with religion. The place's sacredness may well have been enhanced by any memory of earlier Bronze Age ritual use.[54]

Fig 7.22 The rock 'tower' at Dinas Mawr coastal promontory fort, Strumble Head, north Pembrokeshire, is enclosed by two or possibly three ramparts. The larger inner rampart can be seen in the middle distance, with traces of a low innermost third rampart beyond which left little useable space inside for houses. Crude rock-cut steps, probably of historic date but perhaps with prehistoric origins, ascend the outcrop to access its summit. Ledges around the sides of the tower also accessed the rear of the outcrop, looking out to an offshore islet beyond. This unusual promontory fort is a good example of an 'augmented coastal outcrop' where level ground for practical settlement was limited. (T. Driver)

In Wales we also find coastal outcrops which have been enclosed or 'augmented' with ramparts and ditches. Often the coastal outcrop in question is set low down from the surrounding mainland, in a 'bowl-like' depression or natural amphitheatre in the coastal cliffs, forming a singular focus for human activity. These outcrops are frequently concealed from view until the final approaches. Whilst not previously recognised or classed as a distinctive type of prehistoric coastal enclosure, it now appears that these augmented coastal outcrops may have formed the key locales for coastal ceremony or ritual along the western coasts of prehistoric Britain.

Augmented or defended coastal outcrops form some of our most impressive and oft-visited 'coastal promontory forts'. Crocksydam or Moody Nose promontory fort (Fig 1.5) on the Castlemartin peninsula, south Pembrokeshire, is a distinctive outcrop set in a bowl-like and boulder-strewn valley which remains invisible until the last moment. The site is approached by descending through a spectacular rocky canyon of limestone cliffs. In north Pembrokeshire, ramparts enclosing the visually concealed coastal rock tower of Dinas Mawr on Strumble Head (Fig 7.22) could almost have been built by visitors from Treryn Dinas. Again the rocky outcrop is generally invisible until one begins to descend down to it. At the foot of the slope a narrow neck connecting the outcrop to the mainland is crossed by twin ramparts. The inner wall, much like at Treryn Dinas, encloses little usable space for settlement in the shadow of the great rock tower. Rock-cut steps of uncertain age scale the outcrop to its summit. To date we have not discovered prehistoric pottery or offerings in rock crevices at these sites, as at Treryn Dinas, but this is something to be scouted in the future. It is also possible to see these potentially sacred promontories closely paired with more 'domestic' forts nearby, which have more evidence for roundhouses and permanent settlement. Crocksydam faces Flimston Bay promontory fort across a bay while Dinas Mawr sits below the great north Pembrokeshire hillfort of Garn Fawr on Strumble Head.

Fig 7.23 A handful of Welsh coastal promontory forts enclose dangerous chasms and natural blow holes like the Cauldron inside Flimston Bay fort, south Pembrokeshire (see Chapter 8). Such deep chasms may have been seen as sacred locales and perhaps even viewed as portals to otherworlds. During stormy weather waves crash and winds howl in these dark places. Such strange and dangerous portals may have been the main reason why certain promontories were chosen for coastal enclosure. The Cauldron perhaps gave Flimston Bay fort a valued cult focus which was visited by people from miles around at key times of year. The site is more fully discussed in Chapter 8, and lies on the Castlemartin military training area with restricted access. (T. Driver)

Fig 7.24 Striking vertical grooves in the summit of the islet which dominates the bay enclosed by Castell Bach coastal promontory fort, Ceredigion, may have been a particularly special feature of the site. Although the grooves are natural, caused by the bedding planes of the rock, this pyramidal rock is the first feature one sees descending to the promontory fort. Artificial terraces also appear to have been cut into the summit of the islet. (T. Driver)

On the Ceredigion coast to the north, Castell Bach at Cwmtydu has two low ramparts which 'enclose' a distinctive offshore islet in a secluded bay; the offshore stack has artificial terraces cut around its summit. The ramparts at Castell Bach, as with other augmented coastal outcrops, are low and unmonumental yet sit at the base of a great natural amphitheatre in the coast. This is a similar topographic setting to some sacred lakes in Wales like Llyn Fawr, Rhigos, which occupies a great 'amphitheatre' in an escarpment. The Castell Bach islet has three vertical groves in its summit, undoubtedly caused by natural rock strata but presenting an unusual symbol visible across the coastal promontory fort. It may be that this islet was seen as a sacred, liminal place on the Ceredigion coast and was augmented by low defences and terraces on the landward approaches.

Castell Bach, Crocksydam and a number of other coastal sites have benefitted from new detailed surveys and investigations in recent years by the EU-funded CHERISH Project, headed by the Royal Commission. New detailed surveys and photogrammetry provide a permanent record of coastal erosion, against which future change and loss can be measured. Further archaeological work at all these coastal promontory forts should further develop our understanding of them as places for living, defending, meeting and trading. We need to better understand the territories they commanded and whether closely neighbouring coastal forts always saw contemporary occupation. It is also vital to better understand the potential sacred and ceremonial use of some of the more dramatic or unusual locales. These coastal forts at the edge of Wales still have the power to amaze and inspire after two millennia.

8 Visiting the hillforts of Wales: a top ten

Fig 8.1 (PREVIOUS PAGE)
Around Wales, more hillforts are becoming accessible to the public. Finger-post showing waymarked paths at Pen Dinas hillfort and Local Nature Reserve, Penparcau, Aberystwyth.
(T. Driver)

8

A 'LONG LIST' of my favourite Welsh hillforts might well number a hundred sites, if not more. Putting together a shorter gazetteer of hillforts to visit for this final chapter inevitably leaves out many which are equally worthy of recommendation. The 10 monuments described in detail here are a personal selection of some of the more interesting, accessible or unmissable hillforts that I have visited during the writing of this book.

Wales is fortunate in that a good number of its hillforts, and so much of its prehistoric landscape, can be freely visited. The Wales Coast Path immediately opens up more than 100 coastal promontory forts for visitors in all parts of the country. There is also the Countryside and Rights of Way Act, or CROW Act, of 2000 which allows free access to unenclosed countryside; 'open access land' is highlighted on larger-scale Ordnance Survey maps. This is particularly valuable for visiting vast tracts of upland Wales where one can see a wide variety of archaeological sites, from prehistory to the recent past. Through the important work of Wales's three National Parks, in coastal Pembrokeshire, Eryri (Snowdonia) and Bannau Brycheiniog (the Brecon Beacons), together with the extensive land ownership of the National Trust Wales, many more archaeological sites can be freely explored via waymarked paths. Cadw guardianship sites across the country also encompass a fair number of prehistoric monuments, most of which are free to visit.

There are parts of Wales where the hillfort heritage should not be missed. Those with a few days to spare in north Wales should visit the major hillforts of the Clwydian Range and Llantysilio Mountain – homeland of the Deceangli – which fall within the Clwydian Range and Dee Valley Area of Outstanding Natural Beauty, including Moel Famau Country Park. These hillforts include

Fig 8.2 Tredegar Camp on the western edge of Newport in Gwent is one of the most accessible hillforts in south Wales and can be visited via paths from the adjacent housing estate. It is one of the larger and more complex south Wales hillforts but has suffered due to its incorporation in an historic golf course and can be overgrown. The fort commands wide views over the Severn Estuary. (© Crown copyright: RCAHMW. NPRN 93429. DI2006_2004)

Penycloddiau, one of the largest in Britain and also **Moel Arthur**, **Moel y Gaer Llanbedr**, **Moel Fenlli**, **Moel y Gaer Llantysilio** and **Caer Drewyn** (described below). Together with **Moel Hiraddug** (Fig 2.9) further to the north near Dyserth, these hillforts form a coherent group in north-east Wales and are served by nearby car parks, good paths and interpretation panels. One should also visit the giant **Pen-y-corddyn-mawr** hillfort further west along the north Wales coast at Abergele, and **Caer Eini** (Fig 8.5) north-east of Bala.

Anglesey is a rewarding island to visit for its prehistoric heritage. Neolithic chambered tombs aside, there are good hillforts which can be visited at **Caer y Tŵr** (Figs 2.3 and 8.3), above Holyhead, and **Ynys y Fydlyn** coastal promontory fort in the far north-west of the island. There are also lowland hut groups and defended farmsteads, the best of which are Cadw guardianship monuments, open at all reasonable times. These include **Caer Leb** (Fig 4.14) in the south of the island, the Ty Mawr or **Holyhead Mountain hut group** (Fig 6.15) west of Holyhead and

Din Lligwy hut group (Fig 6.4) in the east near Moelfre. The **Melin Llynon Mill** attraction at Llanddeusant north-east of Holyhead includes two reconstructed roundhouses. **Llyn Cerrig Bach** Iron Age votive lake also has an interpretation panel and can be visited near RAF Valley.

The Llŷn Peninsula in north-west Wales, once homeland of the Gangani, is crowded with major hillforts and hut groups; not only **Tre'r Ceiri** hillfort described below, but also **Garn Boduan** (Fig 6.10) and **Carn Fadryn** hillforts inland of Nefyn, **Carn Bentyrch** near Llangybi and **Castell Odo** towards the south-western tip of the peninsula. The **Canolfan Felin Uchaf Centre** near Rhoshirwaun, east of Castell Odo, is a community skills hub and cultural centre with a small **reconstructed roundhouse** available for overnight stays. At the northermost tip of Llŷn is the unmissable National Trust owned **Dinas Dinlle** hillfort (Figs 1.27 and 6.7), recently excavated and now with a roundhouse preserved on view close to the edge of an eroding cliff to chart the future effects of coastal erosion and climate change. As a hillfort it has every modern convenience for the visitor including an adjacent car park, toilets and nearby cafés.

Fig 8.3 The panoramic views from the summit of Caer y Tŵr hillfort on Holy Island, Anglesey, were later harnessed for the construction of a Roman watchtower to guard the western seaways. (T. Driver)

For those visiting central Wales and the borderlands, the upland fringe of Montgomeryshire (now northern Powys) has several hillforts to visit on open access land including the large **Craig Rhiwarth** above Llangynog on the Tanat Valley and **Pen y gaer** hillfort just above the Llyn Clywedog reservoir dam in western Montgomeryshire. Upland Radnorshire, today in southern Powys, has many good hillforts, in particular the group across Gilwern Hill and the Carneddau uplands between Llandrindod Wells and Builth Wells including **Castle Bank**. To the east of Llandrindod the **Llandegley Rocks** hillforts can also be freely visited; the larger summit enclosure may be a Late Bronze Age fortification. The Welsh borderlands contain a particular concentration of larger hillforts to visit and too many to list individually here. **Gaer fawr, Guilsfield** and the **Breiddin** feature in the gazetteer below. **Beacon Ring** hillfort on Long Mountain above Welshpool has been owned by the Clwyd Powys Archaeological Trust since 2008 and is the subject of long-term investigation; it can be visited via a footpath. A borderlands visitor should also not miss Cefn y Castell, **Middletown** near The Breiddin and **Burfa Camp** in forestry to the south near Presteigne. On the English side of the border – south to north – are great hillforts at **Wapley Hill**, Presteigne, **Croft Ambrey** on the National Trust's Croft Castle estate, **Caer Caradoc**, Knighton, **Bury Ditches**, Clun, **Nesscliffe hillfort** and – of course – the unmissable **Old Oswestry** hillfort (Fig 6.8) at Oswestry in the care of English Heritage.

For those travelling in south-west and south Wales some particular hillforts and attractions should not be missed. These include **Castell Henllys** Iron Age Village (Fig 8.4) in north Pembrokeshire where costumed reenactors interpret hillfort life. Whilst in Pembrokeshire, the hillforts of **Carn Alw** (Fig 5.35) and **Foel Trigarn** (Fig 3.6) on the Preseli hills, along with the many coastal promontory forts of the Pembrokeshire coast including that on **St David's Head** (Figs 7.9 and 7.18), are highly recommended. Further north **Pen Dinas hillfort** (Fig 5.21) at Aberystwyth is worth a visit and has a new network of paths and panels to guide people to the summit.

Visitors in south Wales should visit **Caerau hillfort** in Ely (Fig 1.26), Cardiff, which is well signposted and stands at the heart of the CAER Heritage project; footpaths up to the hillfort start from the community centre. The ramparts are overgrown and fenced off but the hillfort gateways and interior are accessible as is the later castle ringwork and ruined church. The new community centre (Fig 1.23) is inspiring. South Wales has several interesting hillforts to visit including – in no particular order – **Crug Hywel** hillfort (Fig 4.16) which is a stiff walk above Crickhowell and **Twyn y Gaer** hillfort (Fig 3.20) above Stanton, both in the southern reaches of the Black Mountains. Bordering the conurbations of south Wales are **Tredegar Camp** (Fig 8.2), a large fort in a suburb of Newport, the spectacular **Twmbarlwm hillfort** and castle high above Cwmbran and **Llanmelin Wood hillfort** (Fig 1.18) near Caerwent which is best visited in the winter months when vegetation is low. The Glamorgan coastline also has several excellent coastal promontory forts and hillforts, particularly at the western end of the Gower peninsula accessible by the Wales Coast Path

Fig 8.4 Castell Henllys Iron Age Village in the Pembrokeshire Coast National Park is an excavated and reconstructed small Iron Age hillfort set within a 12ha estate of river meadows and woodland. It is now run as a major heritage attraction and educational resource, as shown in this excellent illustration by Richard Allen. (© Richard Allen. By kind permission of Pembrokeshire Coast National Park Authority)

Also essential to visit in south Wales is **St Fagans National Museum of History** outside Cardiff, not only for its incredible range of reconstructed buildings including the **Bryn Eyr roundhouses** (Fig 6.13), but also because both the main building and an additional pavilion in the grounds (the Gweithdy/ Workshop) now house the nation's collections of **prehistoric and Roman finds**. Be sure to visit all three different gallery rooms as it is all too easy to miss some famous pieces, and the collections are not well signposted. The Tal-y-llyn hoard and Capel Garmon fire-dogs are on view in the 'Gweithdy' building outdoors among the main reconstructed village. The remaining finds are on display upstairs in the main museum building; the Llyn Cerrig Bach treasure is in the 'Wales Is' gallery and the Pencoed-y-Foel and Boverton (Fig 3.5) neck rings together with the paired Iron Age tankards from Trawsfynydd and Langstone (Fig 3.2) are on display in the 'Life Is' gallery.

Fig 8.5 Caer Eini is a ridge-top hillfort to the north-east of Bala in Gwynedd. The fort was extended over at least two phases and encircled with a deep rock-cut ditch. Caer Eini lies on open access land. (© Crown copyright: RCAHMW. NPRN 93712. AP_2007_4552)

Finally, the archaeology of the Romans in western Britain is an essential part of the story. There are still some notable remains of the works of the invaders who interrupted the Iron Age in Wales and ultimately changed the course of the country's history. The key sites to visit in south Wales include the Cadw guardianship properties of **Caerleon Roman fortress**, ancient *Isca*, and **Caerwent Roman city** (Fig 4.17), ancient *Venta Silurum*, both essential visits and not too far from one another. Other unmissable trips to understand the Roman Conquest of Wales include **Wroxeter Roman city** (English Heritage; Fig 8.7), ancient *Viroconium* in Shropshire on the Welsh borderlands, **Segontium Roman fort** (Fig 4.15) at Caernarfon (Cadw), **Tomen y Mur Roman fort** near Trawsfynydd in upland Eryri (Snowdonia National Park Authority) and **Carmarthen Roman amphitheatre** (alongside the main road on the eastern approach to the town centre).

POINTS TO REMEMBER

All sites are visited at your own risk and, unless otherwise stated, should be assumed to lie on private land. Readers are advised to follow the Countryside Code (see below). The majority of hillforts are Scheduled Monuments in the care of Cadw, and are protected by the 1979 *Ancient Monuments and Archaeological Areas Act* and the *Historic Environment (Wales) Act* 2016. It is against the law to disturb them in any way or to metal detect over them. If you do find anything of archaeological interest you should report it first to the landowner, then to the Portable Antiquities Scheme in Wales (PAS Cymru), or to your local museum. Queries about finds from Wales should be directed to treasure@museumwales.ac.uk. Finds remain the property of the landowner.

TREASURE

In England, Wales and Northern Ireland, all finders of gold and silver objects, and groups of coins from the same finds, over 200 years old, have a legal obligation to report such items under the *Treasure Act* 1996. Prehistoric base-metal assemblages found after 1 January 2003 also qualify as Treasure. Some changes to the present Treasure Law are also expected as this book goes to press. Finders of potential Treasure in Wales should contact their regional Finds Liaison Officer for help in reporting Treasure, and for further advice. By law, finds of potential Treasure must be reported to the Coroner in whose district they were found within 14 days of discovery.

Fig 8.6 An evocative National Park interpretation panel at Garn Goch hillfort, Carmarthenshire. (T. Driver)

REMEMBER THE COUNTRYSIDE CODE 2022

Respect everyone

- Be considerate to those living in, working in and enjoying the countryside
- Leave gates and property as you find them
- Do not block access to gateways or driveways when parking
- Be nice, say hello, share the space
- Follow local signs and keep to marked paths unless wider access is available

Protect the environment

- Take your litter home – leave no trace of your visit
- Do not light fires and only have BBQs where signs say you can
- Always keep dogs under control and in sight
- Care for nature – do not cause damage or disturbance

Enjoy the outdoors

- Check your route and local conditions
- Plan your adventure – know what to expect and what you can do
- Enjoy your visit, have fun, make a memory

Fig 8.7 Urban life after the Conquest. The resettlement of the Cornovii people of the Welsh borders after the Roman Conquest was at ancient Viroconium, now Wroxeter Roman city, where this reconstructed townhouse perfectly evokes the comforts of town life. The site is managed by English Heritage. (T. Driver)

Fig 8.8 The 'top ten' hillforts described in the detailed gazetteer (numbered stars) together with the locations of museums and attractions where reconstructed roundhouses (house symbol) can be seen. The gazetteer lists the forts from north to south. (T. Driver)

Directions: The hillfort lies on open access land within the moorland setting of the Yr Eifl National Nature Reserve. It is best reached by car from Llithfaen village off the B4417 between Llanaelhaearn and Nefyn. A minor lane routes north-east from Llithfaen up to the moorland boundary where there is parking for a few cars. Waymarked paths lead upwards towards the hillfort. Access may be difficult in low cloud or inclement weather. National Grid Reference: SH 373 446

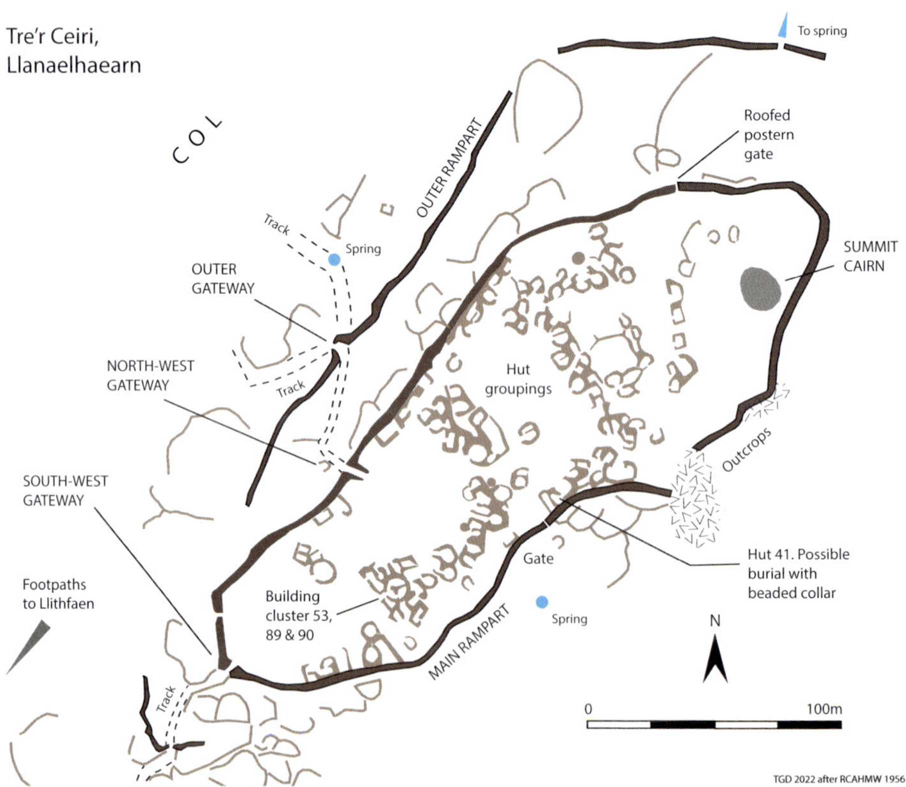

Fig 8.9 Plan of Tre'r Ceiri hillfort, based upon the 1956 Royal Commission survey with additions. Note the multiple dense clusters of buildings inside the fort, but also the open ground between them which may once have been infilled with timber structures. The outer scree-slopes of the hill are covered with additional enclosures and paddocks. (T. Driver)

Crowning a high, rocky summit at the northern end of the Llŷn Peninsula in Gwynedd is one of the most unusual and special hillforts in the whole of southern Britain. The three peaks of Yr Eifl, incorrectly in English 'The Rivals', form a striking three-pronged skyline feature visible for miles around. These peaks no doubt held a special place in the regional geography of later prehistoric Gwynedd and Tre'r Ceiri is the highest hillfort in north-west Wales.

The central peak of the Yr Eifl hills, at 564m above sea level, is crowned by a great summit cairn dating to the Early Bronze Age; there is also a cairn on the northern peak. Only on the steeply-sloping southern peak, at 480m above sea level, do we find signs of permanent settlement in the form of Tre'r Ceiri. This was a long-lived stone-walled hillfort dating from Iron Age and Roman times with sporadic occupation likely to have extended into the Early Medieval period.

Fig 8.10 View out from the south-west gateway at Tre'r Ceiri towards Nefyn and southern Llŷn. Consolidation work in the 1990s revealed that the entrance passage had been remodelled in the Romano-British period, showing that the hillfort continued to evolve after the Iron Age. Scale 1m. (T. Driver)

Although proclaimed in books and on visitor signs as 'The Town of the Giants' (based on a reading of its current name thought to have derived from the plural of 'cawr' for giant), its original name *Tre'r Caeri* meant 'Town of the Fortresses'. In the eighteenth century Thomas Pennant described it as '... the most perfect and magnificent, as well as the most artfully constructed British post I ever beheld'. In 1960 the hillfort archaeologist A.H.A. Hogg wrote that, 'In its present form the fortress is probably unique'.

The great grey walls of scree and stone rise around a sloping summit as one approaches along a moorland valley (Fig 3.3). On the north-west side a second lower wall strikes along the slope and all around and below the main rampart are systems of enclosures and clearings on the hillslopes. The interior of Tre'r Ceiri is crowded with some 158 huts and other structures, the earliest of which appear to be the roundhouses which contained almost exclusively prehistoric finds. Further analysis of the chronology of the structures shows that 62% of the partitioned D-shaped buildings contained Romano-British pottery. House 23, a rectangular building, produced a bone comb of late Roman or early medieval character.[1]

Many archaeologists have sought to understand this special hillfort through surveys and excavations over the last century and more. In the twentieth century much work was directed towards the buildings but excavations were not always carried out to exacting modern standards. In 1903 Reverend Baring-Gould and Robert Burnard, fresh from their early excavations in Pembrokeshire, cleared 32 of the 'cyttiau' or huts inside the fort. Three years later Harold Hughes of the Cambrian Archaeological Association returned to the hilltop to excavate another 32 structures assisted by workmen who, '... laid bare walls and doorways, and enabled the outlines of many 'cyttiau' to be followed accurately'.[2] Both seasons of work produced a range of pottery, stone, bone and metal finds from the houses mostly dated from 150BC to AD 400.

Later, during the 1950s, the Royal Commission conducted further campaigns of excavation and survey to clarify the development of the fort towards the publication of a definitive account for the 1960 *Caernarvonshire Inventory.* Finally, following more than a century of conservation concerns over the condition of the tumbled houses and ramparts, Gwynedd County Council began a programme of excavation and repair to the walls in 1989 supervised by the Gwynedd Archaeological Trust.[3] It is this programme of work we have to thank for the current clarity of the remains. Modern rebuilds are clearly marked with drill-holes showing replaced stones.

The main hillfort forms an elongated oval enclosure built on a sloping site, measuring some 290m from north-east to south-west by 100m, containing around 150 houses and huts. Originally the stone-walled ramparts (Fig 5.14) stood with a rear foundation footing, a wall-walk accessed here and there by internal steps and a low parapet wall. At the higher, eastern end of the fort, surveys of the rampart wall by the Royal Commission suggest its external face originally rose some 3.35m above the ground (Fig 5.16).

At the eastern summit is a great Bronze Age burial cairn, respected during the lifetime of the fort and perhaps re-used for Iron Age burials. The main fort encloses a modest 2.1ha, but the settlement was enlarged to 3.1ha overall with the addition of an annexe on the north and west sides. Further enclosures extended beyond the defences on the hillslopes on the north and south-west approaches showing that, in peacetime at least, the main fort may have acted as a 'hub' of settlement surrounded by informal dwellers, farmers and squatters.

Fig 8.11 Rebuilt and conserved postern gate in the northern rampart of Tre'r Ceiri, which once provided access through the rampart wall to a spring outside the hillfort. (T. Driver)

There were two main gateways: on the north-west, inner and outer gateways gave access up through the annexe into the main hillfort via a zig-zag path. This path not only served to negotiate the steep slopes but would have slowed down any attackers, exposing them side-on to a hail of sling shot and spears from above. Today these north-west gates have been restored as stone-lined passageways to walk through, having previously been blocked by collapsed rubble prior to the start of conservation work in 1993. The other main gate at the south-west point commanded spectacular views across the Llŷn Peninsula but the entrance passage and walls are low and partly obscured by tumbled stone.

There are a handful of smaller postern gateways, as with Garn Goch. The best-preserved example towards the summit of the fort was re-roofed in the recent works. This postern gate provided access out to the hillslopes beyond where a path leads down to a spring. The main rampart walls are still striking today, with the rear rampart-walks restored in places. Originally these walls stood some 3.35m high and could be patrolled as required.

Inside the hillfort we see one of the most clearly visible Iron Age and Roman villages in Britain. Tre'r Ceiri remains an arresting hillfort to visit, almost a 'Welsh Pompeii' considering its levels of preservation. Yet the crowded housing here is unusual. As explained in Chapter 6 (Fig 6.11), the Early Iron Age roundhouses were later subdivided in Romano-British times and later added to again with clusters of D-shaped buildings and crude shelters. At least one house – hut 41 against the southern rampart – may have been used for burial, suggested by the unusual find of a beaded collar from the building (Fig 2.13). Such finds usually accompany Iron Age and Roman burials. A further example is recorded from nearby Clynnog.

Fig 8.12 The heather-clad interior of Tre'r Ceiri looking southwest over the central clusters of interlinked huts. (T. Driver)

In between the clusters of houses there were tracts of open ground, but whether temporary timber or stake-walled structures stood in these open spaces is unclear. Perhaps the population of the hillfort swelled at key times of year, if the hillfort acted as centre for trade and, perhaps, seasonal festivals? Or, was it simply a prestige residence for its various leaders, a proto-town in north-west Wales and seat of the Gangani peoples before the Roman Conquest? Despite a century and more of work, there are still major questions about how this distinctive settlement was constructed, owned and used in its lifetime. It will continue to fascinate visitors and archaeologists for generations to come.

2 A great stone-walled hillfort of the north: Caer Drewyn, Corwen

Directions: The hillfort lies on open access land within the Clwydian Range and Dee Valley Area of Outstanding Natural Beauty just north of Corwen town centre. It is accessible via well signposted footpaths from the B5437 road. Seek safe parking in Corwen or nearby Trewyn Fawr estate. National Grid Reference: SJ 087 444

Caer Drewyn is one of the most interesting hillforts of north-east Wales, being built largely of scree with good sections of Iron Age rampart walling still visible. The hillfort gained its name from the hero or giant Drewyn Gawr to whom its construction was attributed when first mentioned around 1600, at which time it was noted as being occupied as a 'hafod' or summer farm in the Middle Ages. In the seventeenth century antiquarian Edward Lhwyd noted Caer Drewyn as the 'place where they kept their cattle in war time'.[4]

Caer Drewyn is strongly positioned high up on the leading western slope of the Llantysilio Mountain uplands, a block of high ground extending west to visually command a wide lowland valley junction above the Vale of Edeirion. The hillfort occupies a detached 'island spur'[5] of the mountain, as the tiny river of the Morwynion cuts a valley northwards separating Caer Drewyn from higher ground to the east. The great lowland plain below the hillfort was a meeting point for routeways through the hills in prehistory. A Roman marching camp was built just above this valley junction at Penrhos, Druid, 4.5km west of Caer Drewyn, further attesting to the strategic importance of this wide lowland vale during their campaigns. Caer Drewyn hillfort even occupies a 'tipped' or sloping position to look down into, and thus visually command, the valley below.

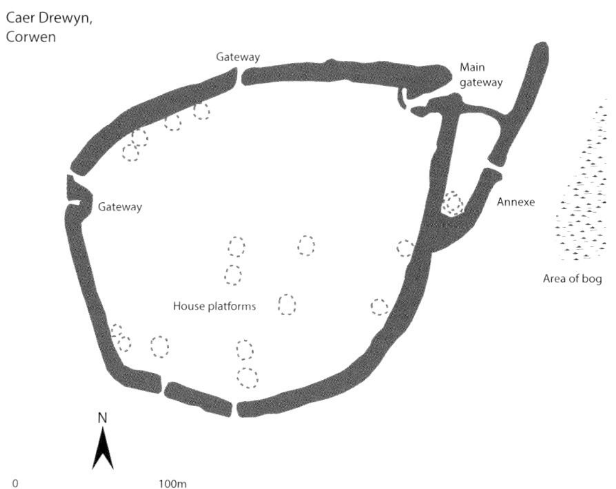

Fig 8.13 Plan of Caer Drewyn hillfort, showing the sites of several house platforms in the sloping interior identified by field survey. Note the area of bog at the top of the slope to the east, which may have been a votive focus for the fort. (T. Driver, after Heather and Hillforts Partnership Board 2011, 59)

Hillforts built of scree are rare in north-east Wales but here the abundant building stone was fully utilised. Much of the lower half of Caer Drewyn's rampart is a broad earthwork rampart with a tumbled outer facing of scree, while the upslope half of the hillfort is almost entirely built of scree. The ramparts form a great oval enclosure with no obvious traces of a ditch. The fort measures 192m north–south by 215m east–west and encloses 3.36ha. It sits on a steep hillslope facing west, with opposing gateways at the top and bottom of the slope separated by 40m of ascent; the ruinous main gateway sits on the level ground of the hill summit. There are around 13 house platforms within the hillfort, identified during survey for the Heather and Hillforts Project. It may be that many more ephemeral buildings and structures once stood here but a geophysical survey did not reveal much more detail. Gardner[6] also notes a water source in the form of a spring below the western gateway.

The hillfort was first explored by an antiquarian archaeologist, the Reverend Hugh Pritchard, who cleared away the 'clatter' from parts of the rampart, publishing his results in 1887.[7] Subsequent clearance and survey by Willoughby Gardner early in the 1920s noted the rampart consisted of, '... a core of rubble stones, faced either side with a wall of dry masonry'.[8] The wall was better built on the outer face, presumably for purposes of display. Gardner found evidence for a stepped profile with an upper platform or wall-walk 1.5m wide, an advanced feature also found at Tre'r Ceiri on Llŷn (Fig 5.16). He proposed the original wall may have stood between 4.2m and 4.6m high. There are many oval shelters within the rubble of the rampart built by farmers, walkers and soldiers on manoeuvres in recent centuries to provide shelter in inclement weather; they were first mentioned by Pennant in the eighteenth century.

The main gateway at the north-east point forms an inturned passageway between the terminals, a type of gate which was common among the hillforts of north-east Wales including at Pen-y-corddyn-mawr and Dinorben. It would have formed an intimidating entrance to this hillfort. In contrast to the visible wall sections around the rampart, the gateway itself is ruinous today and partly infilled with rubble. The siting of the main gate on the level ground of the hill summit may suggest that most visitors and traffic were expected from this direction. In 1922 Willoughby Gardner also noted 'numerous points of rock sticking up across the causeway'[9] which he took to be a natural chevaux-de-frise.

Immediately outside the main gateway on the hill summit is what appears to be a later defended hut group, appended onto the earlier rampart. It may be that the hillfort was entirely defunct when this enclosure was built, or perhaps simply reserved for the penning of livestock. On the hillslopes beyond lie quite extensive remains of prehistoric fields and settlements.

The key to Caer Drewyn's siting and construction probably involved several factors. The availability of scree on the hillslopes provided a novel building material for the Iron Age community. The choice to 'tilt' the hillfort to the west down a 40m slope, may have been influenced partly by the scatter of scree down the slope,

Fig 8.14 (LEFT) Caer Drewyn's north-western rampart, looking downhill towards the western gateway and the wide lowland valley junction beyond. (T. Driver). **Fig 8.15** (RIGHT) Caer Drewyn. Outer face of the north-eastern rampart showing the well-preserved wall face, cleared of collapsed scree by antiquarians to enable viewing. (T. Driver)

but was probably also a strategic decision to allow visibility over the valley below. Perhaps a final critical factor is found outside the eastern ramparts on the hill summit. Just outside the fort is a great wet bog, lying in a gully between the fort on the west and the rocky local summit of the hill above to the east, mentioned by Gardner as a former 'shallow tarn'. This bog must have been a useful source of water and fuel, but was it more than that? Given the importance of wetlands and bogs for religion and ceremony in Iron Age Wales, the fort may well have stood on the edge of a sacred wetland, set only a few metres beyond the gateway to the hillfort and perhaps a key ceremonial focus that underpinned at least some of the function of Caer Drewyn.

3 A centre of ironworking innovation: Bryn y Castell, Llan Ffestiniog

Directions: The fort is accessed off the B4391 minor road running between Llan Ffestiniog and Bala, where a track managed by Dwr Cymru/ Welsh Water leaves the road at SH 723 423. The track is a private road but a public footpath follows it up past the modern waterworks and around to Bryn y Castell hillfort, a short distance further uphill. National Grid Reference: SH 728 429

Bryn y Castell is a small hillfort commanding a narrow mountain pass in the foothills west of Llyn Morwynion above Llan Ffestiniog. It was originally believed to be an early medieval fortress or a *llys* (court or palace) mentioned in the Mabinogion story of Math fab Mathonwy, a king of Gwynedd. Yet complete excavation between 1979 and 1985 by the Eryri National Park Authority revealed instead a later prehistoric hillfort dedicated to iron smelting and working. At the time of excavation, the 1,200kg of waste slag discovered was the most recovered from any prehistoric site in Britain.[10] It is a rewarding site to visit as the rampart, along with the excavated houses and other structures inside, have been reconstructed in stone.

Fig 8.16 Bryn y Castell. High view looking south across the interior of the fort showing the main north gateway (LEFT), with asymmetric terminals, and the 'snail-shaped' roundhouse (RIGHT). (T. Driver)

Bryn y Castell sits atop a steep-sided, impressive crag at 370m above sea level overlooking a well-used mountain pass. To its east and north rise bare mountain slopes but ahead to the north-east, and overlooked from the main gateway, is the upland bog of the Afon Gamallt. It is highly likely that the fort was sited to visually command this bog which was an important source of bog ore for smelting. Pollen analysis has also shown that thick upland woodland here was also a source for oak and alder for charcoal production. Further to the west, on a clear day, there are views across Tremadog Bay and the Llŷn Peninsula. To the south-west the Rhinogydd mountains with their overland trading routes to the coast can be seen, the location of the sister metalworking settlement at Crawcwellt West (Fig 6.20).

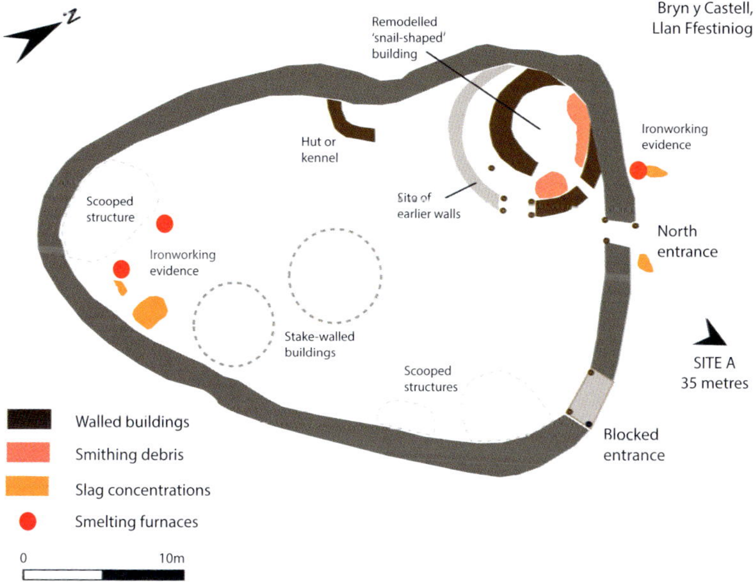

Fig 8.17 Excavation plan of Bryn y Castell hillfort showing areas of ironworking debris and furnaces. (T. Driver, after Crew 2009, Figure 1.)

Bryn y Castell is pear-shaped, the low-walled rampart following the general line of the summit of the crag. It is not large; indeed the interior feels 'family sized' and intimate. The main gateway to the hill lies on the wider, north end of the crag. An earlier gate lay to the east of the present gap but was subsequently blocked.

The main focus of pre-Roman metalworking lay inside the fort. Total excavation of the interior revealed two domestic stake-walled buildings in the central-southern part of the interior and some smaller structures, including a shelter against the western rampart with very high phosphate levels, tentatively interpreted as a dog kennel. The most impressive, and unusual, building here is the 'snail-shaped' roundhouse in the north-west corner just inside the later gateway (Fig 6.22). The building started life as a circular roundhouse before the southern wall was demolished and moved inwards. This created an overlapping entrance wall clearly designed to provide shelter for metal smiths inside, whilst funnelling wind into the furnaces. When excavated, the building was full of smithing debris. There are similar specialised 'snail shaped' structures inside Garn Boduan, Llŷn and inside Tower Point promontory fort, Pembrokeshire (Fig 6.24). Another rich structure for metalworking at Bryn y Castell was a roundhouse some 35m below the gate to the north-east, named Site A.

Radiocarbon dating suggests the main hillfort was in use from around 300BC to the coming of the Romans in around AD 70 at which point metal production within the ramparts ceased. However, the Site A roundhouse outside the fort began to be used for metal production in the 20 to 30 years before the Romans arrived and then, once the Roman garrisons had withdrawn from the region later in the second century AD, ironworking briefly restarted.

The cycle of metal smithing and the production of bar iron at Bryn y Castell mirrors developments at the specialised ironworking roundhouse settlement of Crawcwellt West near Bronaber. Both settlements produced evidence of exotic finds reflecting a relatively wealthy lifestyle when compared with neighbouring hillforts. Finds from Bryn y Castell included glass bangle fragments containing multi-coloured twisted cords, gaming boards scratched into slate with black and white pebbles for game pieces and a group of distinctive whetstones for knife sharpening. It is likely that the arduous, smoky and magical process of smithing ore into iron at this fort attracted kudos and respect from surrounding communities, whilst its reputation for craftsmanship and iron production was carried far and wide along regional trading networks.

4 At the roof of the world: The Breiddin hillfort, Criggion

Directions: The Breiddin hills lie to the north-east of Welshpool and are popular with walkers. Free car parking is provided by the Criggion Estate on the north side of the hill at Criggion village with forest tracks and waymarked trails leading out to the east and south. Steep paths lead up to Rodney's Pillar, a monument which stands on the summit of the hillfort. National Grid Reference: SJ 294 143

Visiting this large hillfort is to experience one of the great hilltop locations of Welsh prehistory. This group of hills, which rises steeply from the virtually flat valley floor of the River Severn, are made of hard igneous dolerite bedrock of an extinct volcano. The stone has long been quarried for hardwearing roadstone. There are four prominent summits in the group: The Breiddin Hill (locally *Breidden*) and hillfort occupies the northernmost ridge rising to 365m above sea level. To the south rises the steeper ridge of Moel y Golfa at 403m above sea level, and just to

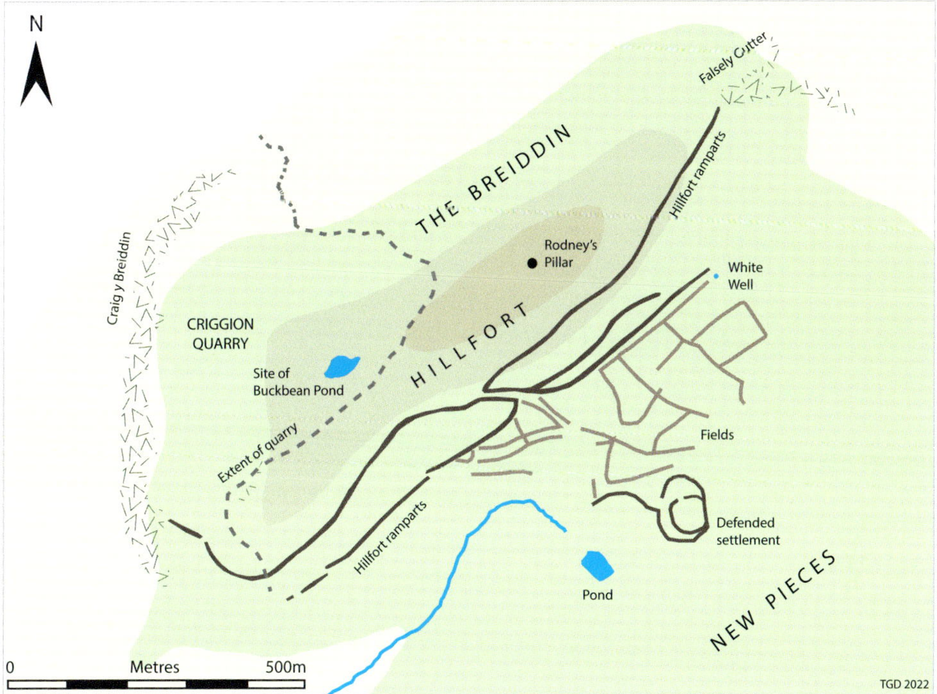

Fig 8.18 Plan of the Breiddin hillfort showing the New Pieces field system and defended settlement beyond the ramparts to the south-east. Large sections of the north-west part of the hillfort interior have now been quarried away, including the site of the excavated Buckbean Pond. (T. Driver; after Musson et al. 1991, Figure 4.)

the south-east, Cefn y Castell hillfort on Middletown Hill stands at 367m above sea level and can be clearly seen from the Breiddin. The intervening lower saddle of hilly ground or col between the Breiddin and Middletown Hill is home to the New Pieces prehistoric defended farmstead and field system, parts of which can be visited when the vegetation is low.

Ascending the Breiddin hill today is quite a task. The author climbed up from the east side alongside Falsely Gutter, described by Chris Musson as a 'dizzying natural fissure which cuts down the cliffs that form the northern bastion of the ridge'. Reaching the col of New Pieces, one enters a tract of productive agricultural land with good soils, watered by the White Well and several springs and ponds. To the north tower the steeper slopes of the hillfort, bounded at their base by a substantial stony rampart. Although this 28ha hillfort is one of the largest in Britain, available space for occupation on the ridge was limited by rocky scarps and steeper slopes.

Fig 8.19 Panoramic views of central Wales and the borderlands are gained from the summit of the Breiddin hillfort: view looking north-east across the triangulation pillar to Rodney's Pillar beyond. (T. Driver)

Excavations at the Breiddin between 1969 and 1976 in advance of quarrying were led by Chris Musson.[11] These were important as they were of a 'rescue' nature at the time before the Welsh Archaeological Trusts came into existence. In the face of quarry expansion several seasons of work investigated the western and southern parts of the interior and defences before they were lost, with an exemplary record of the excavations published in 1991.

The excavations revealed some of the best evidence in Wales for a Late Bronze Age hillfort, bounded by a timber-framed stone rampart dating to around 800BC. Metalworking activity had taken place within this early fort which was enclosed with a rampart of earth and stones, luckily preserved beneath the Iron Age rampart. The hilltop was then abandoned for several centuries and may only have been used for grazing before the construction of a much larger Middle Iron Age hillfort, with new outer ramparts faced inside and out with stone and boulders, around 300BC. Evidence of intense activity just behind the rampart was unearthed in the form of 7–8m diameter Iron Age roundhouses and substantial four-posters for grain storage with supporting posts up to half a metre across. Early Roman material was entirely absent, perhaps suggesting its abandonment in the face of the first century AD invasion and campaigns. The hill was then reoccupied towards the end of the Roman period.

A highlight of the rescue excavations was the exploration of the Buckbean Pond, a boggy area inside the hillfort which is now entirely quarried away. A large cistern had been dug into the pond between 400–200BC to provide water for the fort. It had been backfilled with perishable Iron Age artefacts and debris from daily life which survived remarkably intact in the anaerobic, boggy conditions. The incredible finds included two wooden bowls (Fig 8.20; now on display in St Fagans National Museum of History), a large mallet and a wooden 'sword' (Fig 4.5) which may have been a child's toy, a practice piece or a votive offering as suggested by Miranda Green and Ray Howell, indicating 'water-ritual at the Breiddin'.[12] The pond also produced valuable pollen evidence about the prehistoric environs of the fort which, when considered alongside the structural and artefact evidence, led archaeologists Bill Britnell and Bob Silvester to later conclude, '... the Breiddin was neither densely nor permanently occupied during the Iron Age ... [suggesting] instead an association with seasonal activities such as the exploitation of upland pastures'.[13]

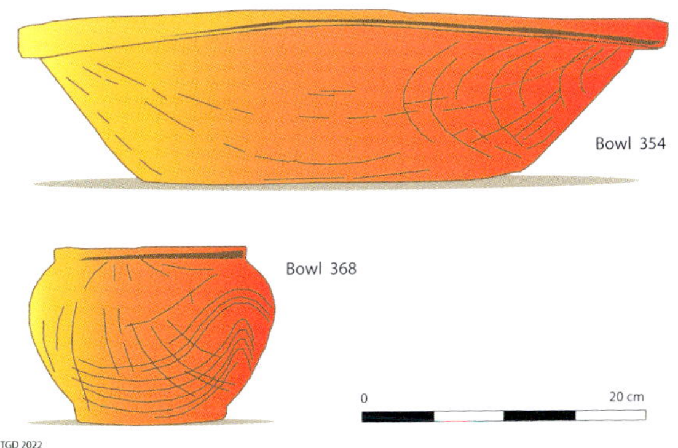

Fig 8.20 Two exceptionally rare Iron Age wooden bowls recovered from the cistern cut into the boggy Buckbean Pond, only preserved because of the anaerobic conditions of the pond deposits. Note the flat base and carved rims of both vessels. The vessels are now on display at the St Fagans National Museum of History. (T. Driver. After Musson et al. 1991, Figure 70)

The Breiddin hillfort remains a rewarding site to visit. The size of the outer, lower rampart is impressive, and one can trace the inner and outer ramparts quite well along the ridge when the vegetation is low. Despite the rocky interior, it is possible to pick out levelled areas sheltered by crags which would have made suitable places for erecting roundhouses. Many springs issue from outcrops across the hillfort.

When standing on the summit one feels to be in a different, upland world far removed from the lowland valley stretching out below. This special location provides an extraordinary 'bird's eye view', particularly to the north as far as Llangollen and Eryri (Snowdonia). Despite this extreme elevation from the lowlands, the high ridge was provided with abundant water, farmland and woodland meeting all the needs of the hillfort community. Any prehistoric visitor, trader or attacker would have been robustly challenged by the journey to the summit and – if they were allowed in – would have been filled with awe at the power and visual command of this great fort at the roof of the world.

5 A borderlands giant: Gaer fawr, Guilsfield

Directions: The hillfort and its woodland are in the care of Coed Cadw/ The Woodland Trust and are accessed from a minor road north of Guilsfield village. There is a small car park and interpretation panels at the foot of the hill from which well-marked woodland trails to the hillfort start and finish. The site is best visited during winter or spring to fully appreciate the earthworks. National Grid Reference: SJ 224 130

Gaer fawr or the 'Great Fort' is a true hidden giant of Welsh hillforts. Concealed beneath thick tree cover it remained out of sight, and largely uninvestigated, until a new detailed survey and study was carried out in 2007.[14] The 2007 survey by Louise Barker for the Royal Commission shed new light on the complexity of the defences of this great borderlands fort, and informed some attractive new interpretation panels on the site. This is a good site to visit to really understand the scale of the engineering of the hillforts of the Welsh Marches on the eve of the Roman Conquest. Whereas some smaller hillforts in western Wales 'aspired' to an appearance of strength through monumentality, Gaer fawr's mighty ramparts would have posed a real military challenge to any invading force.

Gaer fawr is a multivallate hillfort, roughly oval in shape, measuring 426m north-east to south-west by 180m, enclosing just over 6ha. The fort occupies a high ridge at 219m above sea level on a rising tract of hilly ground between the valleys of the Guilsfield brook and River Severn to the south, and the great lowland valley of Dyffryn Meifod which carries the River Vyrnwy to the north. The precipitous south-eastern slopes required few artificial defences, whereas the three other sides of the hill were heavily sculpted with ramparts and scarps, doubtless over several phases.

Just to enter Gaer fawr today is a long uphill journey of twists and turns, following the correct path ever higher up through the woodland to the summit. Every turn reveals more impressive tiers of defence. Gaer fawr's main terraced ramparts define the north and north-west slopes of the hill. Now wooded and invisible, they would once have been striking from afar, appearing as a monumental series of steps topped with timberwork. Indeed, Barker notes: '... on the summit of the hill ... glimpses reveal what once would have been unimpeded and spectacular views'.[15]

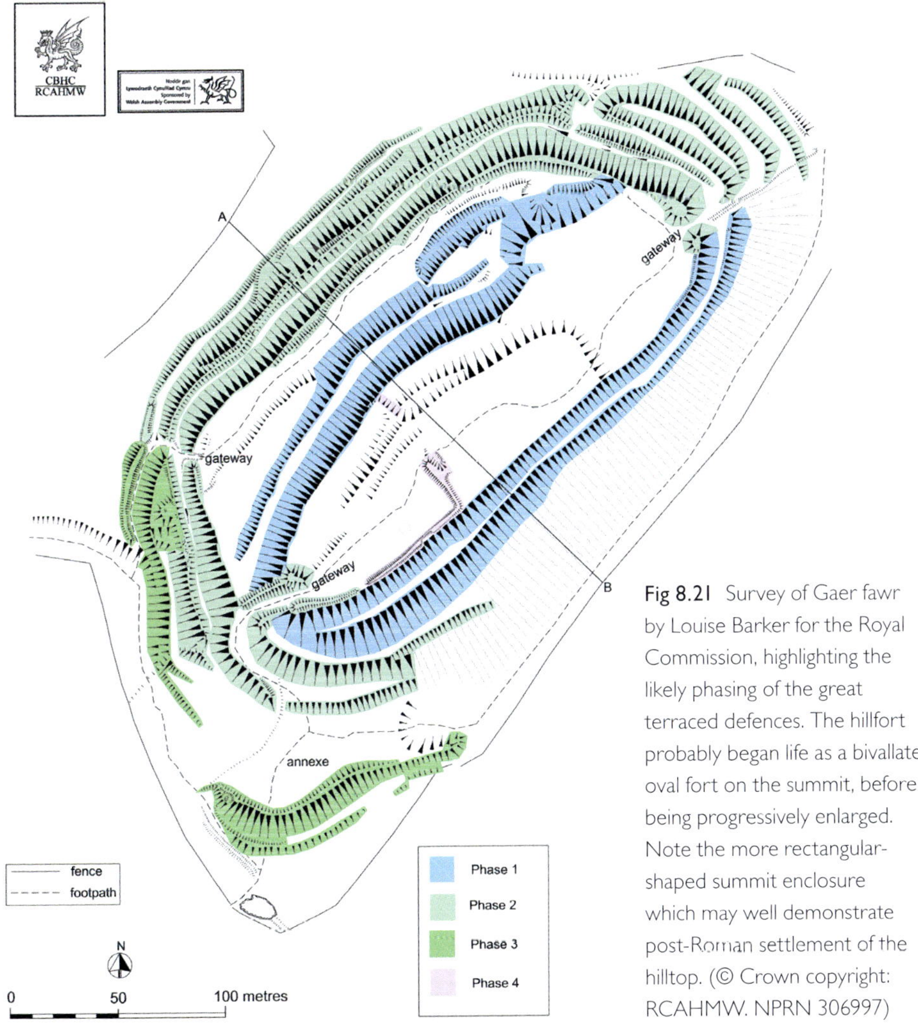

Fig 8.21 Survey of Gaer fawr by Louise Barker for the Royal Commission, highlighting the likely phasing of the great terraced defences. The hillfort probably began life as a bivallate oval fort on the summit, before being progressively enlarged. Note the more rectangular-shaped summit enclosure which may well demonstrate post-Roman settlement of the hilltop. (© Crown copyright: RCAHMW. NPRN 306997)

The defences enclose two main interior spaces. The elongated summit enclosure encompasses around 1.3ha, while a lower terrace within the north-west defences below the summit encloses 0.44ha. A third lower gateway enters the lowest part of the defences on the west side, while a large annexe is appended to the southern side of the fort.

The scale of the Iron Age engineering is impressive even today. The innermost scarped rampart on the east side of the summit enclosure stands around 5.8m high. Looking down from the north-west side of the summit enclosure the topmost rampart drops first some 7.5m downhill to a 4.5m-wide terrace, and then drops a further 6m down. A section of ditch cut on this lower terrace runs for 62m and was originally 13m wide.

Fig 8.22 Gaer fawr. A seat bearing the likeness of Iron Age boars awaits those who make the long climb to the summit. (T. Driver)

Three main gateways can be seen. The lower west gate was approached along a narrow, 50m-long corridor and was overlooked by a platform, newly identified during the 2007 survey, perhaps for slingers to defend the entrance. Slight earthworks suggest a guard chamber at the innermost point of the west gate. Up at the summit there are two gates. The south-west gate is a well-preserved out-turned type similar to those found at Hod Hill and Hambledon hillforts in Dorset. The final 24m approach climbs up through a 5m-corridor set between two high earthworks. The north-east entrance was also approached by a steep approach, first along a curving ramped pathway before turning sharply south-west and climbing up a 38m-long corridor and through the gateway gap.[16] With a combination of long, overlooked approaches and bridges which originally overlooked the main gates, these protected entrances deliberately funnelled unwelcome visitors into a 'killing zone' at the mercy of missiles from above.

Fig 8.23 Drawing of the Guilsfield bronze boar by Arthur Gore.[19] (By kind permission of the Cambrian Archaeological Association)

Were the Iron Age builders influenced by the setting and the shape of the hilltop when they planned the defences on such a scale? Today one sees ridges, valleys and slopes outside the defences which are entirely natural landforms but which nonetheless mimic the later built defences. Perhaps the community building Gaer fawr, whether Cornovii or Ordovices, thought they were rebuilding a long defunct fortress harbouring old ancestral power?

A handful of other small hillforts and cropmarks of lowland defended farms are recorded in the Guilsfield and Welshpool environs, including nearby hillforts of Llwyn Bryn-dinas, Foel Hill or Soldier's Mount to the north, and Crowther's Camp to the south-east. The great Breidden hillfort can be readily seen from the summit of Gaer fawr to the east. This area was already well settled in the Later Bronze Age (1150–800BC) with several Late Bronze hoards known including the famous Guilsfield Hoard. The Guilsfield hoard, comprising some 120 pieces of Late Bronze Age metalwork including palstaves, socketed axes, spearheads, swords and chapes (fittings for sword scabbards), was found by workmen digging below Crowther's Camp, 3km south-east of Gaer fawr. The hoard shows an active Late Bronze Age population in the environs of Gaer fawr, producing and using prestige weapons and metalwork.

A tantalising Iron Age find from the hillfort is a tiny bronze boar found 'within' Gaer fawr in 1833[17] along with 'several ornaments of gold'. The boar is made of hollow bronze and measures 63mm long by 35mm high. A deep incision running the full length of the underside of the animal suggests it was originally mounted, most likely as a helmet emblem.[18]

6 The power of place: Craig yr Aderyn or Birds' Rock, Bryncrug

Directions: On open access land north-east of Tywyn, Gwynedd, and reached via a steep public footpath. There is parking in a layby near Llanllwyda farm on a minor road between Bryncrug and Llanfihangel-y-pennant. Access may be difficult in low cloud or inclement weather. Castell y Bere medieval castle (Cadw; open usual hours, free of charge) is worth a visit 2km further along the valley. National Grid Reference: SH 645 068

The great vale of the Dysynni Valley in southern Eryri (Snowdonia) runs 12km inland from the coast at Tywyn to the foothills of Cader Idris, providing a corridor into the mountains for the movement of people and livestock. In medieval times it was the Welsh castle of Castell y Bere at the head of the valley which controlled cattle movement across the mountains. A thousand years before it was the inhabitants of Craig yr Aderyn or Birds' Rock who did the same.

Craig yr Aderyn is one of the finest inland promontory forts in Eryri, helped not only by its well-preserved defences but also its powerful position, set high on a

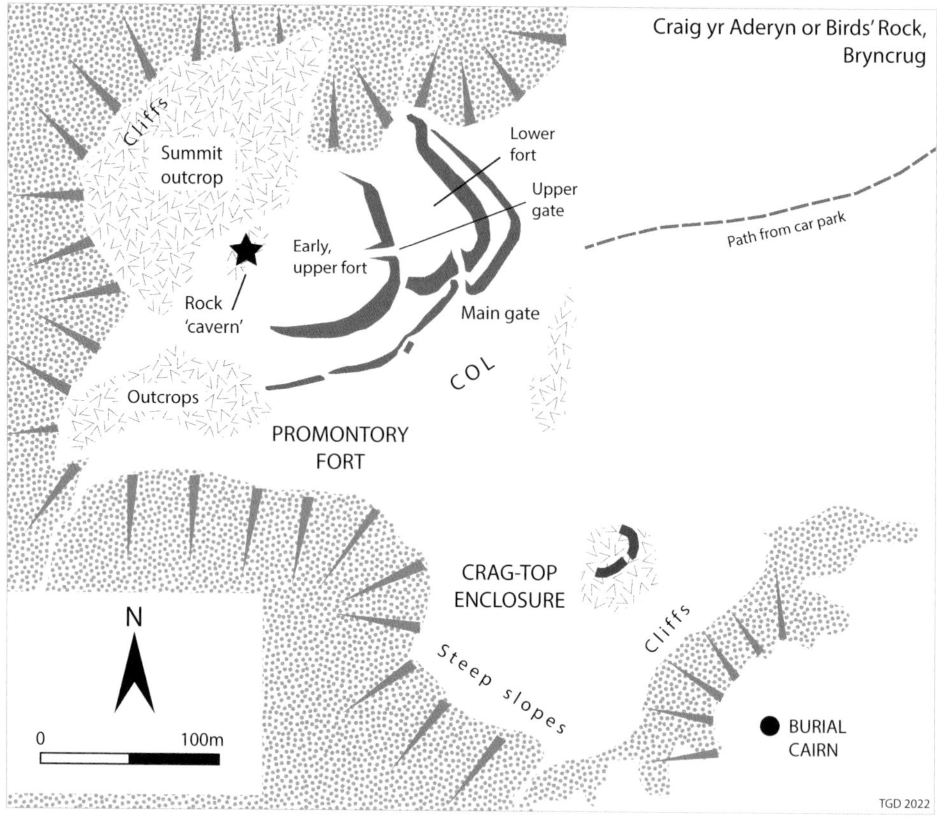

Fig 8.24 Plan of Craig yr Aderyn or Birds' Rock showing location of the main promontory fort (LEFT), with the recently-identified crag-top enclosure and burial cairn (LOWER RIGHT) lying across the col from the promontory fort. (T. Driver)

towering crag which rises 233m above the valley floor. This great crag can be seen from afar as a leaning half-dome of rock (Fig 3.22). This recognisable silhouette no doubt conveyed a considerable sense of 'power of place' and visual command over the surrounding landscape for its inhabitants.

As one approaches the promontory fort today along the steep path from the east (Fig 8.25), the first impression is of a precipitous rocky summit ringed with earth and stone defences. Additional natural scarps in the outcropping rock suggest additional ramparts beyond those built in the Iron Age. The site is essentially unexcavated, although the antiquarian W. Wynne Foulkes did report some cursory digging inside a 'cwt' or hut inside the fort, reported in the journal *Archaeologia Cambrensis* for 1874.[20] He described the discovery of a tightly-rolled lead sheet – possibly a weight – a portion of a round curved leaden bar, perhaps part of an armlet

Fig 8.25 Craig yr Aderyn or Birds' Rock, lit by December sunlight in 2022. View of the inland promontory fort from the south-east, showing the multiple ramparts which enclose the rocky dome. The lowest scarped banks can be seen (RIGHT) with the scree-built rampart of the lower fort and earthen rampart of the upper fort above. Natural terracing of the outcropping rock towards the summit may have suggested further 'ramparts' to prehistoric visitors. (T. Driver)

and some Romano-British pottery. The fort was further described by archaeologist George Smith for a 2009 visitor guide for the Gwynedd Archaeological Trust.[21]

The sequence of development at Craig yr Aderyn appears to be as follows: the earliest defence is probably the substantial upper earthen rampart with one strong inturned main gate facing east. This upper fort encloses a more level area on the west suitable for habitation, but no definite house sites can be made out. Within this upper fort is a great natural rock formation enclosing a restricted cavern (Fig 8.27); was this dark recess perhaps used for Iron Age rituals in the 'inner sanctum' of the fort? Towards the summit of the rock the ground falls away in sheer cliff faces to the valley floor below.

A second stage of enlargement is suggested by the addition of a wide 'lower fort' below and to the east of the upper fort, which was accessed by a new main gateway facing the main approach on the south side. At the outer end of this main gate, vertical slabs of naturally outcropping rock frame the approach to the entrance and may have been interpreted by prehistoric builders as the remnants of an earlier defence. Above and to the right of the outer gateway, a naturally flat rock terrace may have provided a useful slinging platform.

Fig 8.26 Craig yr Aderyn or Birds' Rock. View of the main gateway looking out across the col. The gate passage (RIGHT) would originally have been crossed by a bridge springing from the rampart terminal (LEFT). Note the height difference between the standing figures. In the right background, the flat-topped cone of the crag-top enclosure can be seen, with the burial cairn just visible on the horizon line beyond. (© Crown copyright: RCAHMW. DS2014_357_005. NPRN 302862)

The rampart here is formed by a huge, loose tumbled mass of scree and boulders (Fig 5.8) but in its lower levels coarse Iron Age boulder-walling of the gate passage can still be made out. A quantity of quartz blocks within the tumbled rampart mass suggests that parts of the gate passage may originally have been quartz-walled. The deep gate passage, overlooked by high stony rampart terminals, strongly suggests that a timber crossing bridge was once installed here over a post-lined passage, now infilled with rubble.

Further prehistoric walls were added around and below this great main gate: one running out to the west – the lowest rampart – was a roughly-built boulder-wall which weaves around outcropping rocks. Various later stone buildings and shelters of uncertain date have been built within and around the ruinous outer defences. It is highly likely that this advantageous spot was used in later centuries for occupation and defence.

The environs of Craig yr Aderyn fort have recently begun to reveal more secrets about how this settlement may have functioned in prehistory. The fort faces a 'col' or shallow valley on its south side which is filled with extraordinary rock formations, canyons, scree slopes and quartz veins (Fig 8.26). Overlooking this valley landscape from a hill summit to the south is a prominent burial cairn, around 9m in diameter. Conventionally this cairn would date to the Early Bronze Age, but with increasing recognition of Iron Age burials outside inland promontory forts in Wales, this burial mound may well be contemporary with the fort, or at least have been re-used in the Iron Age.

Of considerable interest is a fortified crag between the promontory fort and the cairn, recently identified by the author. This steep-sided natural crag, marked by stripes of quartz, rises on the south side of the col. At its summit is a low scree rampart of coarse blocks with a simple gateway, entered from the south. At least one rock-cut house platform can be seen inside. If contemporary with the Iron Age settlement, what was the role of this distinct crag-top enclosure? Was it a look-out, a segregated settlement for particular people in society, or a symbolic location where laws were enacted or where Druids foretold the future? Perhaps it is a much later fortification. Without excavation it is impossible to tell, but it shows that additional archaeological sites frequently await discovery just beyond the ramparts of even well-visited monuments, if one searches hard enough.

Fig 8.27 Dark places: a natural 'cavern' high up the interior of Craig yr Aderyn, formed by a stack of glacial rocks, may have provided a ceremonial or ritual space inside the hillfort. Just 10km to the north-east, the famous Tal-y-llyn hoard of Iron Age metalwork (Fig 4.7, Chapter 4 frontispiece) was found interred in a similar rock chamber. Scale 1m. (T. Driver)

Directions: On open access land to the north-west of Brecon town. The hillfort is owned and managed by the Bannau Brycheiniog National Park Authority and is best reached along a footpath which leaves the B4520 road at the Pendre housing estate and climbs the moderate slope to the hillfort. A popular destination for walkers and picnickers. National Grid Reference: SO 029 303

Fig 8.28 Pen y Crug hillfort from the air in winter 2009. The thin blanket of snow makes clear the four or five lines of outer defence which encircle this hilltop. This view shows the fort from the north-east, with the main gateway upper left. Note the curving shadow of the prehistoric holloway approaching the gate across moorland from the east (LEFT), a rare survival which shows the actual path of approach to this hillfort. (© Crown copyright: RCAHMW. NPRN 92058. AP_2009_0832)

Crowning an undulating summit at 330m above sea level, Pen y Crug hillfort is a multivallate masterpiece. This is one of south Wales' larger and more complex hillforts, commanding a prominent hill overlooking the confluence of the rivers Usk and Honddu. Its steep ramparts and deep ditches present a baffling labyrinth to those who explore them. The hillfort is unexcavated but was surveyed by the Royal Commission for their 1986 *Brecknock Inventory*.

The interior of the hillfort encloses around 1.86ha but the true scale of the entire monument is far larger, enclosing 4.7ha to the outer edges of the ramparts. The inner rampart has a steep face which still towers some 4–5m above the partly infilled ditch. Beyond this strong inner defence, between three and four steep outer banks encircle the summit. At times on the west and north these are tightly packed up the steeper slopes, but on the east they extend and spread out to form an impenetrable physical and visual barrier. If only some of these multivallate banks were originally topped with timber palisades, Pen y Crug would have appeared as a spiked 'forest' of fences bristling around the hilltop. It would have been a strange and terrifying sight.

The main approach to the gateway is still marked by a broad, deep holloway heading up towards the gate, worn by centuries of human, cattle and wagon traffic. It veers first left, then kicks back right immediately outside the gateway. Only geophysical survey could test whether this track was once fenced in the style of 'antenna' approaches at other forts or was even flanked by burial mounds. It remains an important prehistoric survival at this site and preserves the 'correct' path of approach.

On reaching the defences at the main gate the visitor is presented first with a 10m-wide gap between the outermost ramparts, certainly wide enough for wagons and chariots to enter. On the right-hand side of this gap are three ramparts, on the left four. Was this asymmetry – at the critical main entrance to the fort – purposely contrived? Perhaps. We see similar asymmetry at other hillfort gateways, and in the decoration of expertly-designed La Tène ornaments and artefacts. The entrance passage climbs uphill, rapidly narrowing to the innermost gate. Today the site of this gate is infilled with rubble but it once would have stood as a deep walled gateway passage crossed by a wooden bridge.

To really experience the size and complexity of Pen y Crug's defences one should set off to explore them. Away from the southern gateway the ramparts quickly steepen. Along the east side they expand along a more gentle slope and are disturbed here and there by more recent stone quarries. At the 'rear' of the fort on the north

Fig 8.29 Pen y Crug, Brecon. The huge scale of the defences as they approach the main gateway is evident in this view. The main inner rampart stands to the right. The ditches, long infilled with tumbled rampart material, would originally have been far deeper. (T. Driver)

side are perhaps the steepest and strongest banks, which presented a visual display of power to all those living in the hills to the north. The inhabitants of Pen y Crug, like those at Twyn y Gaer hillfort to the east, may have seen their greatest threats lying in the rolling uplands to the north at the very edge of Silurian territory.

Even at a large and complex hillfort like this, one can trace the hand of the hillfort's designers and see human-scale decision-making. On the steeper west side, the generous span of four outer ramparts had to be modified into just three. This was achieved by merging a pair of intermediate ramparts into a single bank at two distinct points on the north-west and south sides of the defences. When the vegetation is low these points of convergence can still be seen – and admired.

The interior is featureless today and devoid of any real clue as to where the original roundhouses once stood, having been ploughed in historic times. Modern visitors seeking an obvious source of water on this bare summit may be disappointed, but water for the community was never far away. Whilst visiting during a spring drought in 2022 with dusty ground underfoot, the base of the outer northern ditches was still boggy (Fig 3.25) suggesting a former spring. Other nearby streams still flow freely off the surrounding hillside.

Directions: Both the large (Y Gaer fawr) and small (Y Gaer fach) forts lie on open access land in the care of the Bannau Brycheiniog National Park Authority, with well-marked paths to both. The forts lie on high ground between Llandeilo and Llangadog, Carmarthenshire accessed via steep minor roads from Bethlehem village. From here one follows brown signs to the hillfort and car park at the west end. National Grid Reference: SN 685 242

Garn Goch (alternatively Carn Goch) in Carmarthenshire remains an extraordinary and enigmatic hillfort to visit. It is one of the largest in Wales, enclosing 16.6ha (the main hillfort plus its annexe) and is only surpassed in enclosed size in south Wales by the 22ha Deer Park coastal promontory fort in western Pembrokeshire: the very large 20.5ha Penycloddiau hillfort lies in north-east Wales on the Clwydian Range. As one approaches Garn Goch from the lowland vale of the River Tywi on the north side, there is a steady realisation that most of the long 'whale-back' ridge rising high above you is in fact dominated by a single massive hillfort; its grey scree rampart can be glimpsed in places winding between the bracken on the northern slopes.

There are two other hillforts on this ridge, the small fort (Y Gaer fach) to the west which one passes through on the way to Y Gaer fawr ('The Great or Large Fort') at Garn Goch, and the ridge-top Llwyndu Camp further west, which lies on private land. Clearly this place was important both strategically and, perhaps, for the movement of livestock between the lowlands and the hill country in later prehistory. The co-existence of two well-sized smaller forts, alongside one of the largest in Wales, speaks of centuries of competition, succession and periodic abandonment of these defended settlements during the Bronze and Iron Ages. Or perhaps the two smaller hillforts were for permanent settlement, with Garn Goch itself reserved for trading, meetings and transient activities? Only a long programme of excavation (building on exploratory geophysics carried out in 2009) could disentangle the dates of construction and occupation of the three.

Garn Goch is enclosed by 1,700m of rampart, the majority made from great piles of scree, originally walled on its external faces; here and there, sections of intact Iron Age walling can still be seen. Perhaps only Penycloddiau in Clwyd has a longer

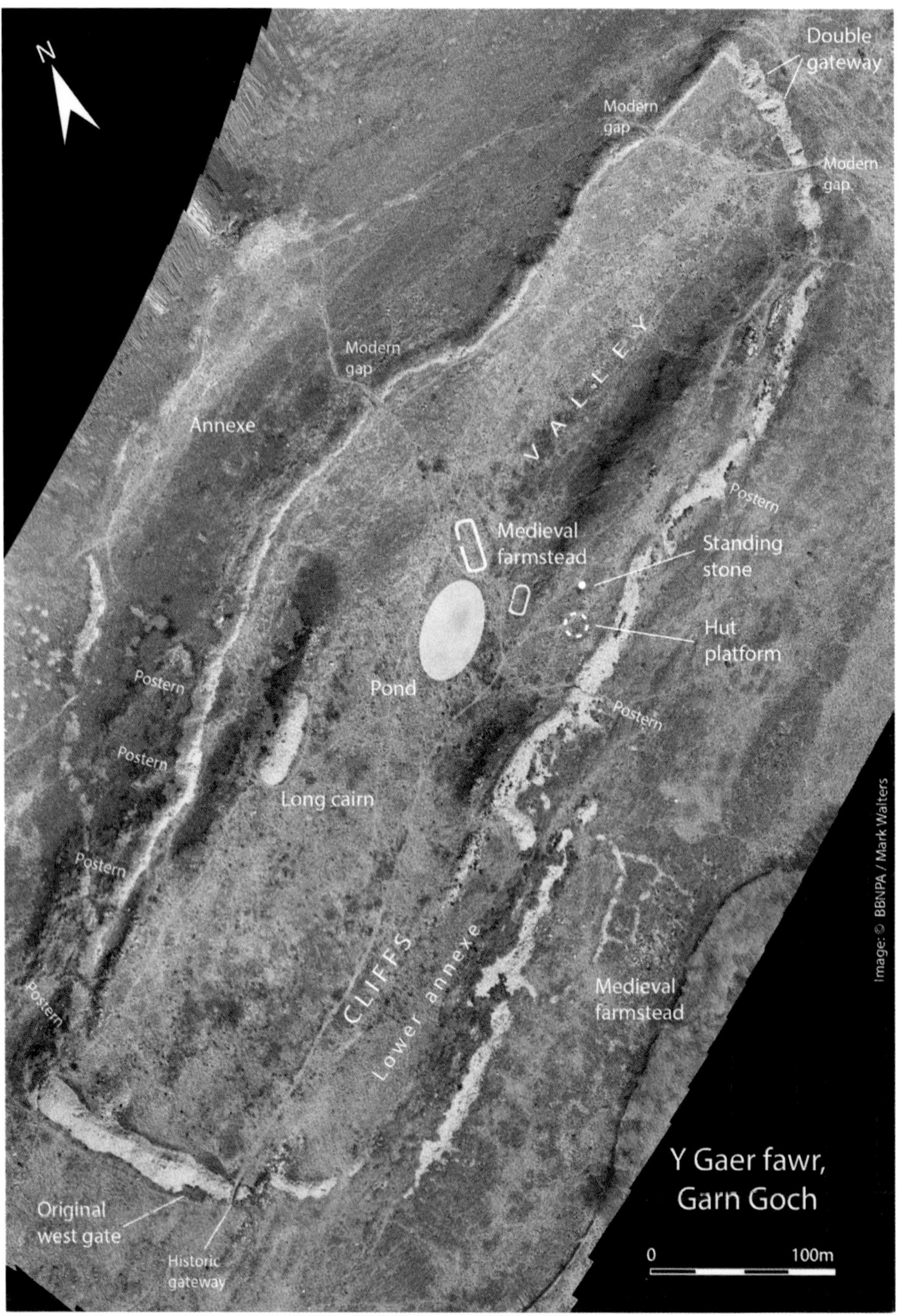

Fig 8.30 Photogrammetric survey of Garn Goch hillfort by Mark Walters for the Bannau Brycheiniog National Park Authority, with key features labelled. (Image: © Bannau Brycheiniog National Park Authority. Imagery by Mark Walters. By kind permission of Alice Thorne. Graphic by T. Driver)

Fig 8.31 The north-western scree rampart of Garn Goch snaking its way across the ridge. In places it was accessed by slab-lined postern gateways, now mostly ruinous. (T. Driver)

set of main ramparts at 1,950m. However an annexe added to the north side of Garn Goch gave an additional 700m of rampart built of earth and scree. The hillfort has at least eight entrances. There are the ruins of two prehistoric main gates: a pair of parallel slab-lined passages at the north-east and the collapsed ruins of a walled and slab-lined gate passage at the south-west. There are also six postern gates or minor doorways ranged along the north and south ramparts, each one apparently built with upright slab walls infilled with drystone walling, some of which still survive. The finest of these, through the central-southern rampart, has much in common with similar gates at Tre'r Ceiri hillfort (Fig 8.11) in north Wales and is one of the best surviving examples to be seen in Wales (Fig 5.26). There are several other more modern gaps in the rampart but at least some of these may have been made or enlarged from medieval times onwards during the later use of the fort.

It is likely that several more gates lie buried within the unexcavated mass of the tumbled ramparts. Only four hillforts in Britain have more entrances than Garn Goch and one of these, Carn-ingli in Pembrokeshire with nine, is an uncertain count due to the ruinous nature of the ramparts.[22]

The definitive archaeological survey of Garn Goch was completed by hillfort specialist A.H.A. Hogg in 1974 for the Royal Commission and published in the journal *Archaeologia Cambrensis*.[23] For greater accuracy his survey was mapped over

Fig 8.32 The site of the ruined south-western entrance into Y Gaer fawr, Garn Goch hillfort, Carmarthenshire, with figures for scale. The walkers are leaving the hillfort interior (RIGHT) and walking downhill along the infilled gateway passage to the exterior (LEFT) of the fort. The gateway passage lay below the enormous 4–5m rampart of mounded scree which was originally stone-walled along the length of the passage. Today the large slabs of the collapsed gateway structure can be seen amongst the rubble. (T. Driver)

specially-flown photogrammetric aerial photography. More recently the Bannau Brycheiniog National Park Authority, which owns the hillfort, commissioned a state-of-the-art drone photogrammetry survey which mapped every part of the monument to an accuracy of a few centimetres (Fig 8.30).

The great puzzle at Garn Goch is its largely empty interior. Judging by other regional hillforts, like Foel Trigarn in Pembrokeshire (Figs 1.14 and 3.6), one would expect at least some traces of Iron Age style roundhouses or clusters of hut terraces but there are few internal settlement features. Only one confirmed circular hut platform can be seen, in the central eastern part of the interior. This lies not far from the well-preserved footing walls of a medieval farmstead comprising a rectangular house and larger 30m-long barn, built at the northern end of the boggy pond which provided a secure water supply inside the hillfort. The proximity of this medieval farm to the well-preserved postern gate through the central eastern

Fig 8.33 A possible Early Bronze Age standing stone inside the fort, with the great long cairn crowning the summit beyond. (T. Driver)

rampart suggests this gateway was kept clear and used into the Middle Ages. There is also a possible prehistoric standing stone (Fig 8.33) to the east of the medieval farm; the squat boulder is certainly prominent and there is no other stone quite like it inside the fort.

The one major internal structural feature is a large cairn which dominates the summit (Fig 8.33). This stands some 3m high and consists of a mass of rubble 55m long with no obvious original walling. It is clearly a prehistoric burial cairn of the Neolithic or Bronze Age and, given its resemblance to Neolithic long cairns, it seems likely to be around 5,500 years old. Although it cannot be firmly dated without excavation, this would be one of the larger surviving Neolithic long cairns in Wales. It was revered and respected by later builders who did not seek to plunder the cairn to construct their ramparts. With the recent discovery of a Neolithic causewayed enclosure inside the great hillfort at Caerau in Ely (see Fig 3.10), the long cairn which stands within Garn Goch may indicate a Neolithic origin for part of this great enclosure. However the construction of a much larger final defended hilltop enclosure with over 2km of ramparts and with sophisticated stone gateways would only have been possible in the Later Bronze or Iron Ages.

There are other questions: whilst superficially Garn Goch's rampart may seem to be a straggling and poorly-planned structure, wandering over the moorland to enclose a great elongated oval valley, it incorporates precise decisions. Unusually for the Iron Age in south-west Wales there are two right-angled corners at the extreme north-west and north-east angles of the fort. Along the southern rampart is another distinct change in direction, where the scree wall angles first south, then west, enclosing an additional lower annexe along a largely stone-free saddle of useful ground. Following the principal of least-effort, where prehistoric

Fig 8.34 The north-eastern rampart of the hillfort with the sharp northern rampart angle (LEFT) and the site of the parallel gateway passages (RIGHT). The view beyond the hillfort looks down to the lowlands of the Tywi valley. (T. Driver)

communities must have had a very good reason to build more elaborate structures than they had to, these distinct angles, directional changes and additional enclosed areas show purpose and design in the completion of Garn Goch's defences.

The final question regarding Garn Goch is what was its likely function? The author does not believe this fort was densely-settled like other hillforts. There simply isn't the evidence, at present, for numerous roundhouses within it although the rough moorland interior could conceal the ephemeral remains of many undiscovered buildings. What the evidence currently tells us is that Garn Goch was an unusual stone enclosure built over decades or centuries by large numbers of people. It encloses an entire upland valley and provides numerous access points to the summit via two formal hillfort gateways and a host of minor postern gateways. If we look beyond the ramparts we may see the answer.

The main gateways sit at the north-east and south-west narrow ends of the fort, 'blocking off' and controlling movement along a great natural valley which rises from east to west. If one was moving livestock up from the lowland Tywi corridor, via the T-junction of the river Sawdde, to hill country above this may have been the best route to higher ground. Enclosing this long hillslope with long scree walls may have harnessed a well-used route, making the site a great meeting and trading locale. It may be no coincidence that one of Carmarthenshire's very few Roman villas, at Llys Brychan, lies just 1.4km to the north-east on a direct line with the north-eastern hillfort gateway; its location is clearly visible from the north-east gateway. Perhaps the prehistoric legacy of power and wealth associated with the movement of people and livestock lasted into Romano-British times, when new landowners chose to site their villa on a long-used route up to Garn Goch hillfort?

9 Cliffs and chasms: Flimston Bay coastal promontory fort, Castlemartin

Directions: The promontory fort is accessed by a road crossing the Castlemartin military training area which is periodically closed for firing. Search 'Castlemartin access' online to find opening times. Follow signposts to 'Stack Rocks and the Green Bridge' off the B4319 minor road between Castlemartin and Bosherston. Flimston bay promontory fort is a short walk to the east of the cliff top car park. Be very careful of unprotected steep cliff drops when accessing the site. National Grid Reference: SR 929 942

Flimston bay coastal promontory fort is one of the finest of its kind in Wales. Its architecture is well conceived, its ramparts and defences impressive and well preserved and its interior quite unlike anything else around the Welsh coast. It was the subject of a detailed survey by the Royal Commission in 2009 and has recently been re-surveyed as part of a new study of coastal erosion and climate change impacts on site by the EU-funded CHERISH Project.[24]

Approaching Flimston Bay coastal promontory fort one is awestruck by the natural spectacle of the geological wonders here along the sheer limestone cliffs. The towering Elegug (Fig 8.36) stacks, a pair of high limestone pillars covered in nesting birds, stand close to the Green Bridge natural arch just to the west. Today visitors marvel at these natural wonders which stand right at the southern edge of Wales. It is also likely that prehistoric visitors to this distant spot marvelled at similar spectacular coastal features. Indeed we should probably consider the entire group of arches, stacks, blowholes and promontory fort together as an integral landscape of drama and spectacle which no doubt enhanced the power, status and possible ceremonial role of the coastal fort in prehistory.

In plan Flimston has three outer lines of ramparts. The outermost is a D-shaped annexe of sorts, perfectly executed as a sweeping curved rampart but with its eastern arm turning sharply in towards the main gate. This D-shaped 'hook' feature is replicated at Buckspool/ The Castle coastal promontory fort 2.5km eastwards along the Castlemartin peninsula and suggests both forts were broadly contemporary, sharing the same cultural affinities in their design.

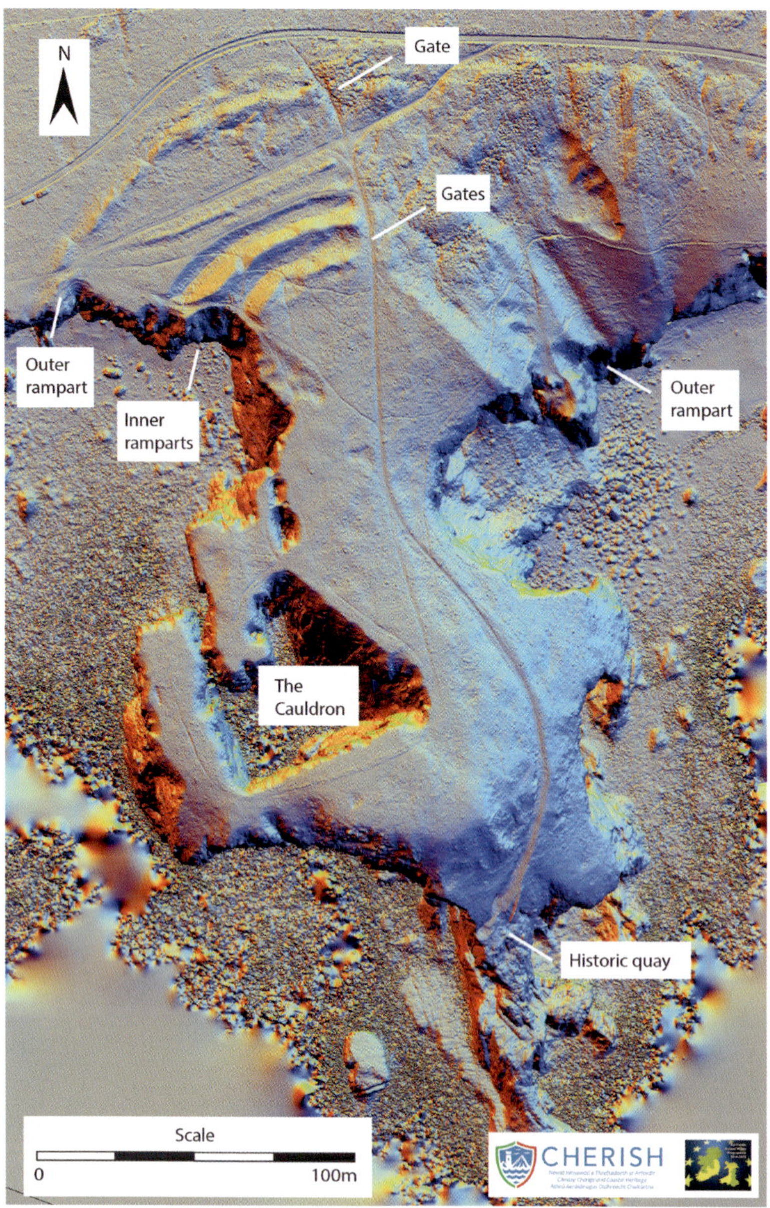

Fig 8.35 Digital survey of Flimston Bay coastal promontory fort, south Pembrokeshire, completed in 2020 using drone photogrammetry by the CHERISH Project. The landward ramparts can be seen at the top of the plan. The interior was well settled with up to 20 house platforms but was entirely dominated by the dangerous chasm of the Cauldron blowhole. On the east side of the fort a more modern rock-cut track winds down to the cliff edge to a nineteenth-century limestone quay. (© Crown: CHERISH PROJECT 2022. Produced with EU funds through the Ireland Wales Co-operation Programme 2014 2023. All material made freely available through the Open Government Licence. NPRN 94227)

Fig 8.36 'Coastal theatre'. Dramatic coastal scenery, like Elegug Stacks (PICTURED) and the nearby Green Bridge natural arch, in south Pembrokeshire would have been no less awe-inspiring in prehistory, although altered in appearance from our modern view. It is likely that the 'coastal theatre' here heightened the experience of visiting Flimston in prehistory and accentuated the kudos of the people who owned the fort. (T. Driver)

The main gate at Flimston is protected by two sets of semi-circular ramparts separating the mainland from the promontory neck. Each neatly curved rampart has a horizontal top and steep outer face suggesting much care and attention was paid towards the internal structuring of the banks during building. Ditches were cut through limestone bedrock. The gateways themselves are unusual. Each is flanked by a right-hand bastion topped with a small platform, conceivably once a tower base or slinging platform. The gates are asymmetric; there were no left-hand terminals or buttresses so timberwork was probably used to build the gate passages. Passing through the gates one enters the fort, but below to the left one sees the enormous eastern defences cascading down the slopes, disturbed here and there by later stone quarrying.

These defences appear carefully designed to baffle and delay the arrival of visitors at the interior for as long as possible, perhaps heightening expectations and intimidating visitors still further. The outer curving rampart makes one's entrance circuitous and difficult. With rampart-top palisades a view of the interior would have been completely blocked on the final approach. Passing through palisades and ramparts towards the gate would have been like entering a maze.

Finally one enters the expansive interior of the fort which is pockmarked with a number of shallow house platforms (see Fig 6.6), shelved into the bedrock of the undulating summit. Flimston's greatest asset is left until last: the heart of the promontory fort is dominated by the enormous chasm – the 'Cauldron' (Fig 7.23). This is a sheer-sided blowhole which drops away into giddying depths. The great age of the Cauldron is clear from the well-weathered rock around its sides. Despite several areas of cliff erosion around the promontory fort, it is very likely that this blowhole stood as an integral feature of the interior in prehistory.

The Cauldron is a dramatic, dangerous, exciting feature of the fort's interior. It seems likely that this enormous chasm was known about and visited before the Iron Age by the many prehistoric communities who left their standing stones, burial chambers and barrows in the south Pembrokeshire hinterland. It is interesting to speculate that this huge blowhole may have been one of the key reasons why people travelled to visit Flimston in the Iron Age and why this particular promontory was chosen for enclosure. The ramparts may have controlled access to this natural wonder.

Whilst undoubtedly the fort had a regular pattern of life focussed around farming, habitation and trading, the Cauldron may well have been perceived as a portal to 'otherworlds' much in the same way as the clear waters of upland lakes, dark

Fig 8.37 A reconstruction of Iron Age life at Flimston Bay coastal promontory fort, south Pembrokeshire. Whilst parts of the Carboniferous Limestone cliffs continue to erode quickly, particularly the eastern (FOREGROUND) parts reconstructed here, other sections of cliff have stood solid and unmoved for centuries. It is likely that the great blowhole within the fort, named the 'Cauldron' by Richard Fenton, was a dangerous cult focus. Wooden totem poles are imaginatively shown in this view on the farthest eroded arm of the fort's interior. (T. Driver)

caves or dangerous tracts of bog. Although there is currently no archaeological evidence to support the theory, this blowhole may well have been used for rituals and ceremonies in front of large crowds during key festivals of the Celtic calendar – perhaps with objects or sacrifices cast into the void.

Fig 8.38 View across the tall ramparts and now infilled rock-cut ditch on the west side of Flimston promontory fort, with a figure showing their scale. The rampart would originally have been steeply faced with bright blocks of limestone walling. (T. Driver)

10 Trading hub on the Severn Estuary: Sudbrook coastal promontory fort, Portskewett

Directions: The promontory fort is used as a public playing field accessed by the Wales Coast Path at the southern edge of Sudbrook village. Parking is available in nearby Sudbrook village. Follow the path alongside the pumping station to coastal cliffs on the east side of fort. There is alternative entry from the north side through a play area. National Grid Reference: ST 505 873

At the far south-east point of Wales, on a headland jutting into the Severn Estuary, is one of the more massive coastal promontory forts in the south of the country. Today Sudbrook promontory fort sits in the shadow of the Second Severn Crossing on the west side and the village of Sudbrook on the east, alongside the water pumping station for the Severn railway tunnel. It was first noted in Camden's Britannia of 1637 as, '... an old Fortification ... compassed with a triple Ditch and three Rampiers as high as an ordinary house, cast in forme of a bowe, the string whereof is the sea-cliffe'.

Fig 8.39 Sudbrook coastal promontory fort from the air, looking north-west, showing the curving ramparts against the edge of the Severn Estuary. The central part of the eroded fort was backfilled with spoil from the Severn Tunnel late in the nineteenth century. (© Crown copyright: RCAHMW. NPRN 94873. AP_2013_5517)

In prehistory this was a critical crossing point on the rapidly narrowing Severn Estuary. After a long, exposed and featureless line of low-lying saltmarsh between the rivers Usk and Wye, now the Gwent Levels, the coast climbs slightly and juts out in a promontory providing strategic views to the east and west. This first narrowing point was a key ferry crossing in Roman times between Black Rock and Aust and was also chosen for the location of this large Iron Age settlement.

Sudbrook promontory fort sat in the vanguard of Silurian territory. It looked boldly across the Severn to the lands of the Dubonni people. An early Roman marching camp lies just 2.8km north of Sudbrook at Killcrow Hill, showing that the promontory fort lay in the heart of contested territory during the 30-year conflict between the Silurians and Romans in the first century AD.

This is an extremely impressive Iron Age fort to visit today. Take some time to appreciate the height and scale of the enclosing ramparts. These enclose a D-shaped space defined by a 300m-sweep of ramparts, enclosing 3.06ha. The north-eastern rampart between the fort and Sudbrook village is huge, standing 5.7m tall. On the west side a triple set of ramparts survive, whereas on the east only two now stand. Excavations in the 1930s[25] showed that a middle rampart stood here but was later levelled. Despite housing having destroyed sections of the northern defences, enough of a plan survives beyond the centrally placed north gate to show that the approach into the fort was made more complex with overlapping ramparts to slow, confuse and impress all those approaching.

Fig 8.40 The main inner rampart of Sudbrook promontory fort looking east towards the Severn pumping station on the horizon and the coast edge to the right. The concrete roof of a Second World War pillbox can just be seen on the summit of the rampart (LEFT) continuing the role of coastal command and defence. (T. Driver)

Along the south the fort was defended by sea cliffs, soft and eroding in the east but bolstered by rock outcrops at the western end. It is highly likely that a greater part of the interior has been lost to erosion over the last two millennia including gateways between the rampart terminals and the cliff edge. An opportunity was taken to shore up some of the eroded interior during construction of the adjacent Severn Tunnel in 1873–86 when spoil from the tunnel was dumped in the south-eastern corner of the fort, also serving to protect the ruins of the medieval Holy Trinity church from being lost.

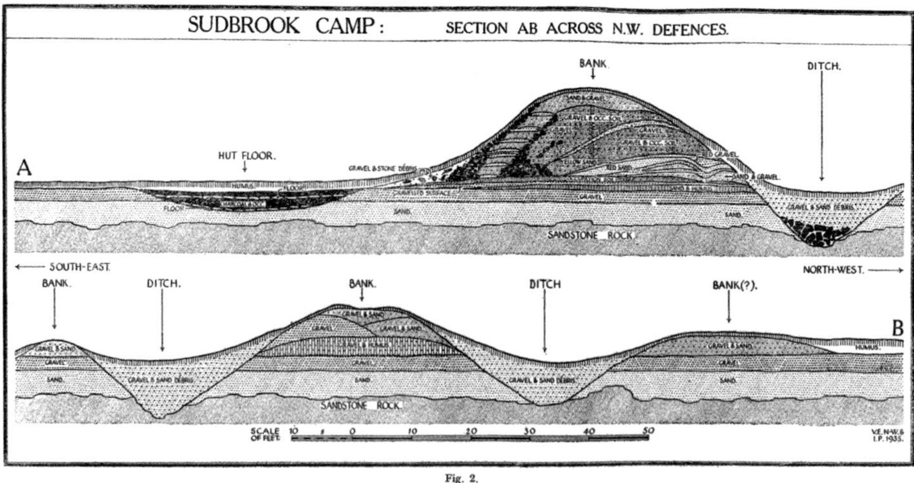

Fig 8.41 Trenching on a military scale: V.E. Nash-Williams' enormous section through the north-west defences of Sudbrook coastal promontory fort revealed the internal structuring of the ramparts, together with the buried profiles of deep V-shaped ditches. The great outer rampart (TOP) stood 4.8m (16ft) tall; rubble tumbled into the ditch below it (UPPER RIGHT) suggests it was originally stone-faced.[26] (By kind permission of the Cambrian Archaeological Association)

Sudbrook promontory fort was excavated between 1934 and 1936 by Victor Erle (or V.E.) Nash-Williams. As was the method of the time, his trenches were on a military scale with great sections cut through the north-west and north-east defences by teams of workmen. These sections revealed careful internal structuring of the ramparts, with stabilising layers of gravel and sand. The sections also show that the deep ditches had originally been V-shaped and far deeper than can be seen today.

Nash-Williams' excavations through the defences and across two house sites in the south-western interior revealed thick occupation deposits and quantities of prehistoric and Roman finds including pottery, brooches, evidence for glass and metal manufacture and Roman coins. His findings suggested Late Iron Age occupation from 100BC with potential reoccupation, and perhaps a takeover of the fort, soon after the Roman Conquest of Britain in the AD 50s or 60s. Finds of quern stones for grinding grain and bones of ox, pig and sheep or goat suggest a thriving agricultural and pastoral economy supporting the fort in Iron Age times. Sudbrook was sporadically occupied in the Mid to Late Roman period and again in Medieval times. In the Second World War this old fort was again used for coastal defence with the installation of a small concrete pillbox on the inner western rampart.

Fig 8.42 View across the Severn Estuary from the rocky crags at the south-western end of the promontory fort with the terminal of the western ramparts (LEFT): a perfect place to draw up boats in the late Iron Age. (T. Driver)

Nash-Williams painted a dramatic scenario for Sudbrook following the Roman Conquest when he suggested its occupation came to an 'abrupt end', with the population possibly being transferred to nearby *Venta Silurum* Roman town at Caerwent (Fig 4.17). In recent years his trenching technique and lack of detailed trench plans have been called into question, along with the accuracy of his excavation findings.[27] It is certain that Sudbrook would repay fresh investigation with modern techniques, potentially telling a new story of prehistoric coastal trade and the impact of the Roman campaigns in south Wales.

~

NOTES

CHAPTER 1

1 Gardner, 1926, 224.

2 information on the Welsh Historic Environment Record via archwilio.org.uk; also Lock and Ralston, 2022 & Davis & Sharples, 2020, Figure 1.

3 Lock and Ralston, 2022, 41.

4 See Ritchie, 2018.

5 Ritchie, 2018.

6 Barker and Driver, 2011, 66.

7 Hughes, 1906, 244–45.

8 O'Kelly, 1970, 50.

9 Gardner, 1926, 228.

10 James January-McCann, pers. comm. 2022.

11 Gardner, 1926, 225.

12 Moore, 1976, 198.

13 Woods, 2016.

14 Barnwell, 1875.

15 *ibid.*, 1875.

16 *ibid.*, 1875, 75.

17 Christison, 1897, 23.

18 Baring-Gould, 1899, 107.

19 *ibid.*, 1899, 115.

20 *ibid.*, 1899, 130.

21 *ibid.*, 1900.

22 *ibid.*, 1900, 189.

23 *ibid.*, 208–9.

24 Baring-Gould and Burnard, 1904.

25 Hughes, 1907.

26 Gardner, 1926.

27 Williams, 1939.

28 Nash Williams, 1939; Guilbert, 2018.

29 Browne and Driver, 2001.

30 Williams, 1939.

31 Dodgshon, 1998, 3.

32 Catling, 2016.

33 Williams and Mytum, 1998.

34 Britnell, 1989.

35 Hill, 1989.

36 Gwilt and Haselgrove, 1997, 2.

37 Haselgrove *et al.,* 2001.

38 CAER Heritage: www.caerheritage.org

CHAPTER 2

1 Collis, 1996.

2 Simon Rodway pers. comm. 2022.

3 Cunliffe, 2002.

4 *ibid.*, 2002, 3.

5 Rivet and Smith, 1979, 247 48.

6 Cunliffe, 2002, 94–95.

7 Strabo, Geography, Book IV, Chapter 5.

8 Strabo, Geography.

9 Mattingly, 1948.

10 Breeze, 2005.

11 Rivet and Smith, 1979, 331.

12 On display: British Museum number: 1856, 0626.1

13 Davies, 1994, 314.

14 Roman inscriptions of Britain website, accessed 2022: romaninscriptionsofbritain.org/inscriptions/311
15 Cunliffe, 2001.
16 Hughes, 1907, 40–42.
17 National Museum of Ireland, Archaeology: Inv. L 1947, 195; see Waddington, 2013, 221.
18 Chapman, 2019.
19 James, 2016, 293–95.
20 Rivet and Smith, 1979, 430.
31 Hogg, 1975, 53.
32 Tacitus: *Annals*, XIV, 30 in Grant, 1978.
33 Waddington, 2013, 99.
34 Armit, 1997, 249–50.
34a *ibid.*, 1997, 250.
35 RCAHMW, 1956, 114 (367).
36 Baring-Gould and Burnard, 1904, 5.
37 Gardner, 1926, 230.
38 RCAHMW, 1986.
39 Bevan, 1997, 185.
40 Dodgshon, 1996, 101.
41 Driver, 2021, 70.

CHAPTER 3

1 Agricola 16 in Mattingly, 1948, 66.
2 Capps, 1975, 18–20.
3 Green and Howell, 2000, 31.
4 Grant, 1978, 330.
5 Steele, 2012, 56.
6 Cunliffe, 1984, 560–62.
7 *ibid.*, 1984, 559.
8 *ibid.*, 1984, 563.
9 Hill, 1995.
10 Lynch *et al.*, 2000, 191.
11 Dodgshon, 1996, 101.
12 Waddington, 2013, 99.
13 Fleming, 2005, 67.
14 Dodgshon, 1996, 108.
15 Burrow, 2006, 40–41.
16 Waddington, 2013, 99.
17 Taylor, 1980.
18 Lynch *et al.*, 2000, 140–41.
19 Davis and Sharples, 2020, 166.
20 Davies and Lynch, 2000, 142.
21 see Murphy, 2016, Figure 3.27.
22 Britnell and Silvester, 2018.
23 Barker, 2009, 5; Savory, 1965; Lynch *et al.*, 2000, 182.
24 Davis & Sharples, 2020, 176.
25 Britnell & Silvester, 2018, 2.
26 Green and Howell, 2000, 31.
27 Cunliffe, 2010, 26.
28 *ibid.*, 2010, 33–34.
29 Green and Howell, 2000, 28–29.
30 Waddington, 2013, 97.

CHAPTER 4

1 Steele, 2012, 54.
2 after Lynch *et al.*, 2000, Figure 4.20.
3 Lynch *et al.*, 2000, 189.
4 Steele, 2012, 54.
5 Green and Howell, 2000, 31.
6 Driver, 2021, 34; 101–2.
7 Hemp, 1928.
8 Green and Howell, 2000, 38.
9 Fox, 1945, Plate 1.
10 Gwilt, 2011, 76.
11 Steele, 2012, 55.
12 Gardner, 1926, 230.
13 Mytum, 2013, 319.
14 Hunter, 2015, 90.
15 nms.ac.uk
16 *ibid.*
17 Carnyx and Co: http://carnyx.org.uk/
18 Steele, 2012, 58–59.
19 Hunter, 2015, 97.
20 NMW Collections Online 2022
21 Howell, 2022, 13.
22 Tacitus: *Agricola*, 12, 62, in Mattingly, 1948.
23 Edwards, 1917, 223.
24 Tacitus: *Annals*, XIV, 34 in Grant, 1978.
25 Tacitus: *Agricola* 5 in Mattingly, 1948.
26 Thomas, 1906, 4.
27 Grant, 1978, XII, 33.
28 Tacitus: *Annals*, XII, 37 in Grant, 1978, 268–9.
29 Tacitus: *Agricola* 18 in Mattingly, 1948.
30 Mattingly, 1948.

CHAPTER 5

1 Mytum, 2013, 319.
2 Manning, 1999.
3 Mytum, 2013, 61–63.
4 *ibid*., 2013, 224.
5 Britnell, 1989, 132–33.
6 Lord *et al*., 201.
7 Musson *et al*., 1991, 35.
8 Mytum, 2013, 220–21.
9 *ibid*., 2013, 224.
10 Bick and Wyn Davies, 1994, 32.
11 Murphy and Mytum, 2012.
12 Bick and Wyn Davies, 1994, 37.
13 Driver, 2018.
14 Avery, 1993, 2.21, 8.
15 Bowden and McOmish, 1989.
16 Hogg, 1975.
17 Mytum, 2013, 319.
18 Mattingly, 1948, 85–86.
19 Mytum, 2013, 214.
20 Ralston, 2006, 45.
21 Mytum, 2013, Figure 10.10.
22 Driver, 2013, 34.
23 Sharples, 1991, 72–76.
24 Waddington, 2013, 98.
25 Mytum, 2013, 138.
26 Barker, 2009, 16.
27 see Murphy, 2016, Figure 3.13,
28 Savory, 1976, 264.
29 Baring-Gould *et al*., 1900, 204–6.
30 Lock and Ralston, 2021, 204.
31 Hogg, 1975, 51.
32 *ibid*., 1975, 52.
33 Pope, R. *et al*., 2020, Fig. 24.
34 Williams and Mytum, 1998.
35 Murphy and Wilson, 2020, 4.
36 Barker, 2009.
37 Mytum, 2013, 69–71.
38 Driver, 2021, 146.
39 Murphy and Mytum, 2012, 40.
40 Driver, 2021, 85.
41 *ibid*., 2021, 86.
42 Fitzpatrick, 2007; Driver, 2021, 99 & 104–7.
43 Driver, 2007, 137–39.
44 Mytum, 2013, 91–102.

CHAPTER 6

1 Baring-Gould, 1899, 107.
2 Rees and Jones, 2017.
3 Ghey *et al*., 2008.
4 Baring-Gould and Bernard, 1904, 3.
5 Roundhouses CS2 and CS3, Davis and Sharples, 2020, Figure 7.
6 Davis and Sharples, 2020, 176.
7 RCAHMW, 1964, Figure 53.
8 Hughes, 1907, 50.
9 RCAHMW, 1960.
10 I am grateful for discussions in 2021 with David Hopewell regarding Tre'r Ceiri.
11 Burrow, 2015.
12 *ibid*., 2015.
13 Longley, 1998.
14 Bennett, in Frodsham, 2004.
15 Butser, Bronze Age Build Blog.
16 Burrow, 2015, 11.
17 RCAHMW, 1964, Fig. 21.
18 Mattingly, 1948.
19 Bick and Wyn Davies, 1994, 23.
20 Williams, R. & Le Carlier de Veslud, C., 2019.
21 *ibid*., 2019.
22 Romilly Allen, 1901, 39–44.
23 Green and Howell, 2000, 30.
24 Crew, 2009, 6.
25 *ibid*., 2009, 7.
26 after Wainwright, 1972, Figure 3.
27 Crew, 2009, 12–16.
28 Waddington, 2013, 214.
29 *ibid*., 2013, 57–8.
30 Crew and Musson, 1997, 21.

CHAPTER 7

1 Baring-Gould, 1899, 107.
2 after Wainwright, 1972, Figure 5.
3 Edwards, 1917, 153–55.
4 Wessex Archaeology, 2012.
5 Murphy and Wilson, 2020.
6 Historic Environment Group, 2020.
7 CHERISH Project, 2020, 24–33.
8 Crane and Murphy, 2010; Murphy and Wilson, 2020.

9 Murphy and Wilson, 2020, 4.
10 Fenton, 1811, 117–18.
11 Fleming, 2005, 93–4.
12 *ibid.*, 2005, 90.
13 Fenton, 1811, 117–18.
14 Lock and Ralston, 2022, 85.
15 Barker and Driver, 2011, 66.
16 *ibid.*, 2011, 66.
17 Edwards, 1917, 147.
18 Cunliffe, 2002, 76.
19 *ibid.*, 2002, 76.
20 Driver, 2021, 151–3.
21 Barker and Driver, 2011, 81.
22 Cunnington, 1920, 251.
23 Savory, 1974.
24 *ibid.*, 1974.
25 Green and Howell, 2000, 25–6.
26 Cunnington, 1920, 253, Plate A.
27 Davies, 1994, 315.
28 Moriarty, 2012.
29 Grant, 1978, 327.
30 Mattingly, 1948, 64.
31 Grant, 1978, 327.
32 Davies, 2012, 377–8.
33 Steele, 2012.
34 Davies, 2012, 371.
35 Cunliffe, 2001, 362.
36 Herring, 1994, 45.
37 Barker and Driver, 2011, 66.
38 Vyner, 2001.
39 Murphy, 2001; Barker *et al.*, 2012.
40 Fenton, 1811, 118.
41 Baring-Gould, 1899.
42 Barker *et al.*, 2012.
43 Plan after Murphy, K., 2001, Figure 2, with additions.
44 Cunliffe, 2010, 27.
45 Herring, 1994.
46 Sharpe, 1992.
47 These include Mount Rushmore in the Black Hills of North America whose human-like rock forms were called 'The Six Grandfathers' and were once sacred to the Lakota Sioux.
48 Herring, 1994, 52.
49 Cunliffe, 2002, 88.
50 Fleming, 2005, 115–7.
51 *ibid.*, 2005, 115–7.
52 Cunliffe, 2001, 362.
53 Green and Howell, 2000, 31.
54 Herring, 1994, 52–5.

CHAPTER 8

1 Waddington, 2013, 220–23.
2 Hughes, 1907, 39.
3 Driver, 2008; Hopewell, 2018.
4 Gardner, 1922, 117; 125.
5 *ibid.*, 1922, 108.
6 *ibid.*, 1922, 114–7.
7 *ibid.*, 1922, 117.
8 *ibid.*, 1922, 117.
9 *ibid.*, 1922, 114.
10 Crew and Musson, 1996, 18; Crew, 2009, 9–11.
11 Musson *et al.*, 1991.
12 Green and Howell, 2000, 31.
13 Britnell and Silvester, 2018, 2.
14 Barker, 2009.
15 *ibid.*, 2009, 3.
16 *ibid.*, 2009.
17 Lewis, 1833.
18 Barker, 2009, 11.
19 for Barnwell, 1871, 163.
20 Ffoulkes, 1874.
21 Smith, 2009.
22 Lock and Ralston, 2021, 204.
23 Hogg, 1974.
24 CHERISH Project, 2021.
25 Nash Williams, 1939.
26 *ibid.*, 1939, Figure 2.
27 Guilbert, 2018.

FURTHER READING:
MAIN SOURCES FOR THE HILLFORTS OF WALES

Those interested in learning more about prehistoric and Roman Wales will find a wealth of academic papers and introductory guides online. These include some 175 years of the Welsh journal *Archaeologia Cambrensis* which can be freely browsed online – an incredible resource for research. Another key online journal article to consult is Issue 48 of *Internet Archaeology*, the special edition on *Iron Age Settlement in Wales* (2018). This is perhaps the most up-to-date academic statement on the subject. Those seeking further detail should also read the Research Framework for the Archaeology of Wales (archaeoleg.org.uk).

There are a handful of very readable books that I would recommend for people looking to find out more about prehistoric and Roman Wales, and prehistoric Britain in general. These include Ian Brown's excellent *Beacons in the Landscape: The hillforts of England, Wales and the Isle of Man* (Windgather Press, 2021), a readable and attractive book on the subject. Barry Cunliffe's various editions of *Iron Age Communities in Britain* (Routledge, fourth edition 2009) are thorough source books for British hillforts. For wider reading around the subject I also recommend Cunliffe's *Facing the Ocean: The Atlantic and its Peoples, 8000BC–AD1500* (Oxford University Press, 2001) and his *The Extraordinary Voyage of Pytheas the Greek* (Penguin Books, 2002); also Simon James' *Exploring the World of the Celts* (Thames and Hudson, 2005). Far older, but still a solid read, is A.H.A. Hogg's *Hill-forts of Britain* (Hart-Davis, Macgibbon, 1975). Readers might find the present author's *The Hillforts of Cardigan Bay* (Logaston Press, 2021) useful for west Wales hillforts and some wider themes. If you can find copies of *Prehistoric Wales* by Lynch, Aldhouse-Green and Davies (Sutton Publishing, 2000) and its companion volume *Roman and Early Medieval Wales* by Chris Arnold and Jeffrey Davies

(Sutton Publishing, 2000), then you will have a very solid overview of several thousand years of Welsh prehistory and history. A more affordable, but highly readable, book on the topic is Miranda Green and Ray Howell's *Celtic Wales* (University of Wales Press/ The Western Mail, 2000); also Ray Howell's new book *Silures: Resistance, Resilience and Revival* (The History Press, 2022). Other good popular accounts of prehistoric and Roman north Wales are Philip Steele's *Llyn Cerrig Bach, Treasure from the Iron Age* (Oriel Ynys Mon/ Llyfrau Magma, 2012) and David Hopewell's *Roman Roads in North-West Wales* (Gwynedd Archaeological Trust, 2013). The definitive account of the Roman army's campaigns in Wales is still Barry Burnham and Jeffrey Davies' 2010 book *Roman Frontiers in Wales and the Marches* (Royal Commission, 2010). Finally, two books I keep going back to, which remain as vivid as ever for their descriptions of the Roman Conquest of Wales, are Mattingly's translation of the '*Agricola*'; *Tacitus on Britain and Germany* (Penguin Books, 1948) and Grant's translation of Tacitus' *The Annals of Imperial Rome* (Penguin Books, 1978) – stirring stuff.

FURTHER READING BY CHAPTER

CHAPTER 1

Barnwell, E.L., 1875. 'Pembrokeshire Cliff Castles'. *Archaeologia Cambrensis*, Fourth Series, No. XXI, 74–86.

Baring-Gould, Revd S., 1899. 'Exploration of the Stone Camp on St David's Head'. *Archaeologia Cambrensis*, Vol. XVI, 105–31.

—, 1900. 'Exploration of Moel Trigarn'. *Archaeologia Cambrensis*, Vol. XVII, Fifth Series, 189–211.

Baring-Gould, Revd S., and Burnard, R., 1904. 'An exploration of some of the Cytiau in Tre'r Ceiri'. *Archaeologia Cambrensis*, Vol. IV, Sixth Series, 1–16.

Barker, L. and Driver, T., 2011. 'Close to the Edge: New Perspectives on the Architecture, Function and Regional Geographies of the Coastal Promontory Forts of the Castlemartin Peninsula, South Pembrokeshire, Wales'. *Proceedings of the Prehistoric Society* 77, 65–87.

Britnell, W., 1989. 'The Collfryn hillslope enclosure, Llansantffraid Deuddwr, Powys: excavations 1980–82'. *Proceedings of the Prehistoric Society* 55, 89–134.

Browne, D. and Driver, T., 2001. *Bryngaer Pen Dinas Hill-fort, A Prehistoric Fortress at Aberystwyth*. RCAHMW.

CAER Heritage: https://www.caerheritage.org/ – accessed 20/09/2022.

Catling, C., 2016. 'Wales in the Vanguard: Pioneering protection of the past'. *Current Archaeology*, 314.

Christison, D., 1897. 'The Prehistoric Fortresses of Treceiri and Eildon'. *Archaeologia Cambrensis*, Vol. XIV, Fifth Series, 17–40.

Davis, O. and Sharples, N., 2020. 'Excavations at Caerau Hillfort, Cardiff: Towards a narrative for the hillforts of south-east Wales' in Defino, D., Coimbra, F., Cardoso, D. and Cruz, Goncalo (eds). *Late Prehistoric Fortifications in Europe: Defensive, Symbolic and Territorial Aspects from the Chalcolithic to the Iron Age*. Archaeopress Archaeology. 163–81.

Dodgshon, R.A., 1998. *Society in Time and Space, A Geographical Perspective on Change*. Cambridge University Press.

Gardner, W., 1926. 'Presidential address. The native hill-forts in north Wales and their defences'. *Archaeologia Cambrensis*, Vol. LXXXI, Seventh Series, Vol. VI, 221–82.

Guilbert, G., 2018 'Historical Excavation and Survey of Hillforts in Wales: some critical issues'. *Internet Archaeology* 48. https://doi.org/10.11141/ia.48.3

Gwilt, A. and Haselgrove, C. (eds), 1997. *Reconstructing Iron Age Societies, New approaches to the British Iron Age.* Oxbow Monograph 71.

Haselgrove, C., Armit, I., Champion, T., Creighton, J., Gwilt, A., Hill, J.D., Hunter, F. and Woodward, A., 2001. *Understanding the British Iron Age: An Agenda for Action.* A report for the Iron Age Research Seminar and the Council of the Prehistoric Society.

Hill, J.D., 1989. 'Re-thinking the Iron Age'. *Scottish Archaeological Review,* Vol. 6, 16–24.

Hughes, H., 1906. 'Exploration of Pen-y-Gaer, above Llanbedr-y-Cenin'. *Archaeologia Cambrensis,* Vol. VI, Sixth Series, 241–56.

—, 1907. 'Report on the excavations carried out at Tre'r Ceiri in 1906'. *Archaeologia Cambrensis,* Volume VII, Sixth Series, 38–62.

Lock, G.R. and Ralston, I., 2022. *Atlas of the Hillforts of Britain and Ireland.* Edinburgh University Press.

Moore, D., 1976. 'Cambrian Antiquity: Precursors of the prehistorians' in Boon, G.C. and Lewis, M. (eds). *Welsh Antiquity. Essays mainly on Prehistoric Topics.* National Museum Wales. 193–221.

Nash-Williams, V.E., 1939. 'An Early Iron Age Coastal Camp at Sudbrook, Near the Severn Tunnel, Monmouthshire'. *Archaeologia Cambrensis,* Vol. XCIV, 42–79.

O'Kelly, M., 1970. 'Problems of Irish Ring-Forts' in Moore, D. (ed.). *The Irish Sea Province in Archaeology and History.* Cambrian Archaeological Association. 50–54.

Ritchie, M., 2018. 'A Brief Introduction to Iron Age Settlement in Wales', *Internet Archaeology* 48. https://doi.org/10.11141/ia.48.2

Woods, J., 2016. 'Of Fires and Giants: Thomas Pennant and Tre'r Ceiri Hillfort'. Curious Travellers blog accessed 14/09/2022: https://curioustravellers.ac.uk/en/of-fires-and-giants-thomas-pennant-and-trer-ceiri-hillfort/

Williams, A., 1939. 'Excavations at The Knave promontory fort, Rhossili, Glamorgan'. *Archaeologia Cambrensis,* Vol. XCIV, 210–19.

Williams, G.H. and Mytum, H., 1998. *Llawhaden, Dyfed, Excavations on a group of small defended enclosures, 1980–4.* BAR British Series 275.

CHAPTER 2

Breeze, A., 2005. 'An Etymology for Dyfed'. *Carmarthenshire Antiquary* 41, 175–6.

Chapman, E., 2019. 'Placing faith in divine aid' in Redknap, M., Rees, S. and Aberg, A. *Wales and the Sea, 10,000 years of Welsh Maritime History.* RCAHMW. 74–75.

Cunliffe, B., 2001. *Facing the Ocean, The Atlantic and its Peoples, 8000BC–AD 1500.* Oxford University Press.

—, 2002. *The Extraordinary Voyage of Pytheas the Greek.* Second edition, Penguin Books.

Collis, J., 1996. 'The Origin and Spread of the Celts'. *Studia Celtica* XXX, 17–34.

Davies, J.L., 1994. 'The Roman Period' in Davies, J.L. and Kirby, D.P. (eds), 1994. *Cardiganshire County History. Volume 1, From the earliest times to the coming of the Normans.* University of Wales Press. 275–317.

Hughes, H., 1907. 'Report on the excavations carried out at Tre'r Ceiri in 1906'. *Archaeologia Cambrensis,* Volume VII, Sixth Series, 38–62.

James, H., 2016. 'Roman Pembrokeshire AD 75–410' in James, H., John, M., Murphy, K. and Wainwright, G. (eds). *Pembrokeshire County History, Volume I. Prehistoric, Roman and Early Medieval Pembrokeshire.* Pembrokeshire County History Trust. 296–339.

Mattingly, H., 1948. *Tacitus on Britain and Germany. A new translation of the 'Agricola' and the 'Germania' by H. Mattingly.* Penguin Books.
Rivet, A.L.F. and Smith, C., 1979. *The Place-Names of Roman Britain.* Batsford Ltd.
Roman inscriptions of Britain website, accessed 2022: *https://romaninscriptionsofbritain.org/inscriptions/311*
Strabo, Geography. Published in Vol. II of the Loeb Classical Library edition, 1923. https://penelope.uchicago.edu/Thayer/e/roman/texts/strabo/4e*.html
Waddington, K., 2013. *The Settlements of Northwest Wales, from the Late Bronze Age to the Early Medieval Period.* University of Wales Press.

CHAPTER 3

Armit, I., 1997. 'Cultural landscapes and identities: a case study in the Scottish Iron Age' in Gwilt and Haslegrove (eds). *Reconstructing Iron Age Societies, New approaches to the British Iron Age.* Oxbow Monograph 71. 248–53.
Baring-Gould, Revd S., and Burnard, R., 1904. 'An exploration of some of the Cytiau in Tre'r Ceiri', *Archaeologia Cambrensis,* Vol. IV, Sixth Series, 1–16.
Barker, L., 2009. *Gaer Fawr hillfort: an analysis of the earthworks.* Royal Commission on the Ancient and Historical Monuments of Wales. Unpublished report, NPRN 306997.
Bevan, B., 1997. 'Bounding the landscape: place and identity during the Yorkshire Wolds Iron Age' in Gwilt and Haslegrove (eds). *Reconstructing Iron Age Societies, New approaches to the British Iron Age.* Oxbow Monograph 71. 181–91.
Britnell, W.J. and Silvester, R.J., 2018. 'Hillforts and Defended Enclosures of the Welsh Borderland', *Internet Archaeology* 48. https://doi.org/10.11141/ia.48.7
Britnell, W.J. and Earwood, C., 1991. 'Wooden artefacts and other worked wood from Buckbean Pond' in Musson, C., 1991. *The Breiddin Hillfort: A later prehistoric settlement in the Welsh Marches.* 161–72.
Burrow, S., 2006. *The tomb builders in Wales 4000–3000BC.* National Museum Wales Books.
Capps, B., 1975. *The Old West: The Great Chiefs.* Time-Life Books.
Cunliffe, B., 1984. *Danebury: an Iron Age hillfort in Hampshire. Vol. 2, The excavations 1969–1978: The finds.* CBA Research Report, No. 52. Council for British Archaeology.
—, 2010. *Druids, A Very Short Introduction.* Oxford University Press.
Davies, J.L., Lynch, F. and Aldhouse-Green, S., 2000. *Prehistoric Wales.* Sutton Publishing.
Davis, O. and Sharples, N., 2020. 'Excavations at Caerau Hillfort, Cardiff: Towards a narrative for the hillforts of south-east Wales' in Defino, D., Coimbra, F., Cardoso, D. and Cruz, Goncalo (eds). *Late Prehistoric Fortifications in Europe: Defensive, Symbolic and Territorial Aspects from the Chalcolithic to the Iron Age.* Archaeopress Archaeology. 163–81
Dodgshon, R.A., 1996. 'Modelling chiefdoms in the Scottish Highlands and islands prior to the '45' in Arnold and Blair Gibson (eds). *Celtic Chiefdom, Celtic State.* Second Edition. Cambridge University Press. 99–109.
Driver, T., 2021. *The Hillforts of Cardigan Bay.* Second Edition. Logaston Press.
Edwards, H.J., 1917. *Caesar, The Gallic War.* Loeb Classical Library, Harvard University Press.
Fleming, A., 2005. *St Kilda and the Wider World: Tales of an Iconic Island.* Windgather Press.
Gardner, W., 1926. Presidential address. 'The native hill-forts in north Wales and their defences'. *Archaeologia Cambrensis,* Vol. LXXXI, Seventh Series, Vol. VI, 221–82.
Grant, M., 1978. *Tacitus: The Annals of Imperial Rome.* Revised Edition. Penguin Books.

Green, M. and Howell, R., 2000. *A Pocket Guide to Celtic Wales.* University of Wales Press.
Hill, J.D., 1995. 'How Should We Understand Iron Age Societies and Hillforts? A Contextual Study from Southern Britain' in Hill and Cumberpatch (eds). *Different Iron Ages, Studies on the Iron Age in Temperate Europe.* BAR International Series 602, Tempus Reparatum. 45–60.
Hogg, A.H.A., 1975. *Hill-forts of Britain.* Hart-Davis, MacGibbon.
Lynch, F., Aldhouse-Green, S. and Davies, J.L., 2000. *Prehistoric Wales.* Sutton Publishing.
Mattingly, H., 1948. *Tacitus on Britain and Germany. A new translation of the 'Agricola' and the 'Germania' by H. Mattingly.* Penguin Books.
Murphy, K., 2016. 'Later Prehistoric Pembrokeshire' in James, H., John, M., Murphy, K. and Wainwright, G. (eds). *Pembrokeshire County History, Volume I. Prehistoric, Roman and Early Medieval Pembrokeshire.* Pembrokeshire County History Trust. 223–92.
Musson, C., 1991. *The Breiddin Hillfort: A later prehistoric settlement in the Welsh Marches.* CBA Research Report No. 76. Council for British Archaeology.
Pearson, T. and Lax, A., 2001. *An Iron Age hillfort on Great Hetha, Northumberland,* English Heritage Survey Report; cited in Hillfort Study Group, 2002.
RCAHMW, 1956. *An Inventory of the Ancient Monuments in Caernarvonshire, Volume I: East.* HMSO.
—, 1986. *Brecknock. Hill-forts and Roman Remains.* (An Inventory of Ancient Monuments in Brecknock (Brycheiniog). HMSO.
Steele, P., 2012. *Llyn Cerrig Bach. Treasure from the Iron Age.* Oriel Ynys Mon/ Llyfrau Magma.
Taylor, J.A. (ed.), 1980. *Culture and Environment in Prehistoric Wales.* BAR British Series 76.
Thomas, Archdeacon, 1906. 'The Ordovices and Ancient Powys'. *Archaeologia Cambrensis,* Vol. VI, Sixth Series, 1–6.
Waddington, K., 2013. *The Settlements of Northwest Wales, from the Late Bronze Age to the Early Medieval Period.* University of Wales Press.
Woods, J., 2016. 'Of Fires and Giants: Thomas Pennant and Tre'r Ceiri Hillfort'. Curious Travellers blog accessed 14/09/2022: https://curioustravellers.ac.uk/en/of-fires-and-giants-thomas-pennant-and-trer-ceiri-hillfort/

CHAPTER 4

Baring-Gould, Revd S., and Burnard, R. 1904. 'An exploration of some of the Cytiau in Tre'r Ceiri'. *Archaeologia Cambrensis,* Vol. IV, Sixth Series, 1–16.
Britnell, W.J. and Earwood, C., 1991. 'Wooden artefacts and other worked wood from Buckbean Pond' in Musson, C., 1991. *The Breiddin Hillfort: A later prehistoric settlement in the Welsh Marches.* 161–72.
Britnell, W.J and Silvester, R.J., 2018. 'Hillforts and Defended Enclosures of the Welsh Borderland'. *Internet Archaeology* 48. https://doi.org/10.11141/ia.48.7
Capps, B., 1975. *The Old West: The Great Chiefs.* Time-Life Books.
Carnyx and Co: http://carnyx.org.uk/
Cunliffe, B., 1984. *Danebury: an Iron Age hillfort in Hampshire. Vol. 2, The excavations 1969–1978: The finds.* CBA Research Report, No. 52. Council for British Archaeology.
Davis, O. and Sharples, N., 2020. 'Excavations at Caerau Hillfort, Cardiff: Towards a narrative for the hillforts of south-east Wales' in Defino, D., Coimbra, F., Cardoso, D. and Cruz, Goncalo (eds). *Late Prehistoric Fortifications in Europe: Defensive, Symbolic and Territorial Aspects from the Chalcolithic to the Iron Age.* Archaeopress Archaeology. 163–81.

Dodgshon, R.A., 1996. 'Modelling chiefdoms in the Scottish Highlands and islands prior to the '45' in Gibson, Arnold and Blair (eds). *Celtic Chiefdom, Celtic State*. Second Edition. Cambridge University Press. 99–109.
Driver, T., 2021. *The Hillforts of Cardigan Bay*. Second Edition. Logaston Press.
Edwards, H.J., 1917. *Caesar, The Gallic War*. Loeb Classical Library, Harvard University Press.
Fleming, A., 2005. *St Kilda and the Wider World: Tales of an Iconic Island*. Windgather Press.
Fox, C., 1945. 'A Shield-boss of the early Iron Age from Anglesey with Ornament Applied by Chasing Tools'. *Archaeologia Cambrensis*, Vol. XCVIII, 199–220.
Gardner, W., 1926. Presidential address. 'The native hill-forts in north Wales and their defences'. *Archaeologia Cambrensis*, Vol. LXXXI, Seventh Series, Vol. VI, 221–82.
Grant, M., 1978. *Tacitus: The Annals of Imperial Rome*. Revised Edition. Penguin Books.
Green, M. and Howell, R., 2000. *A Pocket Guide to Celtic Wales*. University of Wales Press.
Gwilt, A., 2011. 'The Tal-y-llyn shield fittings' in Redknap, M. (ed.). *Discovered in Time, treasures from early Wales*. National Museum Wales Books. 76–7
Hemp, W.J., 1928. 'A La Tène Shield from Moel Hiraddug, Flintshire'. *Archaeologia Cambrensis*, Vol. LXXXIII, Part II, 253–84.
Howell, R., 2022. *Silures: Resistance, Resilience, Revival*. The History Press.
Hunter, F., 2015. 'Powerful Objects: the Uses of Art in the Iron Age' in Farley, J. and Hunter, F. (eds). *Celts: Art and Identity*. The British Museum Press. 82–107.
Lynch, F., Aldhouse-Green, S. and Davies, J.L., 2000. *Prehistoric Wales*. Sutton Publishing.
Mattingly, H., 1948. *Tacitus on Britain and Germany. A new translation of the 'Agricola' and the 'Germania' by H. Mattingly*. Penguin Books.
Musson, C., 1991. *The Breiddin Hillfort: A later prehistoric settlement in the Welsh Marches*. CBA Research Report No. 76. Council for British Archaeology.
Mytum, H., 2013. *Monumentality in Later Prehistory. Building and Rebuilding Castell Henllys Hillfort*. Springer.
nms.ac.uk: https://www.nms.ac.uk/explore-our-collections/stories/scottish-history-and-archaeology/deskford-carnyx/
NMW Collections Online: https://museum.wales/collections/online/
Savory, H.N., 1964. 'The Tal-y-llyn hoard'. *Antiquity* XXXVIII, 18–31.
Slingshot resources website: www.slinging.org
Steele, P., 2012. *Llyn Cerrig Bach. Treasure from the Iron Age*. Oriel Ynys Mon/ Llyfrau Magma.
Thomas, Archdeacon, 1906. 'The Ordovices and Ancient Powys'. *Archaeologia Cambrensis*, Vol. VI, Sixth Series, 1–6.
Waddington, K., 2013. *The Settlements of Northwest Wales, from the Late Bronze Age to the Early Medieval Period*. University of Wales Press.
Woods, J., 2016. 'Of Fires and Giants: Thomas Pennant and Tre'r Ceiri Hillfort'. Curious Travellers blog accessed 14/09/2022: https://curioustravellers.ac.uk/en/of-fires-and-giants-thomas-pennant-and-trer-ceiri-hillfort/

CHAPTER 5

Avery, M., 1993. *Hillfort Defences of Southern Britain*, BAR British Series 231 (three volumes).

Baring-Gould, Revd S., Burnard, R. and Anderson, I.K., 1900. 'Exploration of Moel Trigarn'. *Archaeologia Cambrensis,* Vol. XVII, Fifth Series, 189–211.

Barker, L., 2009. *Gaer Fawr hillfort: an analysis of the earthworks.* Royal Commission on the Ancient and Historical Monuments of Wales. Unpublished report, NPRN 306997.

Bevan, B., 1997. 'Bounding the landscape: place and identity during the Yorkshire Wolds Iron Age' in Gwilt and Haslegrove (eds). *Reconstructing Iron Age Societies, New approaches to the British Iron Age.* Oxbow Monograph 71. 181–91.

Bick, D. and Wyn Davies, P., 1994. *Lewis Morris and the Cardiganshire Mines.* The National Library of Wales.

Bowden, M. and McOmish, D., 1989. 'Little boxes; more on hillforts'. *Scottish Archaeological Review,* 6, 76–84.

Britnell, W., 1989. 'The Collfryn hillslope enclosure, Llansantffraid Deuddwr, Powys: excavations 1980–82'. *Proceedings of the Prehistoric Society* 55, 89–134.

Britnell, W.J. and Silvester, R.J., 2018. 'Hillforts and Defended Enclosures of the Welsh Borderland' in Murphy, K. (ed). 'Iron Age Settlement in Wales'. *Internet Archaeology* 48. https://intarch.ac.uk/journal/issue48/7/toc.html

Burrow, S., 2006. *The Tomb Builders in Wales 4000–3000BC.* National Museum Wales Books.

Capps, B., 1975. *The Old West: The Great Chiefs.* Time-life Books.

Christison, D., 1897. 'The Prehistoric Fortresses of Treceiri and Eildon'. *Archaeologia Cambrensis,* Vol. XIV, Fifth Series, 17–40.

Dodgshon, R.A., 1996. 'Modelling chiefdoms in the Scottish Highlands and islands prior to the '45' in Gibson, Arnold and Blair (eds). *Celtic Chiefdom, Celtic State.* Second Edition. Cambridge University Press. 99–109.

Driver, T., 2007. *Pembrokeshire, historic landscapes from the air.* RCAHMW.

—, 2013. *Architecture, Regional Identity and Power in the Iron Age Landscapes of Mid Wales: The Hillforts of North Ceredigion.* BAR British Series 583, Archaeopress Archaeology.

—, 2018. 'New Perspectives on the Architecture and Function of Welsh Hillforts and Defended Settlements'. *Internet Archaeology* 48. https://doi.org/10.11141/ia.48.4

—, 2021. *The Hillforts of Cardigan Bay.* Second Edition. Logaston Press.

Edwards, H.J., 1917. *Caesar, The Gallic War.* Loeb Classical Library, Harvard University Press.

Fitzpatrick, A.P., 2007. 'Druids: Towards an archaeology' in Gosden, C., Harrow, H., Jersey, P. de and Lock, G. (eds). *Communities and Connections: Essays in honour of Barry Cunliffe.* Oxford University Press. 287–315.

Gardner, W., 1922. 'The ancient hill fort known as Caer Drewyn, Merionethshire'. *Archaeologia Cambrensis,* Volume LXXVII, Seventh Series, Vol. II, 108–23.

Green, M. and Howell, R., 2000. *A Pocket Guide to Celtic Wales.* University of Wales Press.

Hogg, A.H.A., 1975. *Hill-forts of Britain.* Hart-Davis, MacGibbon.

—, 1974. 'Carn Goch, Carmarthenshire'. *Archaeologia Cambrensis*, Vol. CXXIII, 43–53.

Hughes, H., 1906. 'Pen y Gorddyn or Gorddyn Mawr'. *Archaeologia Cambrensis*, Vol. VI, Sixth Series, 268–72.

Lock, G.R. and Ralston, I., 2022. *Atlas of the Hillforts of Britain and Ireland.* Edinburgh University Press.

Lord, I.R., Timberlake, S. and Craddock, B., 2019. 'A Roman spade discovered at Penpompren Mine, Talybont, Ceredigion'. *Archaeology in Wales* 59, 63–66.

Manning, W.H., 1999. 'The Use of Timber in Iron Age Defences'. *Studia Celtica*, Vol. XXXIII, 21–32.
Mattingly, H., 1948. *Tacitus on Britain and Germany. A new translation of the 'Agricola' and the 'Germania' by H. Mattingly.* Penguin Books.
Murphy, K. and Mytum, H., 2012. 'Iron Age Enclosed Settlements in West Wales'. *Proceedings of the Prehistoric Society,* 78 (2011), 263–313.
Murphy, F. and Wilson, H., 2020. *Porth y Rhaw promontory fort, Solva, Pembrokeshire. Interim Report on the 2019 excavation.* Dyfed Archaeological Trust, Report Number 2019/27. Unpublished report.
Murphy, K., 2016. 'Later Prehistoric Pembrokeshire' in James, H., John, M., Murphy, K. and Wainwright, G. (eds). *Pembrokeshire County History, Volume I. Prehistoric, Roman and Early Medieval Pembrokeshire.* Pembrokeshire County History Trust. 223–92.
Musson, C., Britnell, W.J., Smith, A.G. & Casey, P.J., 1991. *The Breiddin Hillfort: A later prehistoric settlement in the Welsh Marches.* Council for British Archaeology.
Mytum, H., 2013. *Monumentality in Later Prehistory. Building and Rebuilding Castell Henllys Hillfort.* Springer.
Pope, R., Mason, R., Hamilton, D., Rule, E. & Swogger, J., 2020. 'Hillfort gate-mechanisms: a contextual, architectural reassessment of Eddisbury, Hembury, and Cadbury hillforts', *Archaeological Journal,* 177:2, 339–407, DOI: 10.1080/00665983.2019.1711301
Ralston, I., 2006. *Celtic Fortifications.* Tempus.
RCAHMW, 1956. *An Inventory of the Ancient Monuments in Caernarvonshire, Volume I: East.* HMSO.
—, 1960. *An Inventory of the Ancient Monuments in Caernarvonshire, Volume II: Central.* HMSO.
—, 1986. *Brecknock. Hill-forts and Roman Remains.* (An Inventory of Ancient Monuments in Brecknock (Brycheiniog). HMSO.
Savory, H.N., 1976. 'Welsh Hillforts: A Reappraisal of Recent Research' in Harding, D.W. (ed.). *Hillforts: Later Prehistoric Earthworks in Britain and Ireland.* Academic Press. 237–92.
Sharples, N., 1991. *Maiden Castle.* English Heritage, Batsford.
Waddington, K., 2013. *The Settlements of Northwest Wales, from the Late Bronze Age to the Early Medieval Period.* University of Wales Press.
Wainwright, G.J., 1972. 'Excavations at Tower Point, St. Brides, Pembrokeshire'. *Archaeologia Cambrensis,* Volume CXX (1972), 84–90.
Wilcox, P., 2009. *Rome's Enemies (2); Gallic and British Celts.* 25th impression. Osprey Publishing.
Williams, G.H. and Mytum, H., 1998. *Llawhaden, Dyfed, Excavations on a group of small defended enclosures, 1980–4.* BAR British Series 275.

CHAPTER 6

Baring-Gould, Revd S., 1899. 'Exploration of the Stone Camp on St David's Head'. *Archaeologia Cambrensis,* Vol. XVI, 105–31.
Baring-Gould, Revd S. and Burnard, R., 1904. 'An Exploration of Some of the Cytiau in Tre'r Ceiri'. *Archaeologia Cambrensis,* Volume IV, Sixth Series, 1–16.
Bick, D. and Wyn Davies, P., 1994. *Lewis Morris and the Cardiganshire Mines.* The National Library of Wales.
Burrow, S., 2015. 'From Celtic Village to Iron Age Farmstead: Lessons Learnt from Twenty Years of Building, Maintaining and Presenting Iron Age Roundhouses at St Fagans National History Museum'. *EXARC Journal* Issue 2015/4.

Butser Bronze Age Build Blog, session 14, 2021.https://www.butserancientfarm.co.uk/blog/2021/10/5/the-bronze-age-build-blog-session-14

Crew, P. and Musson, C., 1997. *Snowdonia from the Air: Patterns in the Landscape.* Snowdonia National Park Authority & Royal Commission on the Ancient and Historical Monuments of Wales.

Crew, P., 2009. *Ironworking in Merioneth from prehistory to the 18th century.* Merfyn Williams Memorial Lectures. Snowdonia National Park/ Plas Tan y Bwlch.

Davis, O. and Sharples, N., 2020. 'Excavations at Caerau Hillfort, Cardiff: Towards a narrative for the hillforts of south-east Wales' in Defino, D., Coimbra, F., Cardoso, D. and Cruz, Goncalo (eds). *Late Prehistoric Fortifications in Europe: Defensive, Symbolic and Territorial Aspects from the Chalcolithic to the Iron Age.* Archaeopress Archaeology. 163–81.

Frodsham, P., 2004. *Interpreting the Ambiguous: Archaeology and Interpretation in Early 21st Century Britain.* Proceedings of a conference session at the 2001 Institute of Field Archaeologists' Annual Conference, held at the University of Newcastle Upon Tyne. Archaeopress Archaeology.

Ghey, Eleanor, Edwards, Nancy and Johnston, Nancy, 2008. 'Categorizing roundhouse settlements in Wales: a critical perspective'. *Studia Celtica* 42, 1–25.

Green, M. and Howell, R., 2000. *A Pocket Guide to Celtic Wales.* University of Wales Press.

Hughes, H., 1907. 'Report on the excavations carried out at Tre'r Ceiri in 1906'. *Archaeologia Cambrensis,* Volume VII, Sixth Series, 38–62.

Longley, D., 1998. 'Bryn Eryr: an enclosed settlement of the Iron Age on Anglesey'. *Proceedings of the Prehistoric Society,* 64, 225–73.

Mattingly, H., 1948. *Tacitus on Britain and Germany. A new translation of the 'Agricola' and the 'Germania' by H. Mattingly.* Penguin Books.

Rees, C. and Jones, M., 2017. 'Exploring a Neolithic neighbourhood at Llanfaethlu'. *Current Archaeology* CA332. Accessed 02/06/2022. https://archaeology.co.uk/articles/features/wales-earliest-village.htm

Romilly Allen, J., 1901. 'Two Kelto-Roman finds in Wales'. *Archaeologia Cambrensis,* Vol 1, Sixth Series, 20–44.

RCAHMW, 1960. *An Inventory of the Ancient Monuments in Caernarvonshire, Volume II: Central.* HMSO.

—, 1964. *An Inventory of the Ancient Monuments in Caernarvonshire. Volume III: West. The Cantref of Lleyn.* HMSO.

Smith, C., 1985. 'Excavations at the Ty Mawr Hut-circles, Holyhead, Anglesey. Part II.' *Archaeologia Cambrensis,* Vol. CXXXIV, 11–52.

Waddington, K., 2013. *The Settlements of Northwest Wales, from the Late Bronze Age to the Early Medieval Period.* University of Wales Press.

Wainwright, G.J., 1972. 'Excavations at Tower Point, St. Brides, Pembrokeshire'. *Archaeologia Cambrensis,* Volume CXX (1972), 84–90.

Williams, R. & Le Carlier de Veslud, C., 2019. 'Boom and bust in Bronze Age Britain: Major copper production from the Great Orme mine and European trade, *c.*1600–1400BC'. *Antiquity,* 93(371), 1178–96. doi:10.15184/aqy.2019.130

CHAPTER 7

Aldhouse-Green, M. and Howell, R., 2000. *Celtic Wales*. University of Wales Press.

Baring-Gould, Revd S., 1899. 'Exploration of the Stone Camp on St David's Head'. *Archaeologia Cambrensis,* Vol. XVI, 105–31.

Barker, L. and Driver, T., 2011. 'Close to the Edge: New Perspectives on the Architecture, Function and Regional Geographies of the Coastal Promontory Forts of the Castlemartin Peninsula, South Pembrokeshire, Wales'. *Proceedings of the Prehistoric Society* 77, 65–87.

Barker, L., Davis, O., Driver, T. and Johnston, R., 2012. 'Puffins amidst prehistory: re-interpreting the complex landscape of Skomer Island' in Britnell, W.J. and Silvester, R.J. (eds). *Reflections on the Past, Essays in Honour of Frances Lynch*. Cambrian Archaeological Association. 280–302.

CHERISH Project, 2020. *CHERISH News*. Issue 5, January 2020 (unpublished newsletter).

Crane, P. and Murphy, K., 2010. 'The excavation of a coastal promontory fort at Porth y Rhaw, Solva, Pembrokeshire, 1995–98'. *Archaeologia Cambrensis,* 159, 53–98.

Cunliffe, B., 2001. *Facing the Ocean, The Atlantic and its Peoples 8000BC–AD 1500*. Oxford University Press.

—, 2002. *The Extraordinary Voyage of Pytheas the Greek*. Second edition. Penguin Books.

—, 2010. *Druids: A very Short Introduction*. Oxford University Press.

Cunnington, M.E., 1920. 'Notes on objects from an inhabited site on the Worms Head, Glamorgan'. *Archaeologia Cambrensis,* Vol. XX, Sixth Series, 251–56.

Davies, J.L. and Kirby, D.P. (eds), 1994. *Cardiganshire County History. Volume 1, From the earliest times to the coming of the Normans*. University of Wales Press.

Davies, J.L., 1994. 'The Roman Period' in Davies, J.L. and Kirby, D.P. (eds). *Cardiganshire County History. Volume 1, From the earliest times to the coming of the Normans*. University of Wales Press. 275–317.

—, 2012. 'Roman Anglesey: a survey and recent research' in Britnell, W.J. and Silvester, R.J. (eds). *Reflections on the Past. Essays in honour of Frances Lynch*. Cambrian Archaeological Association. 369–89.

Driver, T., 2021. *The Hillforts of Cardigan Bay*. Second edition. Logaston Press.

Edwards, H.J., 1917. *Caesar, The Gallic War*. Loeb Classical Library, Harvard University Press.

Fenton, R., 1811. *A Historical Tour Through Pembrokeshire*.

Fleming, A., 2005. *St Kilda and the Wider World: Tales of an Iconic Island*. Windgather Press.

Grant, M., 1978. *Tacitus: The Annals of Imperial Rome*. Revised edition. Penguin Books.

Green, M. and Howell, R., 2000. *A Pocket Guide to Celtic Wales*. University of Wales Press.

Herring, P., 1994. 'The cliff castles and hillforts of West Penwith in the light of recent work at Maen Castle and Treryn Dinas'. *Cornish Archaeology,* No. 33, 40–56.

Historic Environment Group, Climate Change Subgroup, 2020. *Historic Environment and Climate Change in Wales*. Cadw. https://cadw.gov.wales/advice-support/climate-change/adapting-to-climate-change

Lock, G.R. and Ralston, I., 2022. *Atlas of the Hillforts of Britain and Ireland*. Edinburgh University Press.

Moriarty, C., 2012. 'The Broighter hoard'. *Irish Archaeology*: irisharchaeology.ie

Murphy, F. and Wilson, H., 2020. *Porth y Rhaw promontory fort, Solva, Pembrokeshire. Interim Report on the 2019 excavation*. Dyfed Archaeological Trust, Report Number 2019/27 (unpublished report).

Murphy, K., 2001. 'A Prehistoric Field System and Related Monuments on St David's Head and Carn Llidi, Pembrokeshire'. *Proceedings of the Prehistoric Society* 67, 85–99.

RCAHMW, 1976. *An Inventory of the Ancient Monuments in Glamorgan, Volume I: Pre-Norman. Part II. The Iron Age and Roman Occupation*. HMSO.
Savory, H.N., 1974. 'An early Iron Age metalworker's mould from Worms Head'. *Archaeologia Cambrensis*, Vol. CXXIII, 170–74.
Sharpe, A., 1992. 'Treyn Dinas: cliff castles reconsidered'. *Cornish Archaeology*, No. 31, 65–8.
Steele, P., 2012. *Llyn Cerrig Bach, Treasure from the Iron Age*. Oriel Ynys Môn.
Vyner, B., 2001. 'Clegyr Boia: a potential Neolithic enclosure and associated monuments on the St David's peninsula, southwest Wales' in Darvill, T. and Thomas, J. (eds), 2001. *Neolithic Enclosures in Atlantic Northwest Europe. Neolithic Studies Group Seminar Papers 6*, Oxbow Books. 78–90.
Wainwright, G.J., 1972. 'Excavations at Tower Point, St. Brides, Pembrokeshire'. *Archaeologia Cambrensis*, Volume CXX (1971), 84–90.
Wessex Archaeology, 2012. *Watery Bay Rath and Gateholm, Pembrokeshire. Archaeological Evaluation and Assessment of Results*. Report reference 77508.1. Wessex Archaeology (unpublished report).
Williams, A., 1939. 'Excavations at the Knave Promontory fort, Rhossili, Glamorgan'. *Archaeologia Cambrensis*, Volume XCIV, 210–19.

CHAPTER 8

Barker, L., 2009. *Gaer Fawr hillfort: an analysis of the earthworks*. Royal Commission on the Ancient and Historical Monuments of Wales, NPRN 306997 (unpublished report).
Barker, L. and Driver, T., 2011. 'Close to the Edge: New Perspectives on the Architecture, Function and Regional Geographies of the Coastal Promontory Forts of the Castlemartin Peninsula, South Pembrokeshire, Wales'. *Proceedings of the Prehistoric Society* 77, 65–87.
Barnwell, E.L., 1871. 'Bronze Boar', *Archaeologia Cambrensis*, Fourth Series, 2, 163–67.
Britnell, W.J and Silvester, R.J., 2018. 'Hillforts and Defended Enclosures of the Welsh Borderland'. *Internet Archaeology* 48. https://doi.org/10.11141/ia.48.7
CHERISH Project, 2021. *CHERISH News*. Issue 7 (unpublished newsletter).
Crew, P., 2009. *Ironworking in Merioneth from prehistory to the 18th century*. Merfyn Williams Memorial Lectures. Snowdonia National Park/ Plas Tan y Bwlch.
Crew, P. and Musson, C., 1997. *Snowdonia from the Air: Patterns in the Landscape*. Snowdonia National Park Authority & Royal Commission on the Ancient and Historical Monuments of Wales.
Driver, T., 2008. 'Tre'r Ceiri and the Stone Forts of Llŷn' in Wakelin, P. and Griffiths, R.A. (eds). *Hidden Histories. Discovering the Heritage of Wales*. Royal Commission on the Ancient and Historical Monuments of Wales. 78–9.
Ffoulkes, W.W., 1874. 'Tumuli, Merionethshire – Tomen Pentref'. *Archaeologia Cambrensis*, Vol. V, Fourth Series, 313–19.
Gardner, W., 1922. 'The Ancient Hill Fort Known as Caer Drewyn, Merionethshire'. *Archaeologia Cambrensis*, Vol. LXXVII, Seventh Series, Vol. II, 108–25.
Green, M. and Howell, R., 2000. *A Pocket Guide to Celtic Wales*. University of Wales Press.
Guilbert, G., 2018. 'Historical Excavation and Survey of Hillforts in Wales: some critical issues', *Internet Archaeology* 48. https://doi.org/10.11141/ia.48.3
Heather and Hillforts Partnership Board, 2011. *Heather and Hillforts of the Clwydian Range and Llantysilio Mountains* (unpublished booklet).

Hogg, A.H.A., 1974. 'Carn Goch, Carmarthenshire'. *Archaeologia Cambrensis,* Vol. CXXIII, 43–53.
Hopewell, D., 2018. *The Tre'r Ceiri Conservation Project – Re-Examination of an Iconic Hillfort.* Gwynedd Archaeological Trust Report 45136 (unpublished pre-publication report).
Hughes, H., 1907. 'Report on the excavations carried out at Tre'r Ceiri in 1906'. *Archaeologia Cambrensis,* Volume VII, Sixth Series, 38–62.
Lewis, S., 1833. *A Topographical Dictionary of Wales.*
Lock, G.R. and Ralston, I., 2022. *Atlas of the Hillforts of Britain and Ireland.* Edinburgh University Press.
Lynch, F., Aldhouse-Green, S. & Davies, J., 2000. *Prehistoric Wales.* Sutton Publishing.
Musson, C., Britnell, W.J., Smith, A.G. & Casey, P.J., 1991. *The Breiddin Hillfort: A later prehistoric settlement in the Welsh Marches.* Council for British Archaeology. Available at: http://ads.ahds.ac.uk/catalogue/adsdata/cbaresrep/pdf/076/076tl001.pdf
Nash Williams, V.E., 1939. 'An Early Iron Age Coastal Camp at Sudbrook, Near the Severn Tunnel, Monmouthshire'. *Archaeologia Cambrensis,* Vol. XCIV, 42–79.
Prehistoric Society, The, undated. *Signposts to Prehistory: The Breiddin Hillfort.* Online publication available at: https://www.prehistoricsociety.org/sites/prehistoricsociety.org/files/resources/ps-signpost_the-breiddin.pdf
RCAHMW, 1960. *An Inventory of the Ancient Monuments in Caernarvonshire, Volume II: Central.* HMSO. No. 1056, 101–3.
—, 1986. *Brecknock. Hill-forts and Roman Remains.* (An Inventory of Ancient Monuments in Brecknock (Brycheiniog). HMSO.
Savory, H.N., 1965. 'The Guilsfield Hoard'. *Bulletin of the Board of Celtic Studies* 21, 179–96.
Smith, G., 2009. *A visitor guide to the main Iron Age hillforts of Meirionnydd.* Gwynedd Archaeological Trust (unpublished report for Cadw; Project No. G1770, report No. 839).
Waddington, K., 2013. *The Settlements of Northwest Wales, from the Late Bronze Age to the Early Medieval Period.* University of Wales Press.
Whittle, E., 1992. *A Guide to Ancient and Historic Wales: Glamorgan and Gwent.* Cadw. HMSO.
Woods, J., 2016. 'Of Fires and Giants: Thomas Pennant and Tre'r Ceiri Hillfort'. Curious Travellers blog accessed 14/09/2022: https://curioustravellers.ac.uk/en/of-fires-and-giants-thomas-pennant-and-trer-ceiri-hillfort/

FINDING OUT MORE

THE ROYAL COMMISSION ON THE ANCIENT AND HISTORICAL MONUMENTS OF WALES

The Royal Commission is the investigation body and national archive for the historic environment of Wales. It has a lead role in ensuring that Wales' archaeological, built and maritime heritage is authoritatively recorded, and seeks to promote the understanding and appreciation of this heritage nationally and internationally. The **National Monuments Record of Wales** welcomes bilingual enquiries from individuals and organisations interested in the many and varied aspects of the heritage of Wales. The National Monuments Record of Wales is available for consultation via **coflein.gov.uk**. The specialist reference library contains books and journals which may be consulted during public opening hours, based within the National Library of Wales, Aberystwyth. **www.rcahmw.gov.uk**

THE WELSH ARCHAEOLOGICAL TRUSTS

The four Welsh Archaeological Trusts for Gwynedd, Clwyd-Powys, Glamorgan-Gwent and Dyfed each offer a range of commercial archaeological services, heritage and interpretation skills and planning services. Each Welsh Trust also maintains the regional Historic Environment Records (HERs), the contents of which can be searched online via the national online database. **www.archwilio.org.uk**

OPPOSITE: Castle Bank hillfort south of Llandrindod Wells, Radnorshire: one of a group of small but strongly-built hillforts on the linked upland commons of the Carneddau, Gilwern Hill and Llandegley Rocks. The main hillfort is crowded with house platforms, not unlike Foel Trigarn, Pembrokeshire. A later annexe adjoins this fort on the south side (TOP). The main southern gateway between the two shows signs of burning, possibly following attack. (© Crown copyright: RCAHMW. NPRN 305802. AP_2013_0111)

CADW

Cadw is the Welsh Government's Historic Environment Service, and manages historic properties around Wales as well as overseeing various projects and programmes. **Cof Cymru** is the National Historic Assets of Wales website, an online service developed by Cadw. **Cof Cymru** displays information on the Designated Historic Assets in Wales, including scheduled monuments and listed buildings. **cadw.gov.wales/advice-support/cof-cymru** • **www.cadw.gov.wales**

AMGUEDDFA CYMRU/ NATIONAL MUSEUM WALES

The National Museum Wales manages a number of sites around Wales including the National Roman Legion Museum in Caerleon and St Fagans National Museum of History near Cardiff. These two museums house the principal displays of prehistoric and Roman archaeological collections in Wales. The Collections Online website is an excellent way to search for images and information about the museum's archaeology collections. **www.museum.wales/collections/online**

THE ATLAS OF HILLFORTS

The Atlas of Hillforts of Britain and Ireland website was produced as part of a four-year collaborative project between archaeologists at the University of Edinburgh and the University of Oxford, assisted by colleagues at University College Cork for Ireland. The atlas contains data on all hillforts or possible hillforts spread across England, the Isle of Man, Wales, Scotland, Northern Ireland and the Republic of Ireland. **www.hillforts.arch.ox.ac.uk**

THE CAMBRIANS AND THE CBA

Those with a passion for Welsh archaeology and heritage should consider joining the Cambrian Archaeological Association (**www.cambrians.org.uk**) with its annual journal *Archaeologia Cambrensis* and other benefits. Also, the Council for British Archaeology which has a Wales membership and an annual journal, *Archaeology in Wales*. **www.cbawales.org**

INDEX

Numbers appearing in ***bold italics*** in this index refer to images, illustrations and maps and to references in the captions. Those in **bold** relate to main entries. All hillfort sites are listed under 'hillforts, specific sites'.